Jews

Jews

AN ACCOUNT
OF THEIR EXPERIENCE
IN CANADA

Erna Paris

MACMILLAN OF CANADA
A DIVISION OF GAGE PUBLISHING LIMITED
TORONTO, CANADA

Canadian Cataloguing in Publication Data

Paris, Erna, 1938-
  Jews, an account of their experience in Canada

Bibliography: p.
Includes index.

ISBN 0-7715-9574-3

1. Jews in Canada—History. I. Title.

FC106.J5P37   971'.004924   C80-094654-5
F1035.J5P37

Every reasonable care has been taken to trace ownership of
copyrighted material. Information will be welcome which will enable
the publishers to rectify any reference or credit.

Printed in Canada
Macmillan of Canada
A Division of Gage Publishing Limited

This book is dedicated to
four generations of a Jewish family:

to the memory of my grandparents,
Anne Lipkin and Isaac Lipkin,
and Ethel Newman and Benjamin Newman

to my parents,
Christine Lipkin Newman and Jules Newman

to my brother, Peter,
and my sister, Jill

and to my children,
Michelle and Roland

Table of Contents

Acknowledgements

DURING THE PAST THREE YEARS, dozens of individuals have taken the time to share their knowledge and their personal experience with me. In reading this book they will see how deeply I am indebted to them. In particular, I would like to thank David Rome, archivist for the Canadian Jewish Congress in Montreal, Sam Lipshitz of Toronto, and Ben Kayfetz of the Canadian Jewish Congress in Toronto, all of whom were more than generous with their time and kind enough to read parts of the manuscript. Their comments and corrections were of inestimable help to me, although, naturally, I remain solely responsible for all interpretations as well as for any errors that have occurred in the text. I would also like to thank other individuals, including the many librarians and archivists who steered me in interesting directions: in particular, Ronald Finegold of the Jewish Public Library in Montreal, Walter Neutel of the Public Archives of Canada, Ed Morgan of the Provincial Archives of Saskatchewan, and Dorothy Hershfield and Esther Nisenholt of the Jewish Historical Society of Western Canada. To Professor Irving Abella I owe a special debt of thanks for directing me to valuable material dealing with communists. I have also profited from reading Professor Abella's article on the attitudes of the Canadian government to Jewish refugees during the Second World War which was published in the *Canadian Historical Review* in

June 1979, and I look forward to reading the no doubt definitive book on the question which he is currently preparing along with Professor Harold Troper of the University of Toronto.

I am also indebted to the Canada Council Explorations Program and to the Ontario Arts Council for their financial assistance; to Linda Walter and Pat Russo, who transcribed untold hours of taped interviews and typed the manuscript; to Marcia Basman, who allowed me to read and quote from her work in progress, a translation of her uncle Mike Usiskin's remembrances of the Edenbridge colony; to Heather Robertson, who on more than one occasion alerted me to documents relating to Mackenzie King that she thought might be of value; and to the members of my family, who supported me throughout. My deepest appreciation, however, goes to my companion and friend, Tom Robinson, whose love and encouragement consistently buoyed up my spirits and helped renew my resolve when it flagged.

Introduction

I AM A MEMBER OF THAT GENERATION of Canadian Jews who grew up feeling an uneasy combination of pride and embarrassment about my origins. I knew that my relatives had only recently come from the ghettos and muddy shtetls of eastern Europe, but that information did not please me much. I was emphatically a Canadian and a privileged one at that. Although my grandparents were immigrants and still spoke English only imperfectly, my parents had been born here, were identified thoroughly with this country, and had succeeded in lifting themselves into the middle class, where they lived with grace and a distinguished personal style that was apparent to me even in adolescence. I attended Holy Blossom Sunday School, the upper-middle-class Reform Jewish temple of Toronto, and was confirmed there into something I understood to be the Jewish faith.

But there was always something missing in my understanding, something only vaguely apprehended, something, in effect, to be avoided. That something had to do with my ghetto past and the associated trappings of Orthodox Judaism that were my legacy, but as foreign to me as they might have been to any gentile. I had received a strong message, perhaps in a subliminal way, that I (and other young, educated Canadian Jews) must leave all of that behind. To look forward and never backward was imperative. Not to do so would be to remain uncomfortably distinct and perhaps to affect our future in this country.

11

There were, however, other reasons for avoiding those traditions and that past. Since childhood I had been put off by the patriarchal vein that threads through the entire fabric of Jewish life, both secular and religious. I learned early that while Jewish men were the idea-makers and political movers of their communities, their wives and daughters were relegated to a perpetual shadow cabinet, where they contributed hundreds of hours of indispensable and undervalued work, but always in the knowledge that their roles were subordinate and their efforts secondary to those of the men. Historically, the most distinguished accolade a Jewish woman could receive was to be called a "Mother in Israel"; to produce male offspring might be considered her most significant life achievement.

My Canadian-born generation was perhaps the first to have access to widespread higher education and certainly the first in which daughters as well as sons were automatically accorded the privilege. We were educated into equality, and that made it hard, if not impossible, to accept the traditions of inequality in the Jewish community that seemed to some to be as natural as breathing. Faced with ambivalence and a complex heritage, many of us intermarried and "moved out". We hoped we had turned our backs on parochialism.

In my case, however, the uneasiness about the past and my own place in a historical continuum did not dissipate with time. How, I wondered, did one move from the station of my grandmother, who arrived in Canada three-quarters of a century ago as a girl of eighteen, without skills or education, to my assimilated parents, and then to me with my distinctly modern dilemmas? I wondered about the process of assimilation and about the adaptation of values and attitudes from the Old World to this Anglo-Saxon land.

This book was originally born as a study of three generations of several Jewish families: how daughters had resisted their mothers and their mothers' world, and how granddaughters had moved into a new sphere altogether;

how sons had rejected the deeply held dreams of their
fathers and what, of all the baggage brought from centuries
of life in Europe, they had chosen to cherish. But as I
researched background material, the actual history against
which individual dramas were played began to loom larger
and larger. Here was evidence and documentation for all
the wisps of rumour that had floated about my ears for at
least two decades. Here was the man, dead more than forty
years, who was the first Jewish MP of any significance, and
on whose shoulders fell the burden of squeezing Jewish
refugees from pogroms, and then from Hitler's Germany,
into Canada; and here, too, were the men in the public
service of this country who thwarted him at every turn.
Here was a prime minister using this same man's friendship
for political advancement, then turning his back when he
sought even token recognition for a lifetime of service; here
was the very mixed history of Jews in Quebec, an experience quite different from that of Jews anywhere else in
North America; and here were the Jewish Communists—
men and women who had dedicated their entire lives to the
dream of the Russian Revolution. Here were stories of
Jewish pioneers on the prairies of western Canada, survivors of nineteenth-century Russian pogroms, who had
moved into the North West *before* the waves of Poles, Germans, Scandinavians, and Ukrainians. Here also was correspondence between Canada's first Prime Minister and his
High Commissioner in Britain discussing Jewish immigration in the most cynical of terms; here were diaries written
by some of the pioneers themselves; and here were their
children, still living in places like Winnipeg and Saskatoon
and carrying with them a legacy of the land undreamed of
by eastern urban Jews.

The generations of families remained a part of the
story, but they took a back seat to the drama of the times
they lived in. The final result is, however, not intended to be
a comprehensive social history of the Jews in Canada. I have
not traced the religious history of the community, or the

growth of synagogues, for example; nor have I written about the Zionist movement in any detail. Instead, I have concentrated on those periods and events that struck me as most vital and significant; periods and events, often marked by passion, that revealed the clash of internal Jewish politics as the individual and collective struggle to adapt to the new land progressed; periods and events that signalled the converging points of Jewish politics and the larger political happenings of the country itself. I have tried to write about real people who lived and breathed, who felt joy and loss; people with failings as well as strengths, with warts as well as beauty spots. I have, in other words, tried to tell the truth as dispassionately as I could.

I chose to concentrate on Quebec, Toronto, and the Prairies because in those three places I found particularly clear examples of the living experience I wished to describe. Although the Jewish communist movement was important in Winnipeg, it had its seat in Toronto, so it is in Toronto that I have examined it. The social and urban experience of Jewish immigrants took place in all major Canadian cities, but I located it in Montreal because the Jewish community of Canada had its origins in that city. As for the Jewish farmers in the west, the Prairie locale speaks for itself.

The writing of this book has turned out to be a rather happy personal odyssey. I did succeed in answering many of my own questions about the cultural chasm and the historical void that existed between my grandparents' generation and my own. The first generation lived its own history of transition from the Old World to the New. The second generation turned from the foreign "ethnicity" that marked their parents in a desire to identify themselves as native Canadians. It has taken three generations for Canadian Jews to feel confident enough to look back with interest and some dispassion on their past.

I have come to look upon both the bearded, Orthodox immigrant from the shtetl of seventy-five and one hundred years ago and his radical, idealistic brother with caring and respect. I have come to admire the courage and, of course, the optimism they displayed in crossing half a world and producing children to carve a future and, they hoped, recreate their past in a new country. I have also come to realize that one of the challenges facing my generation of assimilated Jews is to search out and cherish the living roots of the past, but only those whose continuance we can honestly defend. In my case that means the ongoing recognition of a historical connection and an attempt to understand the attitudes and the events that have formed us. To chart the emergence of the Canadian Jew through the experience he has undergone in this country has been a part of that quest.

Erna Paris
Toronto, Ontario
June 1980

PART ONE

The Jews, Quebec, and Parliament Hill

But what can one man, however able and advanced, do against the current of his age? History shows us constantly that the great reformers have been those who felt and followed the general feeling of their times, who became mouthpieces for the great mass of thought and effort behind them, not those who struggled against [the] tide.

*Found among the papers of
R. B. Bennett; dated February 1935.*

CHAPTER ONE

Beginnings

CANADIAN JEWISH LIFE began in Quebec as long ago as the struggle for dominance between the English and the French on the bloody Plains of Abraham. It was in Quebec that Jews tasted genuine freedom as well as discrimination. It was in Quebec that Ezekiel Hart became the first Jew in the British Empire to be elected to Parliament and in Quebec that a Jewish "declaration of rights" was agreed to. It was in Quebec that anti-Semitism and fascism grew during the 1920s and 1930s and in Quebec that hundreds of people demonstrated to keep Jewish refugees from Hitler's Germany out of Canada.

In Quebec the Jewish clothing industry had its source, its largest production, and its worst sweatshops. In Quebec the Jews prospered. In Quebec the Canadian Jewish Congress was born, failed, and was born again. And in Quebec in another era, Jews faced new fears over nationalism and worried about just who was and who was not a Québécois.

In the final, decisive days of the battle over New France two men of different language, culture, and allegiance pledged loyalty to their generals. One, a French Jew from Bordeaux called Abraham Gradis, had never set foot in Quebec, for in the Revocation of the Edict of Nantes Louis XIV had proclaimed that neither Jew nor Huguenot might settle in the new colonies. Ironically, the Gradis family became the most important wartime link between France and the new continent. They were wealthy shipowners whose fleet crisscrossed the Atlantic bringing food, supplies, and munitions to Montcalm and his men as they clung to the rocks at Quebec. Through Abraham Gradis, his loyal friend, Montcalm was able to send communications home to France — to his King, to his mother, and to his wife.

Although his ships were shot at and destroyed with depressing regularity, Abraham Gradis never deserted his trust. His fleet plied the waters of the St. Lawrence until July 1759, when one of his ships was captured at the mouth of the river by twenty English vessels carrying 11,000 men.

Second in command of that English fleet was Captain Alexander Schomberg, also of Jewish ancestry, and a member of General Wolfe's staff. Schomberg was the son of an eminent physician and came from a family that had had active and distinguished careers in the British navy. He was an educated and cultured man who could quote French poetry whenever the occasion moved him. On July 22, disturbed by the fact that the English in their ships were vastly outnumbered by the French on land, Schomberg penned a few pessimistic lines about the forthcoming battle into his diary:

Si nous venions en ambassade
nous étions beaucoup
mais si c'était pour combattre
nous étions bien peu.

On July 26, the British attacked. On August 9 Schomberg recorded one line in his diary: "Quebec lower Town on Fire." On September 13 the British attacked again, and this time Montcalm lay dying on the Plains of Abraham.

The English Jew, Alexander Schomberg, had served his country well and brought new honour to his family name. The French Jew, Abraham Gradis, had served *his* country well. In recognition of Gradis's patriotism and courage in the defence of New France, King Louis XV granted the Jews of Bordeaux full rights, including, ironically, the right to settle and to own territories in the remaining French colonies of the New World.

In 1760 General Sir Jeffrey Amherst marched into Montreal and captured the city. With him was a staff member, Aaron Hart, a Jew and a lieutenant in the British army. The establishment of British rule meant that Jews were now permitted to live in the new territory. The land looked promising, and Hart stayed to become the first Jew to settle in the colony. When he took up residence in Three Rivers, he became the first English-speaking settler in the area.

Hart returned briefly to England to marry his cousin, Dorothea Judah, and together they founded a dynasty — a long family line that extends to this day. Single-handed Hart developed the fur trade of Three Rivers — so successfully that he became the wealthiest landowner in the Empire outside Britain. In 1779, during the American Revolution, Hart supplied the American army with blankets, spades, and material for uniforms, as well as 3,070 pounds of bread and 265 gallons of rum. He was also wealthy enough to buy a slave woman on the block in Montreal (he paid forty-five pounds).

Hart was well enough known to warrant a visit from Edward, Duke of Kent, during his trip to the colonies in 1791. He was also an incalculably important creditor. By 1831 the government of the United States was in debt to Hart to the tune of $60,000 and President Andrew Jackson was obliged to write an embarrassed letter in which he acknowledged that only $15,000 of the money owed was immediately available.

Aaron Hart brought such renown to Three Rivers that the second post office in the entire country was opened in his home. His personal wealth grew to inestimable and fabled proportions; but Hart was also a generous man, and when he shrewdly included the Catholic church of Three

Rivers in his philanthropy, the community responded by
naming a street after the family. Indeed, by the end of his
career, his donations to the institutions of Catholicism had
earned him the somewhat dubious designation of "Pope of
Canada".

With his happy good fortune and cheerful policies of
noblesse oblige, Aaron Hart was never called upon to re-
pudiate or even suffer for his Jewish heritage. In fact, he
remained adamant that his children maintain the faith. A
letter to a son who was unable to return home for Passover
has survived.

> I hope you will not risk in any danger if you find that
> you cane not be hear Pesah [Passover]. You will acard-
> ing to my instrucktions go to New Yark and keep
> Pesah.... You will say as leetle as passeble about your
> bussiniss to any of the Jues in New Yark nore to you
> Unkils too. You must remain Pesah in a Jues house.

In quite different ways, the next generation of Harts
were as visible and as flamboyant as their father. Moses,
Aaron's second son, was a notorious libertine who adored
good food and wine and was eventually discovered to have
fathered more illegitimate than legitimate children during
a long, sensual career.* He was also distinctly modern (and
self-serving) in his approach to marriage. Before submit-
ting to a traditional ceremony he drew up a contract which
stipulated that in exchange for a sizable amount of money
to be left to his widow at his death, he would be free "to
separate from her bed and board" whenever he pleased.
"In short, he wants her at the price of a good negro wench,"
the girl's father wrote angrily to Aaron Hart in 1799. Moses
countered by begging his fiancée, Sarah (Sally) Judah, to
run away with him. She did, and they were married; but

*Moses Hart recognized his illegitimate offspring and educated them
with the same care as his legitimate children.

they separated fifteen years later on the predictable grounds of Moses's "poor conduct".

Aaron's oldest son, Ezekiel, also achieved legendary notoriety for his pivotal role in a drama that documented the first instance of outspoken anti-Jewish sentiment in Lower Canada, but ended with an important official acceptance of Jewish rights.

In 1807 Ezekiel Hart was elected to the Assembly of Lower Canada as a delegate from Three Rivers. All seemed to be well, but when the session opened and Hart insisted on taking the oath on the Old Testament, chaos erupted in the Assembly. Member after member rose to claim that a Jew did not have the right to sit as a member of Parliament. Jews, they claimed, were wanderers and had no real homeland; Jews traditionally await the coming of the Messiah, therefore they could not owe allegiance to an earthly kingdom; Jews were not citizens in European countries; therefore, they clearly did not *want* to be citizens anywhere; England did not allow Jews in its Parliament, so as a colony they were under no greater obligation; and, finally, no Jew should be allowed to make laws for Christians. For three weeks they debated. Then they voted, twenty-one to five, to expel Ezekiel Hart from the Assembly.

In May 1808 new elections were held, and Hart was re-elected with a large majority; but when the session opened the tirades resumed and he was expelled once again. This time an angry Assembly proposed a bill to disqualify Jews from sitting in Parliament under any circumstance.

Although the objections to Hart were apparently on religious grounds, there was much more at stake, politically. The French saw the Jewish issue as an opportunity to get rid of a new English-speaking, English-sympathizing member, and after the second expulsion Governor General Sir James Henry Craig began to feel that his authority was being threatened in an intolerable way. Bolstered by a personal petition for help from Ezekiel Hart and another petition from the Jewish community of Lower Canada, Craig descended on the Assembly on May 15, 1809, and unceremoniously dissolved Parliament just as the deputies were preparing to push the bill to disqualify Jews through the formality of a third reading.

Between 1807 and 1809 the issue of the Jewish member of Parliament was bandied around like a rubber ball, debated in newspapers and around dinner tables. The esteem the Harts had enjoyed for over fifty years was threatened, so much so that when a new election was called in 1809, Hart announced his candidacy, only to withdraw it twenty-four hours later. His own quick poll of the community suggested that he couldn't win. Indeed, there was nothing to suggest that, should he be re-elected, he would not be expelled again, as the issue had not been resolved. In any event, Ezekiel Hart's withdrawal from the race put an end to the Jewish problem for the Assembly of Lower Canada. It also ended Hart's political career.

Twenty years later, the mood of Lower Canada had changed dramatically. A wave of liberalism was sweeping the West, blown in by winds of change from the French and the American revolutions. It was a time of optimism in which people fervently believed that humanity had entered a better, more moral phase of existence. Prejudice and discrimination were now frowned upon and editorial writers and ministers preached brotherhood from their respective pulpits with a happy satisfaction at being part of a better world.

In 1831 an English member of the Assembly of Lower Canada introduced a bill that would grant Jews the same rights and privileges enjoyed by everyone else. The bill was strongly supported by the French-Canadian rebel Louis-Joseph Papineau and his followers, who fully agreed that Jews were being discriminated against. Remarkably (given the experience of Ezekiel Hart in the very same Assembly), the bill was adopted by the legislature almost without discussion. In 1832 this Jewish "Magna Carta" of rights became law and Canada became the first country in the Empire legally to emancipate Jews.

Ezekiel Hart was filled with gratitude to Papineau and his rebel Patriotes and in 1835 he held a special dinner for them in Three Rivers. Papineau was present, as were Jacques Viger, a writer and the first mayor of Montreal, Roy de Portilance, and other important figures in the rebel movement. With one exception, all the invited English guests declined the invitation.

Within the Jewish community there was a division of loyalty (there were 107 Jews in Canada in 1831); neverthe-less, during the Papineau Rebellion of 1837 the majority of Jews defended English interests. English was their lan-guage, England was their original home, Victoria was their Queen. But they remained grateful for the generosity of the Patriotes, whose outrage at the status of the French in Lower Canada had spilled over to encompass the cause of discrimination against the Jews.

In the 1850s one William Dawson of Three Rivers took a business trip to England, where he met Baron Lionel de Rothschild, head of the British House of Rothschild. Daw-son informed Rothschild that he came from the first place in the Empire to have elected a Jew to government.

"You are the first person to tell me about it," exclaimed Rothschild. "I myself have passed through four or five similar elections from which I came out victorious, but... the House of Commons always rejects me, in spite of the people. It is understood that Jews will not be deputies."*

"They will be in England as they are in Canada," Daw-son assured him.

"What a good colony," said the Baron. "I love it without knowing it."

---

*Baron Lionel de Rothschild was first elected to the British House of Commons in 1847 but could not take his seat until 1858, when legislation requiring a Christian oath of allegiance was amended.

In an atmosphere of tolerance, with their "Magna Carta" legislation of 1832 still fresh in living memory, Jews in Canada rose to positions of esteem. And all the while the press of the day continued to congratulate itself and everyone else on having the good fortune to live in such wonderful times when human nature had finally and forever rid itself of its warts, and merit was duly rewarded.

CHAPTER TWO

Immigrants: How "Uptown" and "Downtown" Montreal Came To Be

IN THE LATE 1850s AND 1860s several families from Russia and Poland arrived in Canada. Abraham Jacobs, Moses Vineberg, Lazarus Cohen, and the others were directed by immigration agents to the villages along the St. Lawrence. They settled in Lancaster, Maberly, Lanark, and Kingston. Like many Jewish immigrants they peddled wares among the farmers; then, when they had saved enough, they opened general stores.

From this group, Lazarus Cohen would emerge as the most successful and the most dedicated to Jewish life. Cohen was enterprising from the beginning. He looked around and saw trees — the very community where he lived had only recently been claimed from the forest. So he shrewdly went into the lumber business at Sharbot Lake, Ontario.

Children were born to this cluster of men and women pioneering along the St. Lawrence, and their religious education became a worry. Every year Cohen and his friends gathered their families together and made a pilgrimage to Montreal for the holy days of Rosh Hashanah and Yom Kippur; but by the 1880s this began to seem pointless. Lazarus Cohen decided to move to Montreal, and the others soon followed suit.

They couldn't have made the move at a better time. Although originally from eastern Europe, this group of

27

people had already been in Canada for twenty years, long enough to learn to speak English well, and they quickly adopted the anglicized ways of their Jewish co-religionists in Montreal, whose background was quite different from theirs. But the move was also timely because they arrived in Montreal just as Quebec was beginning to industrialize. Some of them moved into the newly emerging needle trades; at least one became a successful cigar manufacturer. Astute as ever, Lazarus Cohen went into a variety of businesses—coal, a brass foundry, and dredging—and became a wealthy man. So did most of the others.

They moved to Westmount and took up residence in great stone mansions alongside the Scottish fur barons. They educated their children, boys and girls, in the best schools, and if the best schools were Catholic schools, well, they compensated with a rigorous Hebrew-school education after hours. Soon the children themselves knit their already closely associated families even more closely through intermarriage.

The new arrivals were deeply committed to Jewish life and to community organization. They appropriated the Shaar Hashomayim synagogue and turned it into the rich man's Orthodox synagogue of Canada (which it remains to this day). Lazarus Cohen took over the Young Men's Hebrew Benevolent Society and later helped to establish the Baron de Hirsch Institute, which would be called upon to provide relief to the thousands of immigrants pouring into Canada after the eastern-European pogroms of the 1880s.

The women worked in Ladies' Auxiliaries as an energetic "shadow" work force in activities that paralleled the men's. The men concerned themselves with the male heads of refugee families; the women worried about the women and the children. The men agitated to build a hospital; the women visited the sick. The men organized charity drives and made speeches about politics and war; the women made clothing for the poor. Their work was understood to be secondary.

At the head of the women's section was Mrs. Clarence I. de Sola, who represented, in her very person, all the virtues of elegance and accomplishment that the new notables of Jewish society aspired to. Mrs. de Sola's father-in-law, the Reverend Abraham de Sola, had been imported from England in 1847 to occupy the position of Rabbi of Montreal. His career was outstanding. In 1853 he became full professor of Hebrew and Oriental literature at McGill University. In 1858 he was awarded an honorary LLD by McGill. In 1872, at the invitation of President Ulysses S. Grant, he opened the U. S. Congress with a prayer. The de Sola sons followed in their father's footsteps. In 1898, just one year after the birth of the world zionist movement in Basle, Switzerland, and two years after the publication of Theodor Herzl's seminal book, *The Jewish State*, Clarence helped found the Canadian Zionist Federation. (He became president of the Federation and remained a strong-minded and sometimes autocratic leader until his death in 1919.) In 1904 Clarence was appointed Belgian consul in Montreal, and in 1915 he chaired the Canadian Jewish Conference, a forerunner of the Canadian Jewish Congress.

Mrs. de Sola was herself a university graduate in philosophy. She was a founder of the Friendly League of Jewish Women and of the Welcome Club for Jewish working girls, as well as being honorary president of the Montreal branch of the Canadian Women's Press Club and something of a journalist in her own right. In 1918 she was decorated by King Albert of Belgium in recognition of wartime services connected with Belgian relief work, and in 1923 she was presented to the King and Queen of Great Britain.

Apart from Mrs. de Sola, nothing indicated the new community's sense of itself more clearly than the building erected in 1880, on the very eve of mass emigration from Europe. The Montefiore Club was established "for the purpose of fostering literary and social intercourse among its members and for the encouragement of amateur dramatic

pursuits", and its décor was an important statement by its
members about themselves. The entrance was floored and
walled in marble; the ceiling was vaulted and frescoed.
"The whole interior is furnished in the Dutch style, with
heavily-beamed ceilings, great fireplaces which reach to the
ceiling, polished floors and leaded windows. . . . The furni-
ture, electrical fixtures, which are of pewter, and [the]
Donegal rugs are especially designed to suit these rooms.
The effect has been studied as a whole and there are no
discordant or startling notes of colour. . . ."

They were self-assured and confident about their high
status in Montreal society; but alongside this vision of themselves as a sort of cultured élite, the new Westmount Jews
also believed in duty. For forty years about twenty families
of these moneyed would-be aristocrats carried the burden
for the resettlement and the welfare of thousands of
Yiddish-speaking immigrants from eastern Europe. By
1881 the number of Jews in Canada had increased to 2,443.
By 1891 there were 6,503; by 1901 the population numbered 16,717; by 1911 it had climbed to 76,199; and by
1921, when Canadian immigration policies had begun to
tighten drastically, 126,196 Jews had arrived in Canada.
The clash of attitudes between the two groups — the
"uptowners", as the old guard of Westmount-dwellers came
to be called, and the "downtowners", as the new immigrants
squashed into slum housing in the streets around St. Lawrence and Main were called — surprised no one. But the
wealthy anglicized Jews were never disloyal to their self-
appointed task of aiding immigrants and refugees. They
occasionally dispensed their help and advice with a condescension not untypical of Victorian society, but they dispensed it all the same.

The different attitudes of uptown and downtown were
most apparent in the newspapers both communities established. In 1897 *The Jewish Times* was created by two sons of
the new notables, Lyon Cohen and Sam Jacobs (who would
later be an MP in the Laurier and King governments). *The*

Jewish Times was the first Jewish-interest paper in Canada and it spoke, in English, with the voice of concerned, anglicized Jewry. The *Times* promoted "Canadianization" and the ways of the British Empire. It looked for leadership to Jewish notables in Britain and to the chief rabbi of France, who was learned and kind. *The Jewish Times* was the perfect vehicle for Lazarus Cohen's son, Lyon, who could be seen of a spring morning strolling down Rosemount Avenue, past the baronial castles of his similarly rich neighbours with their family coats-of-arms impressed into stone over the front portal, the tap-tap of his expensive cane on the pavement breaking the dignified hush of the street. The *Times* spoke for the philanthropists whose job it was to help the needy and advise the shtetl newcomers on how to comport themselves. At the same time it did not hesitate to condemn Jewish clothing manufacturers who were operating sweatshops and exploiting Jewish labour, although these very manufacturers were Westmount neighbours and may have sat in the next pew in the Shaar Hashomayim synagogue.

The *Jewish Times* was emphatically *not* interested in promoting the interests of the Yiddish "masses", who were seething with new ideas and left-wing ideology. This group found expression in the *Kanader Adler (The Jewish Daily Eagle)*, a Yiddish-language paper established in 1907 by Hirsch Wolofsky. The *Eagle*, which attracted many of the brightest minds of the day, maintained a steady opposition to the assimilationist tendencies of *The Jewish Times* and the uptowners, and promoted a deliberate strengthening of Yiddish language and culture in this new land. The uptowners and *The Jewish Times* were restrained and Anglo-Saxon in their behaviour and attitudes; the new immigrants from eastern Europe were not. They were excitedly intellectual and overtly emotional, and their paper reflected their style. Issues and arguments were fought out on its pages with high drama and full-blown rhetoric.

That the uptowners and downtowners communicated at all was itself a minor miracle. What did the downtown immigrants know of Westmount or Outremont or the dignified ways of the Cohens and their friends?

> [They] worked under appalling conditions in sweat shops [wrote Mordecai Richler in *The Street*]. They rented halls over pool rooms and grocery stores to meet and form burial societies and create shuls....Slowly, unfalteringly [they] began to struggle up a ladder of streets, from one where you had to leave your garbage outside your front door to another where you actually had a rear lane as well as a back yard where corn and tomatoes were usually grown....

A half-century later, immigrant life on the downtown streets still stood in approximately the same relation to the elegance of uptown (and the old Montefiore Club) as a street bazaar to Buckingham Palace.

> Of the five streets, St. Urbain was the best [wrote Richler]. Those on the streets below, the out-of-breath ones, the borrowers, the *yentas*, flea-carriers and rent-skippers, *goniffs* from Galicia, couldn't afford a day in the country or tinned fruit for dessert on the High Holidays. They accepted parcels from charity matrons (Outremont bitches) on Passover, and went uninvited to bar-mitzvahs and weddings to carry off cakes, bottles and chicken legs....They were not yet Canadian. *Greeners*, that's what they were....

In the early years of the twentieth century the general atmosphere in Quebec began to change. A wave of French-Canadian nationalism was emerging, and the cheerful optimism of the nineteenth century gave way to a new bitterness. The federal Naval Bill* (which had lost Prime Minister Laurier the election of 1911) had divided the country along racial lines. The mood turned ugly and became uglier still in 1912 when Ontario passed a law limiting the use of French in schools to one hour a day.

As nationalism and self-interest in Quebec intensified, attitudes towards Jews also began to change, and in 1910 a startlingly regressive event took place. Joseph Edouard Plamondon, a Quebec City notary and journalist, made a speech in which he claimed that all Jews were enemies of all Christians. He claimed to quote from the Talmud:

> Jesus is an idol conceived in vice and adultery; those who follow Jesus are idol-worshippers; a Christian is an animal; he thereby strengthens the power of the impious; it is permitted to a Jew to practice usury against a Christian; he who causes to flow the blood of the impious, that is, of non-Jews, thereby offers a sacrifice to God; it is necessary to slaughter the best among the Christians; the Jew who acquires the power should, under any pretext, bring death to heretics; a Jew, accused of having killed a Christian, may swear that he did not kill a human being, thinking and saying to himself that it is an animal that he killed.

Plamondon went on to revive the medieval accusation of Jewish blood murder (the charge was that Jews murdered Christian children to get blood for the baking of Passover matzohs). Plamondon was probably encouraged by the fact that a similar charge had recently been made in Kiev, but before that, the last blood-murder accusation had been heard in the fifteenth century.

When Plamondon's speech was distributed as a pam-

---

*The Naval Bill was introduced into the Canadian Parliament by Prime Minister Laurier in 1910 in order to create a separate Canadian navy that would come to the aid of the British admiralty. French Canada was opposed to the Bill.

phlet, the Jews of Quebec City found themselves under attack. Synagogue windows were broken and businesses were disrupted. Jews were molested and stoned. The day after these violent events, two Jewish shopkeepers filed a suit for damages and hired Sam Jacobs as their lawyer.

The trial was as bizarre as the accusations themselves. Rabbi H. Abramowitz from the Shaar Hashomayim synagogue testified (as a Talmudic scholar) that Plamondon's "quotations" were entirely false. He dredged forth evidence from the Catholic Encyclopedia and reminded the court that popes, cardinals, and archbishops had exhorted Christians not to persecute Jews.

The judge dismissed the case on grounds that Plamondon had incriminated the Jewish race in general without attacking the plaintiffs in particular. But Jacobs appealed, and in December 1914 Plamondon was found guilty. (Five years later, the *Canadian Jewish Chronicle* gleefully printed a letter informing its readers that Mr. Plamondon was serving a prison term for dishonest business practices.)

To Quebec Jews the frightening thing about the Talmud Trial, as it was called, was that it could happen at all in a Quebec that had been liberal and hospitable to Jews. But the Talmud Trial was only a beginning. In the years to come French Canadians would turn inward and, in the warm, damp breeding grounds of frustration, racism would take root.

The Canadian Jewish Congress

In the new, more tense atmosphere of Quebec, Jews felt an urgent need for unity, but the struggling uptown and downtown factions were caught in new contention. In 1915 both groups were worried about the fate of Jews caught in the war zones of Europe, and a combined fund-raising effort in Montreal netted $24,000 in donations. The uptown Jews, whose focus was philanthropic, thought some of the money should be contributed to charities at home as well; the downtowners thought all the money should be sent to help those overseas. Distribution was in the hands of the uptowners, and they duly sent $1,000 to Palestine, $6,000 to the War Victims Committee, and $17,000 to Montreal charitable organizations.

The downtowners saw red. They had had no voice in the distribution of the money they had helped to collect and their priorities were vastly different from those of the Westmounters. From their frustration the idea of a United Jewish Congress was born.

Branch 8 of the Jewish National Workers' Alliance sent out a letter inviting the myriad organizations of Montreal to a meeting. "Dear Organization," the letter began. "As you doubtless know we were completely ignored in the distribution of the Assistance Fund. . . . Thus the voice of those who are suffering was mercilessly suppressed. But the situation is too terrible for us to cease our efforts, as have our Up-Town benefactors. . . . Send your delegates so that together we may develop plans to help those who seek help."

On March 28 seventy-one organizations — including sixteen synagogues, six labour unions, ten sick-benefit societies, eighteen syndicates, eight cultural organizations, five political organizations, and eight charitable societies — held a meeting. The rallying-call for this successful turnout was the emotional letter. "Tens of thousands of young lives have been despoiled. Tens of thousands of new orphans are crying out to their helpless, newly-widowed mothers. . . . Suffering Jewry looks to us. . . . Their fate awaits our response." The new coalition called itself the Canadian Jewish Alliance.

What they dreamed of was a united Jewish voice at the peace talks at the war's eventual end, but a voice that would express *their* political point of view. They were Labour Zionists, left-wing socialists, and Jewish nationalists — and they wanted the creation of an independent Jewish state in Palestine.

The key speaker that day in March was Dr. Yehuda

Kaufman, the newly elected secretary of the Alliance. He spoke of British justice and the dream of Jewish equality.

> The Canadian Jews are citizens of the great British Empire and are therefore in a position to ask their government to protect the rights of our brethren in Russia and Poland. The Canadian Jews are citizens of a pioneer country with great immigration and colonization possibilities. We...want to formulate on the platform of a Jewish Congress our national revindication to the Peace Conference of the world nations. For the above reasons it is absolutely necessary to hold a convention where Canadian Jewry shall publicly declare itself a national entity and organize for political action.

The assembled delegates applauded the man who had just made the impossible sound possible. The longed-for dream of centuries might become a reality. There would be a negotiated end to second-class status when the war ended and perhaps a realization of the homeland that had been prayed for for two thousand years.

But the Canadian Zionist Federation refused to co-operate — for political reasons. The Federation considered itself the national Jewish voice and believed that it alone should represent Canadian Jewry at the eventual peace conference. No one put it more bluntly than did Leon Goldman, the Chairman of the Zionist Bureau, a few years later.

> We Zionists resent [interference] in that work which is peculiarly our own province. To put it mildly, it would be a pretty cool presumption for any party of men to come at this late date to us Zionists and tell us that we are to stand aside and allow them to do our work...when after twenty-one years of hard work we are finally accomplishing the task of regaining Palestine as the national home of the Jews.

The Canadian Zionist Federation believed in colonization and growth in Palestine, but they were opposed to the
Labour Zionist demand that some sort of legal charter
precede such a program. In 1909 Clarence de Sola had
made his position unmistakably clear:

It is not true that Zionism aimed at creating an independent state in Palestine....Look at our Basle pro-
gramme....It simply declares that we seek a "publicly
legally secured home in Palestine"...and as long as that
home is under protection of a strong, just and honest
Turkish government, what more can we possibly ask
for?...Where they may develop their lives on Jewish
lines and live free and untrammelled as one of the
nations that go to make up the Turkish Empire....I am
positive that the Turkish government will find no truer,
no more loyal and no more devoted subjects than the
Jews.

So the Zionist Federation called a counter-conference.
They were joined by wealthy uptown Jews who objected to
the idea that Jews within Canada constituted a national
group, by Orthodox Jews who objected to the irreligious
attitudes of many in the labour-dominated Alliance, and by
Reform Jews who considered Judaism as a religion only and
also rejected Jewish ethnic nationalism. The Conference, as
this disparate group called itself, sent out invitations to *its*
meeting. It was an invitation to open war.

The bitterness and division that the warring factions
caused within the Canadian Jewish community were unpre-
cedented. The Winnipeg Committee wrote to the Conference "strongly disapproving" of being asked to break a still
fragile unity, and to the Alliance demanding the avoidance
of "an inexplicable and inexcusable rupture in our united
forces at this vital moment". At a meeting in London,
Ontario, it was charged that the Conference was using
disruptive techniques to destroy the London branch of the

Alliance. "Our meeting was brought into disorder by our Zionist delegates with the help of the orthodox delegates and their supporters," wrote Richmond, the secretary of the committee. "The issue was voting rights for women. The Zionist and their allies would not permit women to vote....Nor did they permit women to speak in defence of their position. The sense of the meeting was naturally against their stand, so they disrupted the meeting with their shouts until the chairman was forced to adjourn."

The Conference went ahead regardless and held a meeting on November 14, 1915, at the Gayety Theatre in Montreal. The hall was studded with the big names of the Jewish establishment. Clarence de Sola, Lyon Cohen, Michael Hirsch, Maxwell Goldstein, and Nathan Gordon were there. Other delegates arrived from Ottawa, Winnipeg, Hamilton, Vancouver, Calgary, Toronto, Edmonton, Saskatoon, Saint John, and Regina. Excluding the idea of a national homeland for the Jews, their goals were basically the same as those of the Alliance. They wanted to ensure Jewish representation at the peace talks and equal rights for Jews in the countries of their birth.

It was a great event—but nothing came of it. Only the relief committee continued to function after the meeting.

A similar fate awaited the Alliance. Its members met again in Toronto on February 6, 1916, and pledged their efforts towards representation at an eventual peace conference. But in their case as well nothing survived the meeting except the maintenance of relief work.

For almost three years the idea of a united congress lay dormant and it looked as though the historical moment which would certainly occur at the end of the war would bypass Canadian Jews. But the election of American delegates to an American Jewish Congress, just weeks after the war ended, gave the Canadian disputants a needed shot in the arm. H. M. Caiserman was asked by the Alliance to attempt to forge a union between the Zionist Federation and the labour groups of the Alliance. His efforts were successful. Lyon Cohen, always the diplomat and respected mediator, brought in the wealthy community that was fiercely opposed to Jewish nationalism. A. J. Freiman of Ottawa and H. Wolofsky, editor of the *Eagle*, convinced the Zionist Federation to join a single Congress. In the end, the uptown-Zionist-Reform-Orthodox coalition capitulated in face of mass pressure from the Alliance faction for a democratic Congress by elected delegation.

The planning of the first meeting of Congress was a delicate affair. It was to be a strictly democratic organization with one delegate for every 750 Jews across the country (men and women). Every nuance of opinion had to be represented — and that meant a considerable number of opinions. When elections eventually took place all over Canada on March 2 and 3, 1919, 24,866 votes were cast. Almost every adult Jew in Canada had voted.

The air was electric with excitement in the Monument National on March 16, 1919, as 200 delegates and 2,500 visitors milled about waiting for the clock to strike three. The walls of the huge room were brightly decorated with British, Canadian, and Jewish flags. An orchestra played.

At 3 p.m. sharp, Hirsch Cohen, Rabbi of Montreal, walked to the podium. He opened the session with a prayer, an ordinary enough thing to do, but his last sentence was a departure from the words Jews had traditionally uttered. Instead of the famous "Next year in Jerusalem", Cohen cried, *"This* year in Jerusalem!" The dream had never seemed so close. The auditorium of the Monument National rocked with applause, and delegates and guests alike felt their throats tighten with emotion.

The meeting was chaired by Lyon Cohen, the undisputed leader of uptown Jewry (having inherited the position from his father, Lazarus). This was a rapturous moment of unity after years of bitterness and wrangling, but in the midst of joy, Cohen chose to speak of the fear haunting many Jews both in that room and elsewhere in the country. Would a Canadian Jew be seen as disloyal to Canada because he had organized something called the Canadian Jewish Congress which was calling for a national homeland and a declaration of rights for Jews everywhere in the world? No, Cohen answered, for the benefit of those who might have silently phrased such a question. "Abundant loyalty has been shown on many occasions and particularly by the great sacrifices which we have made in common with all sectors of the community in the Great War...."

Later on at a civic reception held by the city of Montreal, Cohen repeated the point. "Those privileges we enjoy here in Canada and which enjoin us to be loyal to Canada is a loyalty which takes second place to no other people in this grand country of ours," he announced to J.J. Creelman, the acting mayor of Montreal, and to the assorted news media. His wording may have been clumsy, but there was no mistaking his concern over the issue.

To initiate an official Jewish Congress with stated nationalistic aims was, after all, a daring act for the many Jews who had been persecuted for their differences and wanted nothing more than to dissolve into a Canadian melting-pot. But the circumstances of Jews in war-ravaged Europe and the chance that Canadians might be able to help end the centuries of oppression had created an overwhelming impetus. They took the risk, and with the birth of Congress, a bold expression of Canadian cultural pluralism came into being.

Two important pro-Zionist resolutions were passed at that first Congress and together they set the tone for the pro-Zionist stance the Canadian Jewish community has espoused ever since. The first was accepted unanimously:

Resolved that the Canadian Jewish Congress instruct its delegation in Europe to cooperate with the representatives of other Jewish Congresses and with the World Zionist Organization to the end that the Peace Conference may recognize the aspirations and historic claims

of the Jewish people in regard to Palestine and that
there shall be established such political, administrative
and economical conditions in Palestine as will assure the
development of Palestine into a Jewish Commonwealth,
it being clearly understood that nothing shall be done
which shall prejudice the civil, national and religious
rights of existing non-Jewish communities in Palestine
or the rights and political status enjoyed by Jews in any
other country.

The second resolution reflected the dominance of the
Labour Zionists in the new Congress:

The Canadian Jewish Congress expresses its desire that
Palestine shall be governed on the principles of social
justice, political freedom and the most progressive
labour laws.
   The Canadian Jewish Congress declares itself in
favour of having the future national home in Palestine
belong to the Nation. The Land and all its resources
shall be nationalized, the railroads and public utilities
shall belong to the state, the drainage systems and
canalization shall be held by the state in the broad sense
of the word.

Then, with a final flourish of pleasure, they also
resolved (well ahead of their time) that a five-day work week
be recognized in Canada.
   The first Congress ended on March 18, 1919, with
applause, handshakes, and cheering as misty-eyed delegates sang "Hatikva" and "God Save the King" from the
bottom of their hearts. But once again a shadow fell
between the idea of unity and the reality. When the Treaty
of Versailles was signed, there was no delegation of Jews
from Canada.
   The American Jewish Congress was there, of course,
represented by Louis Marshall, one of the great lawyers of

his time. The Canadians had asked the Americans to represent their point of view, which they saw as being identical.

After Versailles, the delegates to the Canadian Jewish Congress thought that the issues they had come together to resolve had been resolved. Minority rights had been acknowledged and they expected that the signatures of honourable men would protect Jews from abuse. Relief had been provided for the war victims; and Britain was committed to the Balfour Declaration. So they patted themselves on the back and rested on their presumed laurels; then, as the years passed, they carelessly allowed the idea of a Canadian Jewish Congress to fade into nothing—once again.

The School Question

In the 1920s the conflict between downtown and uptown Jews broke free from the confines of the Jewish world to be played on the wider stage of provincial politics. The issue was Jewish schooling. The downtowners wanted separate Jewish schools within the provincial education system. The uptowners opposed them with angry forcefulness. Intermingled in the argument were the French and the English, in a new mood of intolerance. The field was prepared for battle.

In 1841 education rights had been guaranteed to Catholics and Protestants in Quebec. Jews were excluded from these guarantees, not because Quebec was anti-Semitic in the 1840s, but because there were too few Jews to be noticed. But when the British North America Act gave constitutional confirmation to these guarantees in 1867, the Jews had a problem. Quebec was now thoroughly and officially a Christian society.

In the early years, Jews attended both Catholic and Protestant schools (where they were educated on sufferance only), but they gradually drifted into the Protestant school system. The early Jewish community was anglophile and anglophone, and English-language schools suited it better. All was well until 1901, when a child called Jacob Pinsler won a scholarship to high school but was prevented from picking up his award in the fall. The Protestant School Board of Montreal claimed that he was ineligible because his father was a tenant and not a property owner. The Board had been grumbling about having to subsidize the education of Jewish children since 1870 when legislation was passed allowing Jews to pay their taxes into either the Protestant or the Catholic school system.

Montreal barrister and solicitor S. W. (Sam) Jacobs thought the Board's action was contrary to British justice and took the case to court.

Of the forty scholarship-winners in Montreal that year, ten had been Jews. The Jewish population was increasing at an enormous rate through immigration and a high birth rate (getting married was a priority among Jews, believing as they did that it was God's will that they produce many children), and it was becoming known in the wider community of Montreal that Jewish parents would undergo any amount of personal sacrifice to send their children to high school.

Members of the Protestant School Board shuddered at the prospect of being overrun by Jewish children whose poor immigrant parents paid low school taxes. They also worried about preserving the Christian character of their schools and about whether or not their children would begin to speak English with Yiddish accents. But their knockdown legal argument was that Jews did not come under the provisions of the Quebec School Act.

They were right. Jews did not have a legal right to education. Young Pinsler lost his case, and thus began thirty years of legislation, ill-will, and fighting over the question of who would teach what to whom.

The official court acknowledgement that Jewish children had no legal right to education ironically made the Protestant School Board of Montreal reconsider its stance.

The point had been won, but the Board recognized that the law itself was unjust. For a time Board members and Jewish community leaders worked together to press the Quebec legislature into making changes. The law-makers of Quebec City must have been slightly perplexed by the new alliance, following on the heels of the Pinsler trial, but they were convinced, and in 1903 they legislated three important principles: Jews would pay their taxes to the Protestant panel; no Jewish child would be compelled to take Christian religious instruction; and for the purposes of education "Jews shall be considered as Protestants with the same obligations, rights and privileges."

This system worked well until the early 1920s, when an apparent crisis surfaced. There were now 12,000 Jewish students in the Protestant system out of a total of 32,000, and at the high-school level there were actually more Jews than Protestants. Some schools, such as Baron Byng (known as Fletcher's Field High in the writings of Mordecai Richler), were almost entirely Jewish. The Protestants now worried more than ever about the Christian character of their schools. They charged that Jewish holidays disrupted schooling. They noted that Montreal Jews were still poor and that their school taxes were still low. Then they appealed to the government to overturn the 1903 legislation and its guarantees.

Montreal Jews were humiliated and angry. They pointed out that the noticeable dedication of Jewish students to their studies indicated that the community would not remain poor. They demanded fair employment for their teachers in the school system and elected representation on the school board and commissions.

Suspicion mounted on both sides. The *Eagle* suspected that the taxation issue was a cover for discrimination and ran a highly emotional article invoking images of crying mothers and martyrdom. "Remember you are the grandchildren of those great Jews who sacrificed their lives for their people," exclaimed the writer, in the grandiloquent style of that paper.

In 1909, in a successful attempt to prevent Jews from being represented on the Protestant School Board, a member had made the following statement before a legislative committee: "The Jew is my brother, but so is the infidel my brother and so is the thief my brother...[yet] I would not trust the education of my children to a thief." And in 1910 the rector of St. Mary's Church in Montreal had threatened: "We are determined our schools shall remain Christian schools controlled by Christian men.... It would require very little effort to start a movement...and once that movement were started, it [is] difficult to say where it would stop...."

By 1923 the Protestant community felt even more strongly that its values were under siege. These children in their schools were not acculturated to King, country, and the Protestant ethos. Their folklore was Sholom Aleichem and their history was oppression and poverty. They were "foreign".

For five years the status of Jewish school children hung in a legislative limbo. A Quebec court declared the 1903 Act unlawful and the Supreme Court of Canada and then the Court of the Privy Council in England agreed.

Then, in 1928, with all avenues of just representation sealed shut with the permanent glue of the highest court, a move for a separate Jewish school system mushroomed and intensified among the downtown Jewish population. The uptowners angrily opposed them, and the ensuing struggle laid bare, as nothing else had done, the sharp class divisions in the Jewish community. But this time the battle spilled out of the safe home territory of the Jewish world into the French- and English-language papers of Montreal and the Yiddish press all over North America. It would lead to unimaginable ugliness.

The main contestants in the uptown/downtown battle were, for the uptowners: Peter Bercovitch, MLA in the Quebec Assembly and the first Jew actually to sit in that legislature; Maxwell Goldstein, K.C.; Michael Hirsch, a businessman who was president of the Montefiore Club and a founder of the Federation of Jewish Philanthropies; and Nathan Gordon, rabbi of Temple Emanuel in the uptown, west-end area of the city. Representing the downtown were: Louis Fitch, a lawyer who was so angry at Peter Bercovitch that he ran against him provincially and split the Jewish vote before he withdrew; Shloime Wiseman, principal of the Jewish Folk School; and Rabbi Hirsch Cohen, a younger brother of Lazarus and uncle of Lyon. (Rabbi Cohen wrote into his will that, every year on the anniversary of his death, his children were to meet and remember his dedication to the cause of separate schools.)

The uptowners, who called themselves the Jewish Education Committee, opposed the idea of segregating Jewish students on grounds that a new and irreversible ghetto would be created in Canada. Integration, not separation, was the answer. The children of immigrants must learn the customs, manners, and mores of British Canada and forget that horrible jargon, Yiddish. The downtowners wanted a separate-school system as part of a national, secular movement where they could affirm Jewish cultural rights within a pluralistic society, without assimilating.

The established Jews of the west end were embarrassed. For fifty years they had lived among the English Protestants of Montreal, spoken their language, and been raised in their culture, and now they were distinctly unhappy to hear themselves referred to as a separate breed by the more recent immigrants from the east, the very people to whom they had graciously and devotedly extended the long arm of charity. "Do you wish the Jews to remain foreigners forever?" railed Bram de Sola, a member of the illustrious de Sola family. "If not, let us be done with this prating about a separate panel for the Jews, a suggestion which seems prompted by that spirit which has, in all ages, herded the Jews into Ghettos."

"No!" retorted H. Wolofsky, editor of the *Eagle*. "The uptowners are assimilationists who stand on the threshold between Judaism and Christianity."

Peter Bercovitch countered by rising in the Quebec Assembly. "I [am] opposed to the Jewish panel because you will have children grow up with a Jewish mentality...[in] a Jewish atmosphere," he said. "We have no desire to create a Jewish state in the province of Quebec, but want to be citizens of the Province and of Canada.

"I wonder if the Protestant population of Montreal have thought of what a wonderful asset they have in the opportunity of bringing up some 12,000 potential English-speaking citizens of Protestant mentality?...This is a tremendous asset—to know that they will have soon 12,000 mothers and fathers of English Protestant leanings...."

Louis Fitch rejoined: "These Jews are very active in matters academic and good at things like charities, but apathetic and even hostile to matters constructively Jewish...."

The divisions within the Jewish community made it difficult for the Liberal government of Louis-Alexandre Taschereau to know what to do. A delegation might arrive on Monday and another on Tuesday, both claiming to represent the Jews. And there was no consensus outside the Jewish community. Journalist Henri Bourassa, for example, supported the idea of a separate panel on religious grounds. As a pious Catholic, he thought Jews should be able to educate their children in Jewish schools as did the Catholics and the Protestants. The Protestant School Board, however, was now not in favour of a separate panel. It preferred the idea of segregating Jewish students within its own system. The Catholic community was worried about its own traditional rights should a Jewish panel come into being. And, on the fringes of society, a few individuals began to tap latent anti-Semitic feelings and to mobilize their resources.

In April 1930 Provincial Secretary Athanase David introduced a bill into the Quebec legislature approving a separate Jewish School Commission which would have all the powers of the Catholic and Protestant boards. The bill

was passed into law almost immediately, but Taschereau
had misjudged the climate of outside opinion. Overnight
the small voice of anti-Semitism grew to a roar. Taschereau
and Henri Bourassa were attacked as "Jew lovers" and
Liberalism was equated with "Jew-loving" by papers such as
La Croix, *L'Action Catholique*, and *Le Goglu*, a new French-
language sheet dedicated to smearing Jews.

The direction of events soon suggested, however, that
the careful strategy of the uptowners was working. In late
April the Taschereau Cabinet appointed seven Jewish
school commissioners. Six of them were "Westmount men",
in the words of the *Montreal Star*. In May, Joseph Cohen, a
Quebec MLA, lauded the David bill and the stand of Premier
Taschereau, but suggested that the *real* aim of the commissioners was to reach an agreement with the Protestant
School Board. Between October and December 1930 the
Jewish School Commission and the Protestant School
Board had several meetings, and on December 12 they
announced that an agreement had been signed. Jewish
children would stay in the Protestant system without being
segregated and they would be excused for Jewish holidays.
But Protestants would retain exclusive control and Jews
would not be represented on the school board or commissions.

The downtowners felt betrayed. In April 1931 they
attended a meeting which had been called to express confidence in the Jewish school commissioners. They sat across
the room from the uptown sell-outs and traitors they
despised so passionately. They bitterly condemned the
Westmounters and called for their resignation.

A motion of censure was put to the vote and passed, and
the commissioners resigned.

But their agreement with the Protestant School Board
held. Montreal Jews did not get a separate Jewish school
panel, and before long the David bill was itself repealed
under pressure from the bishops of Quebec.

CHAPTER THREE

Fascism in Quebec

THE GLARING LIGHT OF PUBLICITY that was focused on the Jewish population during the school crisis could not have come at a worse time. Rising nationalism had created a mood that was ripe for the exploitation of anti-Semitic feeling, and, as always, there was a man on the spot for the job. He was a young journalist called Adrien Arcand, and in the late 1920s he entered into partnership with Joseph Ménard, a printer who wanted to propagate the emerging nationalist-patriotic ideologies of Quebec society.

"Arcand made the school issue the departure point for an assault on the legal status of Canadian Jews, whom he wished to see deprived of the rights of a minority in a democratic society," wrote Lita-Rose Betcherman in her book *The Swastika and the Maple Leaf.* "Since French Canadians in particular clung tenaciously to the concept of minority rights in order to stay afloat in a predominantly English Canada, Arcand's solution was to refuse to recognize the Jews as a *bona fide* minority. He maintained that there were only two minorities in Canada — the English in Quebec and the French in the rest of the country. By alleging that Jews were not entitled to minority status... Arcand was able to refute Jewish claims for equal treatment under the law...."

By 1930, Arcand and Ménard were publishing three papers, *Le Goglu, Le Miroir,* and *Le Chameau.* Their editorial stance was nationalist, anti-capitalist, and anti-Semitic; their chief targets were the David bill for a separate Jewish school commission, Premier Taschereau, Henri Bourassa, and Jews in general.

Arcand and Ménard did not originate ideas of racial nationalism, nor did they invent fascism in Quebec. They merely dipped into a stream of Quebec intellectual life that had been on the rise since about the time of the First World War. Perhaps Jewish "Anglos" were easier targets for the resentment of French Quebecers like Arcand than were the powerful Anglo-Saxon barons themselves, particularly when wave after wave of immigration brought penniless Jewish peddlers who threw packs on their backs and travelled into the countryside competing directly with French-Canadian merchants.

Overt anti-Semitism had been surfacing since about 1913 when a small, expensively produced book of anti-Semitic cartoons called *Montréal Juif: Dessins Gais* was published in Montreal. Although the Jews were stereotyped as physically ugly in a style not unlike the later work of Nazi cartoonist Julius Streicher, the focus of the J. Charlebois cartoons was economic rivalry. The local Jewish haberdasher (who probably started with a pack on his back) was depicted in one cartoon as robbing the innocent young Frenchman from the farm. Another cartoon represented an idea that still cuts into the raw nerve of Québécois sensibilities — the fear of being overrun, overtaken, of becoming second-class citizens in their own province. Two wealthy men wearing top hats and black frock-coats look over a Quebec countryside which is empty except for one church and a couple of buildings. "Isaac," says one of these unsavoury characters to the other, "in fifty years we will be the masters."

Nine years later, in 1922, an important novel was published in French Canada called, significantly, *L'Appel de la Race*. The book first appeared under a pseudonym, but the real author was soon discovered to be Lionel Groulx, a

Catholic priest. The abbé Groulx's story, a political allegory, caused a sensation and became the most talked-about event in Quebec until well into the summer of 1923.

L'Appel de la Race portrayed a mystical form of nationalism in which the spiritual well-being of the hero is tied to his rejection of everything foreign (he is married to a Protestant) and a return to his roots in the breast and soul of French Canada. There was no room for the Jew or any other "foreigner" in this vision of Quebec, and Groulx's views provided fertile soil for the later development of fascism. (In 1933, the abbé himself began to publish a paper called *L'Action Nationale*, in which the idea of dictatorship was praised.)

Adrien Arcand and Joseph Ménard found themselves closely in tune with the ideas of the abbé and his disciples, and in 1929 they expanded their publishing interests to form a political movement known as L'Ordre Patriotique des Goglus. Its platform was the usual collection of values cherished by the political right, but tailored to Quebec. The *Goglus* promoted the conservation of "our Latin character", the purification of society, the cleansing of politics, and the promotion of the keep-the-money-at-home ("achat chez nous") movement. By 1930 they claimed to have 50,000 members and had devised an organizational structure based on Mussolini's fascist Italian state. As for the abbé, his *L'Action Nationale* alleged that politicians had turned Jews into a privileged caste by giving them two seats in the provincial legislature instead of amalgamating the Jewish district into one seat, then suggested that Jews had tampered with election returns. *L'Action Nationale* also charged that Jewish merchants had a monopoly over commerce, that they had taken over the professions, and that a tougher quota in the universities ought to be established. It argued that Jews had no right to seek representation on the Protestant School Board and that all Jews were pro-communist in their sympathies.

But the most important single article concerning Jews

in *L'Action Nationale* was written by one of the directors, Anatole Vanier, and published in September 1933, the year Hitler became Chancellor of Germany. Vanier argued that the Jews of Germany deserved what they were getting. "The problem posed by the Jews in Quebec is the same problem they pose everywhere," he wrote.

> ... They are a people within a people and that's the way they like it.... They want the top jobs in Germany, the United States, in Canada and in Quebec and in order to obtain their desire, they lean, at will, on "principles" of liberalism which impress some of our own people if they are naïve and lacking in nationalism. But who is responsible for problems if Germans [and] French Canadians want to live in their own way and be masters in their own house?...Why don't [Jews] meditate on the tragic struggle...of people who are pushed around by newcomers? Why don't they think about the impudent cry thrown out by their fathers 1900 years ago..."His blood be upon us and upon our children"? By their dispersion and their persistent habit of elbowing others out of the way, they are the authors of their own misfortune.... What is happening in the new Germany is germinating everywhere where Jews are considered as intruders. And where, one may well ask, are they considered otherwise?

That same year a group of militant young students created an organization called Le Jeune Canada. One of their first activities was the publication of a pamphlet called *Politiciens et Juifs* (Politicians and Jews), in which the familiar themes of Jewish financial domination, Jewish communism, and the terrors of Jewish immigration were expounded. One of the contributors to *Politiciens et Juifs* was the young André Laurendeau, who, in another era, would head the Royal Commission on Bilingualism and Biculturalism. While allowing that Jews were peaceful citizens,

Laurendeau assured his readers that "Jews aspire...to the happy day when their race will dominate the world."*

Jews were unpopular in Quebec not least because they promoted liberal ideas such as egalitarianism and secularism (they had been liberated from the ghettos of western Europe by just such ideas), and Pope Pius XI had made it quite clear that the Catholic Church and liberalism were at cross-purposes. Jews were disliked because they were militantly anti-fascist. And the fact of the Great Depression did not enhance their popularity. In Quebec in the 1930s it wasn't difficult to blame one's misery on the "Anglo" in general and the Jew in particular.

On the political front, Arcand and Ménard claimed the growing successes of German fascism as proof of the justness of their anti-Semitic campaigns, and they took credit for the repeal of the bill for a separate Jewish panel, calling it "a triumph for the *Goglus*". Indeed, they became so effective that Conservative leader R. B. Bennett guaranteed them $25,000 if they could help his party win more than twelve Quebec seats in the 1930 general election.†

Arcand began to make speeches. "At a mass meeting in November 1930 at the Monument National in Montreal, his [Arcand's] audience was told that Jews isolated themselves, were materialistic, controlled the means of communication including the film industry, regarded themselves as the chosen people, promoted such 'evil' ideas as internationalism and liberalism, and were the cause of the Bolshevik Revolution. (Ménard contributed lasciviousness to the list.)" wrote Lita-Rose Betcherman.

The *Goglus* movement fanned into Ontario, and to a minor degree into the West. The anti-Semitism in their

*To his credit, Laurendeau changed his mind after seeing Hitlerism in operation.

†Bennett won twenty-four seats in Quebec, but according to Lita-Rose Betcherman, Arcand and Ménard were paid only $18,000. However, by 1936 "a Conservative organizer estimated that the party had spent $27,000 on *Le Goglu* and its affiliates."

papers became more and more virulent, turning off sophis-
ticated readers with articles on "The Drinkers of Blood"
and "Jewish Cannibalism", but succeeding in its appeal to
the credulous and the uneducated. In 1938 a letter from
Quebec arrived on Mackenzie King's desk. "Without the
Jewish argument, Arcand will get nowhere in Quebec.
French-Canadians are educated in their early childhood to
hate the Jews," wrote the author, a French Canadian.

Widespread, organized fascism died in Quebec in 1939,
athough not from moral repugnance. It died because Canada entered a war against a fascist country. The *Goglus* went
underground or disappeared, and the anti-Semitic, pro-
fascist newspapers stopped publishing. Adrien Arcand was
arrested as a threat to national security and interned for the
duration of the war.

CHAPTER FOUR

The Department of Immigration and the Rise of Hitler

XENOPHOBIA AND ANTI-SEMITISM were less blatant elsewhere in Canada during the 1930s, but they were there all the same and most acutely visible in changing attitudes towards immigration.

By 1933 the bottom had dropped out of the Canadian economy. Twenty-nine per cent of the work force was unemployed and one out of every ten people in the country was on direct relief. No more immigration, shouted the Canadian labour movement; what few jobs exist must go to Canadians. So, in 1929, then again in 1930, and in 1931, new orders-in-council were passed, and with a bang and a clatter the doors to Canada slammed shut. With the exception of citizens from Britain, the other Dominions in the British Empire, and the United States, only three categories of immigrants would be allowed into the country: farmers with enough money to start work right away; wives and unmarried children under the age of eighteen whose "head of the family" was already in Canada; and girls coming to be married. Everyone else would be admitted only by individual order-in-council.

Although over 48,000 Jews had migrated to Canada during the 1920s (3.9 per cent of total immigration), Jewish immigration had never been quite like the rest. Jews were not able to enter Canada along with other immigrants from the same countries of birth—from Poland, or from

Lithuania, or from Romania. They were identified not as nationals but according to racial orgin, as Hebrews, and they needed a special permit which was issued by the Department of Immigration before they were allowed to buy a steamship ticket. Immigrants who were ignorant of these special considerations were turned back at the end of their voyage. Sometimes the special treatment emerged during the entrance medical examination. One doctor in the late 1920s had a habit of asking Jews to race around a room at top speed; then he would disallow them on the grounds that their hearts weren't strong enough. And the 1931 order-in-council regarding the immigration of farmers specifically excluded Jewish farmers. They were obliged to apply for a special permit.

In the decade after the war and before the Depression it was recognized that Canada needed immigration to settle its empty spaces, but attitudes to foreigners were becoming increasingly racist. The anti-immigration lobby accused foreigners of belonging to inferior racial stock, of being unassimilable (a favourite word of the day), or of being a menace (another favourite word) to unquestionably superior British institutions and values. Immigrants were also accused of lowering the standard of living, of creating crime, and of filling insane asylums.

Such accusations were found not only in the gutter press but in more respectable places as well. In the late 1920s the *Queen's Quarterly*, then as now a reputable university journal, published two articles, one entitled "The Immigration Problem In Canada", by W. A. Carrothers, and the other, "The Case for a Quota", by W. Burton Hurd. For these writers, non-white immigration was written off as "impossible". "We cannot assimilate the yellow, black or brown races... any race that cannot blend satisfactorily is a menace," wrote Carrothers. Hurd moved even closer to the emotional crux of the matter when he worried about "the high fertility of certain foreign stocks".

The fear-of-foreign-stock arguments were reflected in

Britain as late as 1938, ironically on the very eve of the collapse of the Empire. At the New Empire Development Conference in Glasgow in July of that year, Vice-Admiral E. A. Taylor "warned...against the consequence of failure to populate the vacant cultivatable areas of the Empire by men and women of British speaking stock. 'The only alternative,' he said, 'is to have an ever-increasing proportion of foreign nationals settling there, nationals who in so many instances have not the same democratic outlook, the same mentality and the same ideals of language. It will mean that sooner or later, these ideals which we hold so dear may be so watered down by direct foreign influence that our Empire will lose its character, and in my humble opinion, its great influence and power for good in the world.'"*

Across the sea in Germany the rise of Hitlerism was creating a new urgency for Jews. They were being deprived of citizenship and driven out of public life. They were hunted, humiliated, and stripped of prestige, their possessions, and all rights. By 1939 a million European Jews had left or escaped their countries of birth and were wandering in the no-man's-land between the borders of European states. The question was, where to go?

Canada's official attitude to events in Europe was isolationist and smug. Europe's problems should remain Europe's problems. As early as 1924 Senator Raoul Dandurand was boasting to the League of Nations in Geneva that "we [in Canada] think in terms of peace while Europe...thinks in terms of war." In September 1936 Prime Minister Mackenzie King advised the League of Nations to be more civilized, more like Canada and the United States, who had ceased "to rely on force [and now] looked to reason as a method of solving their differences."

*This report from the *Glasgow Herald* found its way into the files of the Leader of the Opposition, R. B. Bennett.

Nations, like people, should improve themselves, King believed.

Mackenzie King's attitude to the League of Nations was "one of studied neglect", according to his official biographer, W. A. Riddell. King embraced the disease theory of politics. The virulent infection ravaging Europe might turn out to be contagious. Safety lay in keeping the distasteful messes of lesser nations at a distance.

As a consensus politician, King found plenty of support for his policy. Quebec was anti-immigration on religious and cultural grounds; Anglo-Saxons were anti-immigration on cultural grounds; and everyone was caught in the tight squeeze of an economic depression. "Never was Mackenzie King more satisfied than when enunciating the dictum that his country was difficult to govern...," historian James Eayrs has commented. "Canada's policy was reduced to the lowest common denominator of public agreement."

Ordinary Canadians were not unaware of the desperate Jewish refugees across the Atlantic, but if immigration was generally undesirable, Jewish immigration — refugees or no — was particularly undesirable. Although the real peril of the day was fascism, people worried mainly about communism. And Jews were thought to be communists. The total number of Jews in the Communist Party of Canada in 1937 has been estimated at about four hundred and fifty. But the label stuck.

In Europe, Canada was perceived as a remote, mysterious, red Commonwealth blob on a school map. For refugees clinging to life by their fingernails, Canada was the country whose doors seemed to be most tightly shut of all. When Auschwitz concentration camp became an extermination centre, "Canada" was the name given to the area where victims' belongings were squirrelled away. In inmates' slang, "Canada" meant "an abundance of everything, off limits and closely guarded".

That Canada was anti-Semitic in attitude at a time when

the Jews of Europe were most desperate is unmistakably demonstrated by an opinion poll taken in 1946, after the war had ended and after the concentration camps had thrown up their ghoulish remains to public view. The question asked was: If Canada allows more immigration, are there any of these nationalities which you would like to keep out? Forty-nine per cent of those polled named the Jews. That figure was less than the sixty per cent who picked the Japanese (who had been interned in Canada during the war), but significantly more than the thirty-four per cent who named the Germans, against whom the war had been fought. The results looked like this:

	%		%
Japanese	60	Middle European	16
Jewish	49	Ukrainian	15
German	34	Polish	14
Russian	33	Others	3
Negro	31	None	18
Italian	25	No answer	7
Chinese	24		

Behind the Scenes on Parliament Hill

By 1936 the economy had begun to recover and the federal government cautiously allowed a modest increase in immigration. But Jews were an exception to the new rule; Jewish immigration continued to decrease. In 1935, 880 Jews entered Canada through special orders-in-council; in 1936 only 619 squeezed through; in 1937 the total number had dropped to 584, representing 3.7 per cent of total immigration that year. In 1938–39, at the final hour before war, the figure rose slightly to 890 as the King government was prevailed upon to accept several hundred families who were slated to take up farming under the financial guarantee of the Canadian Jewish Congress.

The fact that Canada's Jewish immigration decreased while a tragedy was being enacted across the sea, and while over-all immigration was increasing, can be traced to indifference and moral cowardice at the seat of power. Directly involved were two prime ministers, R. B. Bennett and Mackenzie King; Mackenzie King's trusted Quebec advisor, Ernest Lapointe (Lapointe was King's Minister of Justice and probably closer to him than anyone else in Ottawa); two immigration ministers, W. A. Gordon and Thomas Crerar; and several individuals in the civil service — O. D. Skelton, Under-Secretary of State for External Affairs, who, by his quiet acquiescence, allowed official positions to harden; Vincent Massey, Canada's High Commissioner in London, whose opposition to the immigration of Jewish refugees was influenced by his "appeaser" friends in the fashionable Cliveden set; and W. J. Egan, J. Magladery, and F. C. Blair, all deputy ministers of immigration during the 1930s. Elected ministers came and went according to the vagaries of public whim and prime-ministerial favour, but it was the top civil servants who remained and who knew the workings of their departments. It was they who advised and were heeded.

Fighting a losing battle for the admittance of Jewish refugees were three elected Jews in the federal House of Commons: S. W. (Sam) Jacobs, Liberal from Montreal; A. A. Heaps, CCF from Winnipeg; and Sam Factor, Liberal from Toronto. Also active in this cause were the Canadian Jewish Congress (which reconvened in 1934 and elected Jacobs president), and the Canadian National Committee on Refugees (formed in the late 1930s under the chairmanship of Senator Cairine Wilson).

The pressure to admit refugees began almost simultaneously with Hitler's ascent to power in January 1933. In April, the Montreal Jewish community held a public rally to protest the treatment of Jews in Germany. The mayor of Montreal presided. The very popular senator Raoul Dandurand was present, as was a representative of the

Taschereau government who spoke, perhaps wistfully, of the legacy of tolerance in Quebec. The Protestant clergy also turned up. The Catholic clergy did not.

The tone of the rally was shocked disbelief that such things could happen in the modern world, but the meeting did not go unnoticed by Le Jeune Canada, which held a counter-protest on April 21. The news out of Germany and the possibility that refugees might be admitted to Canada served to mobilize much of right-wing Quebec, and organizations quickly passed anti-Semitic resolutions which were hurriedly forwarded to Ottawa. One organization, La Fédération des Clubs Ouvriers, was so admiring of German fascism that its members began to sport brown shirts and paste anti-Semitic signs on store windows. La Ligue de l'Action Nationale sent a resolution (signed by Anatole Vanier) asking that Canadian immigration be stopped altogether so that "the government of Canada can remain perfectly resistant before Jewish pressure...so that no favour be shown to that element which the German government has accused of being communists and Marxists...and which, by their faith, their customs, and their unassimilable character are a source of division, dispute and weakness for Canada." The St. Jean Baptiste Society and the Association des Voyageurs de Commerce du Canada sent a protest which asserted confidently, "We know that you don't want Jews any more than we do, but we are sending this letter so you'll know that we all share the same opinion on this point." The St. Jean Baptiste Society also took an active role in sponsoring public meetings on "The Jewish Question" throughout Quebec at which Arcand or Ménard were featured.

In May, the Jewish Immigrant Aid Society of Montreal received a cable from HICEM* (a central body created in

*HICEM. The name was composed of three acronyms. HI stood for HIAS (Hebrew Immigrant Aid Society); IC represented the phonetic pronunciation of the JCA (Jewish Colonization Association); and EM stood for "emig-direkt", an organization that originated in Russia.

1927 in Paris to deal with Jewish migration in Europe) requesting that the Canadian government be asked to admit refugees from Germany. A delegation met with the acting Minister of Immigration, W. A. Gordon, but they were told that no special consideration would be allowed and that, in accordance with the regulations, only individual cases would be considered.

The Department of Immigration also received protests from Jewish organizations across Canada, from Jewish and gentile individuals, from the Council of the City of Winnipeg, and from the Winnipeg Trades and Labour Council, among others. But from a political point of view, the voice of French Canada carried the most weight, and that voice, when it reached Ottawa, was almost uniformly negative.

None of the opposition to Jewish immigration was lost on the chief officers of the departments of Immigration and External Affairs, both of whom advised Prime Minister R. B. Bennett. On November 6, 1933, W. J. Egan wrote to O. D. Skelton consolidating the tone for the decade, as far as Jewish refugees were concerned. "The matter of admitting refugees is, of course, a matter of government policy," he wrote with necessary caution. "[However] we have a considerable file of papers on which there are many protests from organizations and individuals in Canada against a movement to this country of German Jews reported to be coming our way."

Skelton had already been approached directly by the German consul in Montreal, L. Kempff. In October 1933 Kempff had sent Skelton a pamphlet which, he explained, "shows the reasons for which the anti-Jewish policy has been inaugurated in my country." He also noted that he had sent a copy to Prime Minister Bennett and would like to send more material to "other gentlemen who can read German and might be interested".

In 1934 J. Magladery took over from Egan as deputy minister of immigration. Magladery's approach was to continue the policy of his predecessor, and he now had even more official ammunition. Germany had deprived Jews of citizenship, which meant that they had no passports and, if admitted to Canada, could not be deported to their country of origin should such a need arise. Magladery claimed that this new turn made it impossible to consider seriously the immigration of refugees. By July 1934 Magladery could also claim in a letter to Skelton that the "economic, financial and social problems" that large numbers of migrating Jews were creating in Europe "would merely be transferred to Canada by the transfer of refugees." Then, with a reference to existing immigration regulations, he concluded, "I cannot see that we can offer any solution."

Although Frederick Charles Blair did not create the attitudes and policies of the Department of Immigration, he expanded them with enthusiastic determination, as Professors Irving Abella and Harold Troper have pointed out in an article entitled "'The Line Must Be Drawn Somewhere'; Canada and Jewish Refugees, 1933-9". It was not a coincidence that Jewish immigration decreased and other immigration increased when Blair took over the post of director of the immigration branch. Blair was a stern man who loved rules, a man who was called "a holy terror" and "the single most difficult individual I had to deal with the whole time I was a public servant" by a former official of External Affairs. His approach to immigration was to keep out as many people as possible, especially Jews. And he was successful. Towards the end of the decade he wrote proudly to a friend: "Pressure on the part of the Jewish people to get into Canada has never been greater than it is now, and I am glad to be able to add, after 35 years experience here, that it was never so well controlled."

Blair was a religious man, a Baptist, and he once confided (to the same friend) that "it might be a very good thing if the [Jews] would call a conference and have a day of humiliation and prayer...which would honestly try and answer the question of why they are so unpopular everywhere.... If they could divest themselves of certain of their habits I am sure they could be just as popular in Canada as our Scandinavians...." The "habits" included the familiar charge that Jews were "unassimilable". Jews in Canada were called self-interested hypocrites who lustily sang "'Onward Christian Soldiers', but [are] content to stay here and grab up all the opportunities."

The job of deputy minister of immigration consisted of interpreting the regulations and reviewing each case that was put forward for decision under order-in-council; but even under existing rules that could have allowed this or that Jewish refugee entry into Canada, Blair and Magladery found ways to block applications.

A poignant set of letters lies buried in the papers of R. B. Bennett. In 1935 the Davidman family of Calgary and Mrs. Davidman's parents, who lived with them, were attempting to get their sixteen-year-old niece and granddaughter, Figa Birenbaum, out of Poland. They wrote to Bennett, then Leader of the Opposition, through their family doctor. The letter was referred to Magladery, who replied through Bennett's secretary that when bond arrangements had been made, the case would be considered. But Magladery soon changed his mind and concluded that "the file was built up for the purpose of securing the admission to Canada of a person prohibited by law."

Six months later, a letter was sent to Mr. Bennett, handwritten in a Yiddish-English script.

Dear Mr. Bennet,

I don't think you know me. Because Dr. Stanley always wrote to you about that.... I am sure you remember the case of Figa Birenbaum the girl we tried to get papers for from Poland. As you will see we didn't get very far with them. Im sure its because you werent there.... Please Mr. Bennet Im sure you can get the papers if you try and please do try as you know whots going on in Poland now.... Please Mr. Bennet dont be mad at me

Aaron Hart, circa 1759. The first Jew to settle in Canada, Hart opened the fur trade in Three Rivers and became the wealthiest landowner in the Empire outside of Britain. (Canadian Jewish Congress Archives)

In 1807, Hart's son Ezekiel was elected to the Assembly of Lower Canada, but the other delegates expelled him because, they said, Jews were wanderers, and because "no Jew should be allowed to make laws for Christians." (Canadian Jewish Congress Archives)

Ezekiel Bronfman, patriarch of the Montreal Bronfman family, came to Canada from Russia in the 1880s and settled in the Jewish farm colony of Wapella, Saskatchewan. (Jewish Historical Society of Western Canada)

Lazarus Cohen arrived in Canada in the mid-nineteenth century and soon became the leading figure in the Montreal Jewish community. The Cohen family maintained their position until they were replaced by the Bronfmans. (Canadian Jewish Congress Archives)

This first pictorial representation of Jewish life in Canada appeared in a Montreal publication in 1874. (Jewish Public Library, Montreal)

Services at the Shaar Hashomayim synagogue around 1890. In accordance with Orthodox tradition, the men occupy the downstairs pews and the women watch from the upstairs balcony. (Jewish Public Library, Montreal)

Mrs. Clarence I. de Sola represented all the virtues of elegance and accomplishment that the new notables of Jewish society aspired to. She was a university graduate in philosophy and the founder of the Friendly League of Jewish Women. In 1918 she was decorated by King Albert of Belgium for her wartime relief work, and in 1923 she was presented to the King and Queen of England. (Photo from *The Jew in Canada*, edited by A. Hart. Courtesy of Earl Kliman)

The crucial work of settling thousands of East European Jewish refugees escaping from Russian pogroms was carried out from this base. The Institute was founded in 1891 with a grant of $20,000 from Baron Maurice de Hirsch. (Jewish Historical Society of Western Canada)

The interior of the Art Needle Shop on St. Lawrence Boulevard in 1925. During the 1920s and 1930s many Jewish girls prepared a trousseau from materials purchased in this shop and others like it in the area. (Multicultural History Society of Ontario)

Lazarus Cohen's son, Lyon Cohen, inherited the leadership of the uptown Jewish community. He was widely respected as a mediator and a diplomat and was the chairman of the first Canadian Jewish Congress in 1919.

S. W. Jacobs represented the mainly Jewish Montreal riding of George Etienne Cartier in the House of Commons from 1917 until his death in 1938. During the 1930s, Jacobs fought desperately (and unsuccessfully) for the admittance of Jewish refugees from Nazi Germany into Canada.

Lillian Freiman was the most outstanding Jewish woman of her day. She was internationally recognized for her philanthropic work and was active politically (though behind the scenes). After the election of 1925, Mackenzie King credited (or blamed) her for having convinced the Ottawa Jewish community to vote Conservative. (All photos on this page are from *The Jew in Canada*, edited by A. Hart. Courtesy of Earl Kliman)

A. J. Freiman was one of the most influential Jews of his time. In 1920 he succeeded Clarence I. de Sola as president of the Zionist Organization of Canada. He was a friend of Mackenzie King and a significant contributor to the coffers of the Liberal Party.

"Now, with a beaver hat, you will look like my friend the Duke of Connaught."

"Isaac, in fifty years, we will be the masters."

These anti-Semitic cartoons were published in Montreal in 1913. The focus is economic rivalry in which the Jew is depicted as exploiting the innocent French Canadian (*top*) and plotting to take over the countryside (*bottom*). (Jewish Public Library, Montreal)

The first Canadian Jewish Congress was held at the Monument National in Montreal in 1919. Lyon Cohen is in the front row, eighth from the left. (Canadian Jewish Congress Archives)

Le Goglu was founded by Adrien Arcand in 1930 and was dedicated to smearing Jews. In this picture Mayor Houde and Premier Taschereau are being attacked for their support of the David bill, which would have given Jews a separate school panel. During the 1930s Arcand led a small but vital fascist movement in Quebec. (Jewish Public Library, Montreal)

Women from the Jewish Immigrant Aid Society (JIAS) in the 1950s welcoming a refugee from a displaced-persons camp (Jewish Public Library, Montreal)

A family that didn't make it. Saul Sigler's sister, her husband, and their baby, in Vienna, 1938. Sigler's application on behalf of his family was blocked by Frederick C. Blair, director of the Department of Immigration in Ottawa. (Courtesy of Saul Sigler)

Moroccan immigrants arriving at Dorval airport in the 1950s. At least 15,000 North African Jews settled in Montreal. (Jewish Public Library, Montreal)

Community Meeting

The Impact of the Election on the Jewish Community

Sunday, November 14
10:00 A.M.

Jewish Public Library Auditorium
Cummings House.   5151 Côte St. Catherine Road.

Main Speaker: Charles Bronfman...

A hastily written notice advertising the famous meeting at which Charles Bronfman called the Parti Québécois "a bunch of bastards" and threatened to move Seagrams out of Quebec. When the P.Q. was elected, Bronfman went to Jonquière to study French.

for bothering you. . . . Ive been waiting for this for a long time. You dont know what it means to us, especially my old parents. . . .

Bennett's secretary replied:

Dear Mrs. Davidman,

I do not know whether the Department of Immigration has altered their decision with respect to Miss Figa Birenbaum [but] it did not appear clear to the Department that Miss Birenbaum would not eventually seek employment in this country if she were admitted. . . .

The truth is, at the time I communicated with the Department they did not favour her entry into this country.

In view of the decision of the officials of the Department, I am afraid there is really nothing Mr. Bennett could do to be of assistance to you in this matter. . . .

Yours faithfully,
secretary

To Mr. Bennet
Ottawa

Dear Sir

Im sorry to bother you again but you musnt get tired of me, because you must do me a favor, and when somebody wants a favor he dont get tired of writing so Im going to keep up writing to you because I know you are the only man that can help us. Please let this mater be one of so many things you have to atend to, as you know how Poland is now, we must get this girl out of there, and if you dont help us there is no chence. . . .

Yours very truly,
Mrs. A. Davidman

Dear Mrs. Davidman,

... Much as Mr. Bennett would like to be of assistance to you with respect to your niece, he is unable to give her permission to enter this country.

I greatly regret that it was not possible to secure the required consent for the entry of your niece into this country.

Yours faithfully,
secretary

The correspondence ended on March 29, 1937. In 1939 Hitler invaded Poland.

Figa Birenbaum lived in the city of Radom. Before the war's end, ninety per cent of the 30,000 Jews of Radom had been exterminated at Auschwitz, Treblinka, and Maidanek.

CHAPTER FIVE

Fighting a Losing Battle— a Portrait of Sam Jacobs

OF THE THREE MPS engaged in the battle for the admittance of Jewish refugees, Sam Jacobs was the senior member. He had first been elected in 1917 and, with the exception of Henry Nathan, who had sat on the government benches of Sir John A. Macdonald as a representative from British Columbia in 1871, he was the first Jew elected to Ottawa. His constituents were the "downtown" Yiddish-speaking immigrants of Montreal and they adored him, electing and re-electing him with huge majorities while other candidates fell around him like mosquitoes in a storm of Raid.

Jacobs was a Liberal—naturally.

Before the First World War, would-be Jewish immigrants knew in advance that in "America" the Democratic Party was better for the Jews than the Republican Party (any party that had the word "democratic" in its name must be good for the Jews), and that in Canada the Liberal Party was like the Democratic Party and therefore it, too, was good for the Jews. In the old country, "liberals" were for reform while "conservatives" supported the old traditions and the established order. The established order was the enemy; it was what they were escaping from. Eastern-European Jews were also deeply grateful for the Laurier open-door immigration policy that allowed them to come to Canada with their families. They were told, and they believed, that Sir Wilfrid championed civil and religious freedom·and was

opposed to sectarianism and racialism. They were told, and
they believed, that the Conservative Party was primarily
interested in the Empire and the large monied interests of
the Anglo-establishment.

There was evidence to back their faith in Sir Wilfrid. In
November 1905 at a meeting held in Ottawa to protest the
pogroms in Russia, he had thrilled his largely Jewish audience by saying, "We cannot bring all of the survivors here,
but, whoever chooses to come will be sure of a hearty
welcome."

So when it came time to vote, the choice was easy. They
voted for Mr. Laurier, who had brought them here.

Before the election of 1917, it was pointed out to Sir Wilfrid
that there was a large pocket of potential Jewish-Liberal
votes on the island of Montreal. Laurier was interested and
began to cast around for a likely candidate.

It is possible that he first noted Sam Jacobs through the
pro-Liberal stance of Jacobs' paper, *The Jewish Times*. Jacobs
looked like an ideal Jewish candidate. He was forty-six years
old and a well-known courtroom lawyer. His father,
Abraham Jacobs, was one of the original group that had
settled along the St. Lawrence in the mid-1800s. The family
was now well-established and ensconced in uptown
Westmount. They were assimilated and anglophile. Jacobs
had married well. His wife was Amy Stein of Baltimore, the
daughter of a respected family and the cousin of Gertrude
Stein. But before offering him the nomination in the newly
created constituency of George Etienne Cartier, the Liberal
leader tested Jacobs with a monumental task. He asked him
to help organize Montreal for the Liberal Party—which
Jacobs did by convincing five thousand potential voters in
the Jewish St. Lawrence–Main district to become naturalized so they could vote Liberal. "I can safely say that ninety-
five per cent of those placed on the list will go to the polls,
and we need not fear the colour of their vote," Jacobs
reported to Laurier in December 1916.

Jacobs admired Laurier intensely — considered him, in fact, one of the greatest men he had ever met. Once, when Laurier asked him to go somewhere to do a job on his behalf, Jacobs told him openly of his affection. "Sir Wilfrid, I love you so much I'd go to hell for you," he said.

The esteem was reciprocated. Laurier soon saw how popular Jacobs was with the Jewish working class and lost no time in offering him the nomination. And to ensure that nothing would stand in Jacobs' way, Laurier personally insisted that no one else enter the race in opposition. His efforts paid off. On election day 7,250 votes were cast in George Etienne Cartier, of which 6,130 were in support of Sam Jacobs.

Jacobs' election was hailed as the beginning of an important career. The Toronto *Globe and Mail* referred to him as "The growing hope of Liberalism in Canada", but the Montreal immigrant community itself lost no time in reminding Jacobs just who had elected him. The morning after the election, the *Jewish Daily Eagle* sermonized its quid pro quo.

> Montreal Jewry have... elected a Jewish representative in the highest parliament of the land. Now it remains for the elected one to fulfill his part in the "bargain"....
>
> Remember that you were not elected by the wealthy "Uptown" Jews but the common masses of the "Downtown" and with the help and support of their Yiddish paper. Remember that the support of this paper was given you readily and gratuitously with the sole aim that we should have a representative and spokesman in Ottawa.

The editor then moved in with specific instructions on the question that was foremost in the minds of many Jews in 1917.

> Remember, Mr. Jacobs, that Jews are now living

through the dawn of their deliverance. In all parliaments of the world will be discussed the question of a Jewish state in Palestine and therefore we expect of you that on this question you should rise to the heights of Jewish duty and act in such a way as if this were your sole interest in life. You must be our champion as well as our defender.

But Mr. Jacobs, as it happened, had two different obsessions....

During his early years in the House of Commons, Jacobs sat on the benches of the Liberal Opposition. He acted as his party's expert on railway law, an important function at a time when rail communication had finally linked the remote pockets of civilization in this huge land; but essentially he was biding his time until the Liberals were returned to power. Then, he was convinced, the tight new immigration restrictions introduced after the fall of the Laurier government in 1911 would be relaxed. Immigration was Jacobs' first obsession. It had begun as a deeply felt concern for the victims of pogroms who were seeking admittance to Canada, then intensified as a steady stream of people poured through his Montreal law office pleading for help in getting family members out of Europe and into Canada. But Jewish immigration had slowed down even further after the war ended, and in October 1921 Jacobs wrote angrily to a friend in Winnipeg: "Should this government be returned, it is all up with Jewish immigration to Canada as I am satisfied that everyone in the Department [of Immigration] is strongly and bitterly opposed to our people. I am, however, confident that things will right themselves in a few weeks."

Jacobs' hopes lay in the young, untried William Lyon Mackenzie King, who would soon be contesting his first election as leader of the Liberal Party. The death of Laurier in 1919 had been a blow to Jacobs, for Laurier had stood for all he held dear, but he had shifted his loyalty to King without question and had, in fact, actively supported him in his bid for the leadership. Jacobs and King were friends, visiting each other frequently in Ottawa and in Montreal. After one evening with the Jacobs family, King confided his loneliness to his diary. "The sight of Jacobs' little child smiling at his father on Sunday revealed to me the security there can be in an infant's faith and trust in its parents. To go into politics without marrying would be folly. . . . Marry, I must." In 1918 King had invited Jacobs to dinner to meet his good friend John D. Rockefeller, Jr. And in August 1919, weeks after the leadership convention which hailed King as a successor to Sir Wilfrid Laurier, King asked Jacobs to meet with him and a few others to discuss policy for the coming session of Parliament.

In December 1921 the moment Jacobs had been waiting for arrived. The Liberals were once again in power. They had campaigned on a platform of more open immigration. And Jacobs' friend, Mackenzie King, was Prime Minister of Canada.

Jacobs was re-elected in George Etienne Cartier with a majority of over four thousand votes, and so confident was everyone that the "rising star of Montreal" would have a place in the new Cabinet that the *Montreal Star* purred with satisfaction. "The addition of the name of S. W. Jacobs, K. C., member-elect from George Etienne Cartier, to the list of possible ministers in Hon. Mackenzie King's cabinet has brought into the spotlight Quebec's distinction of being the cradle of Jewish political emancipation in the British Empire," the paper cooed happily, referring to the 1832 Jewish bill of rights.

But the Cabinet was sworn in without the presence of the honourable member from Cartier.

Jacobs' disappointment was compounded by a bitter and cruel blow. The government of Mackenzie King was no more open to immigration than its predecessor had been.

Soon a new order-in-council was passed further restricting immigration from "non-preferred" countries (essentially everywhere outside the British Isles and the countries of northern Europe).

By 1922 Jacobs was on his feet in the House of Commons criticizing the Liberal Party's immigration policy. Wages were higher in the United States and Canadians were streaming across the border, he argued. The government needed to step up immigration if that creature called a Canadian were not to disappear entirely from the surface of the earth. He attacked Anglo-Saxon nativism and the concept of "non-preferred" immigration, claiming, rather boldly for the times, that the poor immigrant from the south and the east of Europe worked harder than the remittance men from the British Isles who "thought they owned this country". But his immigration speeches fell stillborn from his lips. His colleagues in the House were simply not interested.

Jacobs repeatedly announced, both inside and outside the House of Commons, that he would cross the floor to sit with any party that would promise to pry open the narrow gates of immigration. He even claimed he would start a new party to be composed of supporters of his views, of whom there were few indeed. But there was one person in the House who appeared to sympathize and that was Arthur Meighen, Leader of the Opposition. Meighen had done nothing whatsoever to promote immigration when he was prime-minister-for-a-day before the election of 1921. Under his leadership the doors to Canada had actually closed even more tightly, but he had apparently changed his thinking. By 1924 Jacobs actually believed that Meighen might introduce a bill which would open the gates once again. "Should this be the case, I will immediately go over to Mr. Meighen's side," he told a constituency meeting at the Prince Arthur Hall in Montreal.

Following that remark, Meighen made Jacobs an offer through an intermediary, George Jones, MP for Kings County, New Brunswick. Jacobs was told that if he agreed to cross the floor of the House, Meighen would appoint him to the prestigious portfolio of Justice if the Conservatives won the next election.

To be appointed to the Cabinet or to the Senate was Jacobs' second obsession — he hoped that, through him, the contribution of Jews to public life in Canada would be recognized — but he mysteriously turned down Meighen's offer, saying that he would not become a "turncoat" and that "One Judas in the family is enough."

One can only guess at his reasons. It is possible that the political traditions of Montreal Jews were so deeply rooted in the stated values of the Liberal Party (regardless of realities) that to become a Conservative, with all the overtones of Empire, big business, and Anglo-Saxon supremacy that the word held at the time, was simply unthinkable. It is possible that Jacobs did not believe Meighen would actually act on the immigration question and that in the long run his move would be futile. It is possible that his personal loyalty to Mackenzie King precluded such a move. But the most likely reason of all is that when the Liberals got wind of Meighen's offer to Jacobs, they in turn promised him a Cabinet or a Senate post. According to Jacobs' friend and neighbour, A. Kirk Cameron, that promise was made publicly at a 1926 election rally for Jacobs by James A. Robb, Minister of Finance and Acting Minister of Trade and Commerce in the King government. Robb's promise at a public meeting would naturally be understood to have the support of King and his advisors.

Jacobs stayed in the Liberal camp, but no Cabinet post came his way.

Jacobs also felt another person had betrayed him — his friend A. J. (Archie) Freiman. Freiman was also a friend of Mackenzie King and a contributor to the coffers of the Liberal Party. He was, as well, president of the Zionist Organization of Canada* and one of the most important

*The Canadian Zionist Federation was renamed in 1920 and Freiman replaced the late Clarence de Sola as president.

and influential Jews in Canada. But Archie Freiman was as ambitious as Jacobs, and he also wanted to be the first Jewish senator in Canada.

During the election campaign of October 1925 Freiman's wife, Lillian,* actively campaigned for the Conservatives in the Jewish communities of Ottawa and Winnipeg on grounds that the King government had kept Jews out of important posts for long enough. She was successful, and at 3 a.m. on October 30, at a party celebrating the election results, Arthur Meighen toasted her through the intermediary of her brother, Bilsky, and offered her credit for the defeat of the Liberal government. In the first flush of victory, Meighen also promised to make Archie Freiman a senator.†

"Isn't that a fine spectacle, a fine way to win a political victory and celebrate it!" Mackenzie King sputtered into his diary on October 30. "The cry was that our government had tried to keep out the Jews. Bilsky says he believes had I gone and called on Mrs. Freiman, this might have been prevented; she wanted recognition and adulation from those in authority. I am told that the Jewish vote in Ottawa numbers 4,000 and went straight to Chevrier...."

By the time of the 1926 election, Freiman had become doubtful about his prospects for a Conservative senator-

---

*Lillian Frieman was easily the most outstanding Jewish woman of her day. She organized the relief immigration of Ukrainian war orphans into Canada in the early 1920s and was internationally recognized for her philanthropic work.

†The 1925 election and its aftermath was one of the strangest in Canadian history. Neither the Conservatives nor the Liberals won a majority, and the tiny Progressive Party held the balance of power, but the Conservatives more than doubled their seats and made a virtual sweep of English Canada.

By June 1926, reeling from the Customs scandal, King asked Baron Byng, the Governor General, to dissolve Parliament. Byng refused, King resigned, and Meighen was sworn in as prime minister. Meighen and the Conservatives governed until they were defeated in the House of Commons on July 2, 1926, and in the ensuing election the Liberals were returned to power.

ship, so he made a practical decision which he hoped would further his case. When Parliament was dissolved he told Arthur Meighen that he would finance the election campaigns of Conservative candidates in four Liberal constituencies (including Jacobs' Cartier riding) in return for a Conservative appointment to the Senate. Meighen was delighted. Freiman also had a large financial stake in the *Jewish Daily Eagle*, and during the subsequent election campaign, the *Eagle* editorials went to the Conservatives for the first time in its history.

Unfortunately for Freiman, the Conservatives lost the election. Freiman turned his attention back to the Liberals, but Sam Jacobs never forgave his erstwhile friend. In 1930 he learned that Freiman's name had been proposed for a Senate position that had opened in Ontario. He wrote to Mackenzie King: "You know, of course, that Freiman made a condition as the price of his 'conversion' to Meighen in 1926, a seat in the Senate, and it certainly would seem to me a grotesque situation if, within a short time after, he were to obtain the seat from the Party whose defeat he did his best to bring about." A week later Jacobs sent off two more letters detailing Freiman's "treachery", one to Senator A. C. Hardy, a Liberal Party organizer, and the other to Max Clavir, editor of the *Toronto Daily Hebrew Journal*.

Jacobs need not have worried. Mackenzie King was not seriously planning to appoint a Jew to the Senate, then or later. But the Prime Minister was quite capable of dangling bait. In June 1933 he invited Archie and Lillian Freiman to Kingsmere for dinner and recorded the following conversation in his diary:

> ...I said I personally...had wanted to see...recognition given him and Mrs. Freiman for their public service & thro' them recognition of the minority they represented. [I said] that I had to stand by Sam Jacobs, who was an M.P. of long standing, that I cld [could] and wd [would] do nothing that was not agreeable to him

[and] that perhaps he wd welcome being made a judge, quite as much as a senator, in which event when opportunity came it might be possible to appoint him (Freiman) to the senate. He was obviously pleased. [He] said Jacobs was a fine fellow, thought his partner (Phillips?) was ambitious. Wd like J. [to] go to Senate & he wd run for H. of C. I said Mr. Freiman, we need not consider the partner.*. . . I spoke of my interest in politics arising out of desire to see Justice done minorities etc. . . . Mrs. Freiman was exceedingly nice, they are both, I think, solid friends & and will be an immense help when the time comes. . . . I was surprised to hear him say he was only 54. He looks much older than I do.

When Freiman's name was proposed publicly for a Senate position and his name was not, Sam Jacobs seemed to lose heart. After 1926 he spoke in the House of Commons only rarely and began to intimate to his friends his desire to leave politics. But in 1929 one last hope for recognition flared briefly then flickered into oblivion. A. A. Heaps (who had developed a truly personal relationship with King) confided that the Prime Minister had said Jacobs was entitled to almost immediate consideration in terms of "a Jewish appointment", but King hesitated to create a senatorship at that time for fear of opening Jacobs' seat in a by-election. Jacobs was emboldened by this news and began to speak openly of his desires. "I wish I were in your place, but the gods have decreed otherwise and I am obliged to go to the mat July 28, I trust for the last time," he wrote to a colleague who had recently been appointed to the august chamber. "Perhaps after the election something along the same lines may be done for me. 'Hope deferred maketh the

*Neither Freiman nor Jacobs ever made it to the Senate, but Lazarus Phillips did — thirty-five years after this conversation — under Prime Minister Lester Pearson. He was seventy-three years old and would serve only two years before compulsory retirement in 1970.

heart sick.' And that is the feeling that sometimes overtakes
me...."

But the Liberals lost the election of 1930 — booted out
by the Depression — and the final hope was buried with the
rest.

On the immigration front, things looked equally grim. The
Conservatives never did introduce a new bill and Anglo-
Saxon nativism was becoming a stronger force daily. Back
in the mid-1920s the Bessarabia Hebrew Sick Benefit Society had made application for the admittance of ninety-four
Jews, all but two of whom were refused entry. Around the
same time, immigration minister Robert Forke planned a
visit to Britain hoping to encourage 300,000 prospective
settlers of the proper "British breed", as he put it, to emi-
grate to Canada.

By the end of the decade Jacobs was writing angrily to
the bureaucrats of the Department of Immigration.

> W. J. Egan Esq.
> Deputy Minister of Immigration
> Ottawa
>
> Dear Mr. Egan —
>
> As you are aware the stringent rules...regarding immi-
> grants have made it practically impossible for [Jews] to
> come forward....Our experience with Jewish immi-
> grants, as you know, has always been satisfactory and it
> would be preferable for the Department to declare
> openly that these people are not to be allowed in the
> country for reasons which are not given by the Depart-
> ment, rather than that subterfuges should be resorted
> to in order to keep them out of Canada....
>
> ...My own district contains more than half of the
> entire Jewish population of Canada and unless some-
> thing is done for my people, and to a lesser degree this

applies to Mr. Heaps' Division, the sooner he and I retire from our present positions, the better all around.

Sometimes the Department of Immigration would throw the Jewish community a pacifying crumb, a special favour to head off the most public criticism and perhaps co-opt the noisiest voices. A particular case might be stamped through, probably someone who had appealed directly to Jacobs through his Montreal constituency office or a relative of someone who was close to him. For example, the family of Senator H. Carl Goldenberg was admitted into Canada from Vienna because Goldenberg was a student and a special friend of Jacobs.

But Jacobs' efforts to bring about a change in policy were now looking thin and slightly pathetic. He had always sent Christmas cards and gift boxes of State Express cigars to his friends in government, and more particularly to the officials in the departments whose favour he wished to curry. (He was also careful to maintain contact with Mac-kenzie King by sending greetings and usually a gift.) But as the 1920s drew to a close and the usual channels of persua-sion and diplomacy dried into dust, Jacobs began to send his important colleagues little gifts that would, he hoped, jog their consciences. He gave R. B. Bennett a book on Jewish history called *The Life of the People in Biblical Times*, and at Passover in 1929 he sent boxes of matzohs to several individuals, including the Minister of Immigration. The House of Commons was a club of Scots Presbyterians who knew their Bible well, and Jacobs hoped they would make the connection between the ancient Israelites escaping from the slavery of Egypt and the sorry Jewish immigrants of the day who hoped to escape into a new land of milk and honey. But all he got for his pains were puzzled thank-you notes. "Thank you very much for the Passover biscuits. They were very good," said one of them.

In 1933 Hitler became Chancellor of Germany and the Canadian Jewish community turned to Sam Jacobs for help. But Jacobs was depressed and powerless and could offer only the rhetoric of leadership. He was sixty-one years old and approaching the end of his career. Now, in this mounting crisis, he was called upon to do what he had been trying, but failing, to accomplish for sixteen years.

Correspondence from the central refugee committee in Paris (HICEM) began to arrive. The Canadian Jewish Immigrant Aid Society must hurry. Quick entreaties must be made to the Canadian government to rescue some of the thousands of homeless German Jews. "The future is very dark....Nothing is impossible," a French acquaintance wrote, ominously, to Jacobs.

The JIAS heaved and strained to keep its head above the growing deluge of desperate appeals. Jews from all over Canada with relatives in Germany anxiously sought aid, and letters poured in from all over Europe from homeless Jews desperately trying to trace family in Canada who might help them. The JIAS turned to Jacobs, but Jacobs' "insider" role had become distinctly and irreversibly that of the outsider. He tried, unsuccessfully, to see R. B. Bennett. He met with W. A. Gordon, the Minister of Immigration, and was informed that German Jews were not farmers, and only farmers could be admitted into Canada. But organizations in Quebec were lobbying too. The Quebec City Council passed a resolution stating that it was "in the interest of the two mother Christian races of this country to prevent the immigration of non-Christian persons".

In December 1933 Jacobs wrote to a friend in Baltimore:

> In the period covering my whole life, I have never seen anything as virulent as the campaign which is being propagated against Jews in the Province of Quebec....
> The language used by the American Jew-baiters is mild compared to that here.... I have little doubt, though, that we are but going through a phase of insanity, and that we shall, in due time, return to normal conditions. "The moon is near the earth and drives men mad."

In 1936 Jacobs and Ben Robinson, the director of the JIAS, met with the new immigration minister, Thomas Crerar, to plead for the admission of one hundred Jewish families. They promised that the refugees would be distributed right across Canada in order to "avoid congestion" in any one place. But their entreaties were to no avail.

Jacobs fought his last election campaign in 1936 against Salluste Lavery, an anti-Semitic candidate who had been parachuted into the riding to fight the Jew. He won easily, as always, although his career was clearly coming to an end. But in spite of his many troubles, Jacobs never lost his widely reputed sense of humour. When the new Cabinet was named (without him) he wrote to a friend: "I am seriously thinking of agitating for the creation of an Embassy to Addis Ababa. Being descended from a common ancestor — King Solomon — I am inclined to think that I might be acceptable on racial grounds, if for nothing else...." And when Arthur Meighen expressed disappointment that Jacobs had been passed over for a new Senate opening, Jacobs told him why. "Mr. King gave me Jew consideration," he explained, "but he gave the seat to a Gentile."

In itself the event that hastened his death was not of world-shaking importance. It was a small thing he hoped for — nothing so significant as a Cabinet post, a Senate seat, or even an appointment to the bench in district court. In 1936 he wanted to go to the Coronation of George VI as part of the parliamentary delegation from Canada. He wrote to the Prime Minister:

My dear King,

Mrs. Jacobs and I are thinking of going to London for the Coronation...and we are wondering whether there is a possibility of our forming part of the Parliamentary delegation from Canada. In the past it has been the custom to select from the House a few of the senior

members and as I can qualify in this respect, I am
writing in good time so that the objection that I did not
apply at the proper time might not arise....

King was going away and he advised Jacobs to write
directly to Arthur Beauchesne, who was Clerk of the House
and Honorary Secretary for the Parliamentary Association.

My dear Beauchesne,

I have been as you know a member of the Association
for many years and as this is the first occasion on which I
am putting myself forward, I do not think that my
claims can be overlooked, particularly in the matter of
seniority....

Beauchesne referred him to Pierre Casgrain, Speaker
of the House.

"Dear Sir, Your representations have been carefully
noted..." was Casgrain's formal reply.

Jacobs was turned down in favour of Jean-François
Pouliot, a French-Canadian Liberal. He was heart-broken
and resigned from the Association. A few weeks later the
Association reconsidered and offered him a place, but he
refused. His many friends sympathized with his public
humiliation, but the Montreal *Gazette* was outraged. "Jewry
rests under no stigma in this country... a fact which those
responsible for the selection of delegates ought to have kept
uppermost in their minds," it editorialized.

"My dear Jacobs," began the note from Thomas
Cantley, a friend who had recently been appointed to the
Senate. "From the front pages of the Montreal Star... I see
that at last you face the Wailing Wall. There is no mistake
this time as to the voice of Jacob. As to Esau — if you look to
the Speaker's Chair, I think you may see him there...."

Pierre Casgrain had, indeed, made the choice, in consultation with Ernest Lapointe. Quebec, they decided, ought not to be represented by a Jew.

"To represent Canada at the Coronation is not the height of my ambition, but to have my name struck from the list was the greatest insult that I have suffered in my political career," Jacobs told his friend Harry Budyk one day after the event. Then he spoke of his efforts for the Liberal Party and of his loyalty to Mackenzie King at the time of the 1919 leadership convention, during King's first election in 1921, and throughout the low ebbs of King's leadership. He said that it was he who had encouraged Jews to apply for citizenship in the days of Sir Wilfrid Laurier, and that his was the first effort made to turn out a large-scale Jewish vote for the Liberals. His parting remark to Budyk was, "Don't go into politics; it will break your heart."

Sam Jacobs died on August 21, 1938. Had he been an observer at his own funeral, he might have smiled, ironically, at two of the sad-faced men who bore his coffin to its last resting place. Indeed, the Honourable Thomas Crerar, Minister of Immigration, and the Honourable Pierre F. Casgrain, Speaker of the House, might have themselves pondered, as they walked those last steps, over the things some men live and die for.

Found among the Papers of Sam Jacobs

Sir Wilfrid Laurier has said that the 20th is Canada's century [and] I make the prediction that in this prosperity Jews will participate. . . . Who can say that we may not produce a colonial Disraeli, who will not consider it necessary to abjure his faith because no barriers will be placed between him and his ambition by religious bigotry and intolerance? May we not aspire to the placing on the Bench of men like Jessel, or be represented in the legislative halls of the country by [a] colonial Sir John Simons and Sir Rufus Isaacs? Perhaps it is too much to expect anything of the kind in our day, but could we be assured of the coming to pass of such a time, many of us would be willing to continue as we are, on the edge, so to speak, of civil and religious tolerance, knowing that the time is not far off when there will be one law for the stranger and the native-born, one rule for the Jew and the Gentile, and that no man's religious views shall stand in his way when he seeks the highest position which his country can bestow and to which his ambition aspires.

CHAPTER SIX

Behind Closed Doors

WHILE JACOBS SAT FRUSTRATED and impotent in the antechamber of power, the real business of decision-making was taking place behind closed doors.

Pressure was building to do something about the situation of German-Jewish refugees, but Frederick Blair remained firm. His response to the loud knocking on the doors of the Department of Immigration was to devise new arguments for keeping refugees out of the country. Canada couldn't possibly admit refugees, he explained to O. D. Skelton, because, as they were stateless people, "no other country will recognize their right of return." This argument had been used by J. Magladery, Blair's predecessor, some years earlier and it became one of Blair's favourites. What if Canada wanted to deport any of these people? It would be stuck with them forever.

In March 1938 Blair and Skelton had a bit of a scare. Hitler's march into Austria had created several hundred thousand more Jewish refugees, and additional pressure was being applied to western governments to help. A request arrived from the United States Embassy in Ottawa inviting Canada to join a special meeting of several nations at Évian, France, to discuss solutions to the crisis.

Blair and Skelton prepared a draft reply for the United States with two endings—one declining and the other accepting, with reservations, "in case it is concluded that it would not look well to be the only country except Fascist Italy declining even to sit on a committee," as Skelton pointed out in a memo to Mackenzie King. King reluctantly agreed to Canada's participation on the committee, but only after being informed that there was general international support for the idea of the conference at Évian.

Had the four players, Blair, Skelton, Thomas Crerar, and Mackenzie King, been aware that the American call for a meeting at Évian was in itself a cover for inaction, they would have breathed more freely. But they did not know. As a result, King made sure there would be no question about the purpose of Canada's presence at the conference. It was to be "for information only", he insisted. According to Abella and Troper, Blair then decided on a neat little trick that would allow Canada to make a gesture, if such a thing proved necessary, without actually bringing in any extra refugees. He held up the admission of a few individual Jews with substantial amounts of money whose applications had already been approved by his department but not yet stamped by Cabinet order-in-council. If a gesture was called for, he would bring these names forward publicly.

Such gestures were not called for. The American delegate set the tone at Évian by announcing proudly that the United States would help resolve the crisis by filling its quota for German-Austrian immigrants with Jewish refugees.* The other delegates were stunned into confused silence — but their surprise soon gave way to understanding and relief. One after another they stood to say, sadly, that they wished their country could do more but immigration restrictions made it impossible. The conference ended. It had been a great public-relations success, for the United States in particular; but for millions of anxious Jews it was a disaster and the shattering of last hopes. The Nazis were especially encouraged. As one German paper put it: "The

*i.e., not one extra person, outside an already established national quota, would be admitted.

Évian conference serves to justify Germany's policy against
Jewry."

On August 26, 1938, five days after the death of Sam
Jacobs, Crerar met with Blair. Perhaps he had, indeed,
pondered the sense of Jacobs' life. In any event, he was
clearly troubled by the reports from Germany and by Canada's policy. Perhaps more people should be admitted on
humanitarian grounds, he suggested to the deputy minister. Crerar's doubts were genuine but vague, and he was
easily overruled. "By the time the meeting was over, the
thoroughly confused Crerar had agreed...to tighten
restrictions even further. Apparently unaware of the regulations, Crerar agreed to raise the necessary capital require-
ment of prospective Jewish immigrants from $10,000 to
$15,000...." In doing so, Blair, through Crerar, succeeded
in eliminating practically everyone.

In the few instances where the money was available and
the conditions of immigration had been met, Blair would
intervene to prevent the entry of Jewish refugees whenever
possible. In 1938 Saul Sigler of Toronto applied to the
Department of Immigration to bring eight members of his
family to Canada from Vienna. They were: his brother, his
brother's wife, and their three children; and his sister, her
husband, and one child. Saul, his brother, and his sister had
left Poland for Austria in the 1920s. The latter two married.
Saul Sigler decided to leave Europe. In 1929 he arrived in
Canada.

In answer to his application to the Department of Immigration, Sigler received a letter from F. C. Blair explaining
that only farmers were allowed into Canada. Since it was
well known that Jews were not farmers, there was little
point in pursuing the application, Blair continued. "I
pleaded with him by letter and by telephone. I asked why he
was so cruel. I said it was a question of life and death," Sigler
recalled later. "He did not disagree. He said, 'You people
will have to learn to live with your neighbours in Europe.'"
Blair then quoted the Bible to Sigler, and said that no

matter what happened, the Jews would eventually have to convert to Christianity.

Sigler got in touch with an acquaintance who had connections in the Liberal Party. "Can you buy a farm?" the man asked after listening to Sigler's story. Sigler went to Newmarket, a few miles north of Toronto, and invested all the money he could dig up—$25,000—in a farm. Then he bought eight tickets from Vienna to Toronto.

Each ticket, however, had to be attached to a permit—a special order-in council; and only the Prime Minister could sign such a document. But it was now 1939. The King and Queen of England were visiting Canada and Mackenzie King was travelling with them. By the time King returned to Ottawa the allotted time had almost expired, but he did sign and it looked as though the family would be saved.

But tragedy had already struck. Sigler received a letter from his sister saying that her husband had been sent to Dachau and had been killed there. She asked Sigler to revise the application for seven rather than eight people.

The documents had to be processed through Blair, and when he heard about Sigler's brother-in-law, he refused to issue the permit. "He let me know that I could not bring my sister and her child into Canada because the 'breadwinner' was not alive, but I could still bring my brother and his family. But my brother refused to leave my sister in Vienna. I called Mr. Blair and I broke down and cried. But he didn't care. I said that in some cultures, if a husband dies, they bury the wife with him. I asked him if that was what he was trying to do. But it didn't help. Then the war broke out and it was too late."

In 1941 when rumours of German concentration camps had begun to spread around the world, Sigler called Blair on the telephone. "Are you satisfied now, Mr. Blair?" he asked. "This is a war, Mr. Sigler," Blair replied. "We all have to sacrifice. Canada has sacrificed more than you have."

After the war Saul Sigler learned that his brother and

his brother's oldest son had died in Auschwitz. There never has been any word about where the others met their fate.

The saga of Canada and the Jewish refugees climaxed in a frenzy of activity on the part of the Canadian Jewish Congress and the revitalized League of Nations Society, now called the Canadian National Committee on Refugees. In November 1938 mass meetings were held across Canada deploring government policy, and petitions poured into the offices of the Department of Immigration. A memo was prepared for the Prime Minister which showed that sixty-six organizations and individuals had sent protest letters. The sixty-six included mass meetings of thousands of people in Toronto, Hamilton, Halifax, Kingston, Sherbrooke, Winnipeg, Vancouver, Moncton, Humboldt (Saskatchewan), and Vegreville (Alberta), to name only a few. Nine organizations had written to demand retaliatory action against Germany. The memo also included a list of those who opposed help for refugees. It numbered only nineteen individuals and organizations, nine of which came from Quebec.

But political action of this sort came too late. As president of Congress, Sam Jacobs had held to a low-profile strategy. He feared that loud Jewish protests would produce louder anti-Semitic protests. He was even afraid of the American-initiated World Jewish Congress and complained that "they" would probably hold a World Anti-Jewish Congress. Jacobs and his colleagues thought they'd achieve more with a quiet diplomacy along the inside track. And their policy remained in force until Jacobs' death in 1938.

On November 23, 1938, King and Crerar met with a delegation of twelve Jewish leaders which included the two surviving Jewish MPs, A. A. Heaps of Winnipeg and Sam Factor of Toronto. The delegation had been shaken by the events of *Kristallnacht*,* when German- and Austrian-

*"the night the glass was shattered".

Jewish businesses and homes had been destroyed, families dragged into the streets, and thousands arrested. King had also been upset and had written in his diary, "The sorrows which the Jews have to bear at this time are almost beyond comprehension...."

The delegation suggested that Canada accept ten thousand refugees, Jewish *and* non-Jewish, they were careful to add, and, in deference to the spirit of anti-Semitism in the land, they recommended that no Jews be settled in districts where there was "strong racial feeling". On behalf of the Jews of Canada, they guaranteed that not one refugee would become a public charge and they offered to do everything possible to help the government in any effort it might make. Then they pointed out that there was considerable Christian support in the country for their stand.

Mackenzie King did not let his private sentiments influence his judgment. He expressed sympathy, but spoke of the importance of unity in the country and of his strong wish not to aggravate the feelings of what he called "separatism" in Quebec. Crerar didn't let his private sentiments influence his judgment either. He spoke of the many administrative problems that such a scheme would create and he reminded the delegation that Canada had already accepted several hundred refugees during the past year. King closed the meeting by promising to consult the Cabinet, which he did the following day. But they were opposed, predictably, and King dropped the issue.

Jewish leaders refused to believe their number was up with the King government as, day after day, the accounts from Germany became more terrible. Canada's immigration regulations were now widely considered to be among the strictest and most unrelenting of all nations. All humanitarian considerations were shunted aside, culminating in the now infamous case of the *St. Louis*. In 1939 the ship, loaded with nine hundred Jewish refugees, sailed up and down the coast of North America and was refused right of entry everywhere. Desperate passengers threatened suicide. In Canada, Blair and Skelton and Ernest Lapoint (who was Acting Prime Minister while King was away with the royal family in Washington) rapidly made a decision about the situation. "Since most of these refugees were obviously making their way to the United States it is not clear why Canada should go out of her way to offer them a home in this country....If Canada had invited these refugees it is probable they would have been followed by others. It is manifestly impossible for any country to open its doors wide enough to take in the hundreds of thousands of Jewish people who want to leave Europe: the line must be drawn somewhere. We are already receiving far more applications from Jewish residents of this country than can be granted, in view of which it was unreasonable to expect Canada to take favourable action on the 'St. Louis' group," Blair wrote to Skelton.

There are two postscripts to the events of the 1930s, the first to the case of the *St. Louis*.

POSTSCRIPT NUMBER ONE
In August 1939 a Vancouver businessman called Hugh E. Arnold wrote to the Prime Minister. He had been passing through France and by chance had seen some of the passengers of the *St. Louis* being returned to that country. He wrote:

> These people would have been an asset to Canada.... They consisted of the best type of business and professional people....They were well-dressed, had expensive luggage and were obviously of the intelligent business and professional class....I think that when the decision was made by your government that these St. Louis refugees were not to be admitted in Canada, there must have been some misunderstanding as to their character....

Mr. Arnold proclaimed his objectivity by stating that he was not a Jew.

He got an official reply, but he could not forget what he had seen. He wrote again in November 1939 and once more in July 1941. Each time he was answered by Blair, who denied Arnold's accusations that Canada had closed its doors to people who could have made a valuable and necessary contribution to Canada. Eventually Arnold stopped writing.

Years later, in the same place but in another era, two Ottawa civil servants came across the *St. Louis* correspondence and put the pieces together. Their memo of dismay somehow found its way into the file itself.

> PEQ: Here, at last, is the background to the St. Louis shipload of German-Jewish refugees.... A brief glance indicates that the merits of admitting them were decided strictly on policy, and that humanitarian needs, although admitted as "distressing", could not decide the issue.
>
> F. Freedman
>
> FF: I have read this with surprise and shame. There was no apparent effort to determine qualifications of the persons on the St. Louis. Mr. Arnold's letters are intelligent and suggest that we missed a golden opportunity —not to provide refuge—but to acquire a group of skilled, educated and moneyed people as Canadian citizens.
>
> P.E.Q.
> November 29, 1965

POSTSCRIPT NUMBER TWO

While the power brokers of Ottawa made sure that the gates of Canada remained closed to Jewish refugees, the West was clamouring for immigrants. As early as 1936 the North Battleford Board of Trade resolved that the time was ripe for a resumption of "selective" (i.e. British) immigration. "Send them out to Saskatchewan" was their call to Ottawa.

The following year Saskatchewan presented immigration minister Thomas Crerar with an official appeal "for the resumption of British immigration on a considerable scale". And in 1938, as King and Crerar shook their heads sadly at the Jewish delegation which had asked them to admit ten thousand refugees, a British delegation was tramping through the interior of British Columbia looking for a suitable location for the proposed migration of ten thousand British settlers. The delegation, headed by Sir Henry Page Croft, MP, marvelled at the massive stands of spruce timber and the unpopulated spaces of Canada; then Sir Henry made a speech about the binding spiritual bonds of Empire. He spoke of "freedom of the individual, our ideals of justice, our toleration, freedom of speech and the press [and] the right of man to worship the God in whom he believes. . . ." But he also spoke of the limitations—those same limitations which had, in that decade, betrayed the trust of generations of Jewish Canadians who had given their hearts to those very ideals of British justice. Sir Henry put it all very neatly. "I have always felt that he is a poor kind of brother who does not prefer the goods of his kinsmen to those produced by the stranger without his gates," he said. "It is even more unnatural to bar the door upon our kinsmen when they seek to move from one British territory to another. . . ."

Mackenzie King and the Jews

The bureaucrats of the federal departments of Immigration and External Affairs did more than implement government policy. In their careful way, through their persuasively worded advice to successive ministers of immigration and the two prime ministers of the decade, they were to a large degree responsible for creating Canada's policy. But, in the final analysis, the blame for Canada's record must rest with the elected politicians and with the heads of government, in particular Mackenzie King.

As C. P. Stacey has pointed out, King compartmentalized his personality into neat, self-contained boxes and could operate on at least two parallel levels with little if any cross-interference. So in any twenty-four-hour period he could consult his Cabinet, the hands of his clock, and his dream world. During a state visit to London, he could slip into his private world to consult a spiritualist medium, then return to the conference table or the reception without batting an eye.

King's attitude towards Jews was but another reflection of his segmented personality. As a student in his twenties, he wrote a series of articles for the Toronto *Mail and Empire* detailing the terrible conditions of Jewish sweatshop labour in the needle trades. His writing was sympathetic and angry enough in tone to provoke an official investigation into the clothing industry. But privately Jews repelled him. "There is something in a Jew's nature which is detestable, the sucking of blood," he wrote in his diary on February 3, 1900. Three months later he added, "For the most part, the ordinary run of them have to learn what politeness is, they have little manners in act or dress, are wanting in the delicate refinements of a nice life, have gross tastes and are a selfish, sluggish lot."

Although this revulsion may have softened with time, King was never able to convince himself that Jews were ordinary folks, deserving of the same rights and privileges as anyone else. His ambivalence turned him into the personification of the old joke, "Some of my best friends are Jews." Some of King's best friends *were* Jews, but the friendships were curiously truncated and two-dimensional. Sam Jacobs was a mentor and a friend during King's early years of leadership. King could (and did) reject him crushingly where it counted, but he never forgot to send a personal note when Jacobs had a cold.* A. J. Freiman was a friend.

*When Jacobs lay dying in July 1938, King wrote to recommend that he have all his teeth X-rayed immediately. He also reminded Jacobs that he was keeping a bottle of Kruschen Salts for him which would soon return him to health.

He dined often at Kingsmere and made hefty donations to the Liberal Party which were accepted without qualms. King led him on, but ultimately he turned his back on the recognition Freiman so openly sought. When Freiman died, however, King made a point of attending his funeral even though it fell on D-Day—June 6, 1944. A. A. Heaps was a truly personal friend and when Heaps's wife died, King (who was not particularly well himself) climbed several flights of stairs to mourn with the family. But when Heaps stood before him to plead for the lives of refugee Jews, King remained unmoved—even though he had recently confided to his diary his horror at the treatment of Jews in Germany.

King's general prejudice was such that in 1935 he offered to buy his neighbour's property at Kingsmere for a higher than ordinary price "to save the wrong class of person acquiring it... McLeod said he had it from Joe who says he got it from Francis that Jews were going to buy the property to put up cottages there. This has been started to get me to purchase, but is too palpable. . . ." (The seller was an Irish Catholic and King had a few choice words for him as well.)

Mackenzie King was a man who bypassed psychological roadblocks like a radar-guided bat, and he was never troubled by personal contradictions. At the first sign of impending trouble the spirit of his mother or of a mentor such as Sir Wilfrid Laurier would appear to tell him what an excellent job he was doing. With such august assurance, worry seemed superfluous.

Jewish Canadians knew that Mackenzie King had visited Hitler in 1937, but had the Jewish delegations in his office realized just how deeply that meeting had affected the Prime Minister, they might have recoiled in horror.

King was profoundly impressed with Hitler "as a man of deep sincerity and a genuine patriot". He had had reservations about many things, including Hitler's treatment of

Jews, but after meeting the Führer he wrote, "I felt increasingly in the course of my stay that there were conditions in Germany itself which accounted for much that had been done there which was difficult to understand beyond its borders."

Less mystically minded men than King had been fascinated by Hitler — in fact, King had been warned by a friend not to become "hypnotized". But King did rely heavily on symbols and impressions, and it was particularly important to him that Hitler "did not appear to be the least excited in anything he said" and that Hitler "spoke with great calmness, moderation and logically and in a convincing manner...."

At the end of their two-hour interview, Hitler presented Mackenzie King with a photograph of himself mounted in a silver frame.

On June 30, 1937, the day after their meeting, King wrote directly to the Führer: "We who wish to see the highest good of our fellow man must cooperate in every possible way toward that end. You, I believe, can do more than any man living today to help your own and other countries along the path to peace and progress. What [that] may come to mean to the world, no man can say...."

Until the outbreak of the war King retained his warm associations with the German government through the consul-general, Erich Windels. Windels and his wife dined at Kingsmere as late as July 1938. Several weeks later, King sent a message through Windels to Hitler and to Ribbentrop, the German ambassador to Britain. "[Please] let them know," he said, "that I am thinking of them and have faith that their love for the well-being of humanity will prevail over all other considerations...."

In August 1939, as the spectre of war loomed large and inevitable on a narrowing horizon, King sent a desperate telegram to Hitler. "Force is not a substitute for reason," he chided, peevishly.

But admiration for Hitler was not the reason for King's

ultimate refusal to come to the aid of German-Jewish
refugees. The final reason was domestic unity. And once
again the deciding factor was Quebec.

The federal Liberal Party had its traditional base in
Quebec, and solid border-to-border Liberal votes kept the
Party in office. Public attitudes in Quebec mattered to Liberals, and in the 1930s Quebec was opposed to Jewish
immigration. Then, of course, there was Ernest Lapointe,
King's friend and Quebec advisor. At the November 1938
Cabinet meeting where King, slightly chastened after having met the Jewish delegation, suggested that Canada do its
part in spite of opposition in Quebec, Lapointe had only to
"look glum", as King recorded in his diary, and the entire
subject was dropped.

King made his own personal statement on the Jewish
refugee problem in March 1938. "My own feeling is that
nothing is to be gained by creating an internal problem in
an effort to meet an international one," he wrote in his
diary.

And that was that.

Between the rise of Hitler in 1933 and the outbreak of
war in 1939, close to one million European Jews fled their
homes and sought refuge elsewhere. Of that number an
estimated four thousand were admitted to Canada.

At the war's end, faced with the alarming strength of
the CCF and even the communists, the government of Mackenzie King turned towards reform. In a remarkable
reversal of law, Canada became the first non-European
country to approve emergency measures for the admittance of refugees from the camps.

But for millions of Jews the gesture came too late. And
some say that on the night of King's announcement, Sam
Jacobs turned ever so slightly in his grave.

CHAPTER SEVEN

Modern Times

For almost thirty years Montreal Jews experienced a second period of easy acceptance and expansion. Distorted attitudes about Jews may have remained—a poll taken at Three Rivers in 1960 showed that people believed Jews controlled commerce and were ten times more numerous than they actually were. But the public voice of anti-Semitism was effectively silenced by the shocking reality of the holocaust that had happened in Europe. Even Adrien Arcand was unsuccessful in his attempts to recreate anti-Semitism. He died, a despised man, in 1967.

The children of the downtown immigrants graduated from the Protestant schools and from McGill University and moved uptown into the west-end districts of the city. Quota barriers in the university faculties of medicine, dentistry, and law broke down and the second generation began to enter the professions; a few succeeded in breaking through the fortress walls of the Anglo business establishment. The Bronfmans expanded Seagram's into a billion-dollar empire and, in doing so, effectively displaced the Cohen family as the leaders of the Jewish community.

The community itself began to change. New Canadian immigration policies brought thousands of refugees and displaced persons to Montreal, including thirty-five thousand survivors of the holocaust. More survivors came to Montreal than to any other city in North America and they

soon represented one-third of the entire Jewish population. In the mid-1950s, French-speaking North African
Jews, fleeing Moslem rule after the breakdown of European colonial government, began to arrive, and at least
fifteen thousand of them settled in Montreal.

By 1971 the Jewish population of Quebec numbered
109,000 (most of whom were in Montreal), but more than
fifty per cent of these had been born outside North
America, and only one out of six had a parent who had been
born in North America.

The organizations and institutions of the community
grew and expanded like a living organism, until the Jews of
Montreal were internationally famous for providing the
best social and community services per size of population of
any Jewish community in the world. They created health
services, chronic-care facilities, recreation services, highly
developed immigrant-reception agencies, dozens of
synagogues, and a whole network of elementary and secondary Jewish day schools that ran the entire gamut from
the secular Yiddish school to the ultra-Orthodox Hasidic.

But the kind of concentrated energy needed to develop
such effective structures could come only from a population that was insular and determinedly unassimilated. The
initial reasons for their isolation were obvious. In other
North American cities, Jews who wished to move to the
outer edges of the community or out of it altogether had
somewhere to go. Not so in Quebec. Would a Jew have
assimilated into the world of the French Catholic? Hardly.
He would not have been welcome had he tried, and questions of language and religion would have doomed the
attempt to failure. Could he have assimilated into the tiny
ghetto of the Anglo-Protestant minority which had also
historically rejected him? Hardly. So, like the French and
the Anglo-Saxon, the Montreal Jew stayed within the narrow world of his own community—the third solitude. As a
result, he has remained more traditional in his attitudes
than other Canadian Jews and more orthodox in his reli-

gious practice. His rabbis have maintained an authority they do not have elsewhere and his behaviour is more closely monitored. As one member of the community in his fifties put it, "The Jewish community is like the Alamo and we are our own guards. This is where the attitudes of the shtetl have survived."

Isolation and their experience of anti-Semitism during the 1930s have made the Jews of Montreal highly sensitive, a tendency that has been intensified by the presence of holocaust survivors. In 1972, survivor associations forced the Saidye Bronfman Centre to cancel a production of *The Man in the Glass Booth* by Robert Shaw, a play about the trial of Adolf Eichmann that had been performed, without an outcry, in Israel itself.

Given the fact that almost one-third of Montreal Jews are holocaust survivors, the choice of *The Man in the Glass Booth* was perhaps largely naïve. As A. James Rudin of the American Jewish Committee describes the play, "the central character is the German Jew, Goldman, who lost his wife and three children in the Holocaust, but somehow manages to survive. After the war, he becomes an immensely coarse and crude New York millionaire; but a man obsessed with his own searing memories and the guilt of one who has survived the Nazi death camps. Shaw portrays Goldman as a schizophrenic who assumes the identity of a distant, dead cousin, Dorff, who had been an SS officer during the war. Dorff's function was to murder large numbers of Jews."

Believing Goldman to be Dorff, Israeli agents take him to Israel to stand trial, during which his deranged obsessions "lead him to justify and even celebrate Hitler and Hitlerism."

Goldman's controversial cry is that the emotional appeal of Hitler to twentieth-century Germans is, in fact, timeless, universal, and human. "People of Israel, if he had chosen you...*you* would have followed where he led," he shouts from his glass booth, dressed in his SS uniform.

Shaw's play was little more than a concretization of the controversial theories of Hannah Arendt on the ultimate banality of evil. She argued that every human carries within him the potential for corruption and the ability to commit unspeakable atrocities. In *The Man in the Glass Booth*, "it is simply a question of history that determines who murders and who is murdered. Hitler found his murdering instrument in the German people, but any other people can be energized to do likewise," wrote Rudin in his commentary.

The play was scheduled to open at the Saidye Bronfman Centre on February 28, 1972, and it was suggested by Saul Hayes, then executive vice-president of the Canadian Jewish Congress, that the Association of Survivors of Nazi Oppression actually might want to sponsor the first performance. The Association was interested and took the script away for study. They didn't take long to make up their minds. Five days later they met with Marion André, the artistic director, Harry Kosansky, the executive director of the Montreal YM-YWHA, and Sam Shriar, the chairman of the Saidye Bronfman Centre, and asked that the production be cancelled. They called the script "insulting", "offensive", "obscene", and "an anti-Semite's paradise". They were especially furious that "an anti-Semitic spectacle should be performed in and produced by a Jewish institution."

The officers of the YM-YWHA and the Centre disagreed with this assessment, but they did agree to hold a private reading of the play for about forty Jewish community leaders.

On February 16 the audience included Manny Batshaw, executive director of the Allied Jewish Community Services, Murray Spiegel, chairman of the eastern division of Congress, and Rabbi Leonard Poller of the Jewish Board of Ministers, as well as officers from the Survivors' Association; but the real drama took place during the intermission. "The survivors put on their own performance. They screamed and howled and cried," recalled Sam Shriar.

After the reading the Survivors' Association publicly denounced the play. Eventually they succeeded in winning over all the Jewish organizations in Montreal, including Congress. According to Shriar, only B'nai Brith stood behind Marion André and the directors of the Saidye Bronfman Centre.

When the directors still refused to cancel, the survivors announced their intention to don concentration-camp prison uniforms on opening night. Then they asked people not to cross the picket lines they planned to set up in front of the theatre.

The controversy had escalated out of control and the small voices calling for artistic freedom were drowning in a roar of angry protest. André, Kosansky, and Shriar were increasingly isolated, and on February 24, 1972, they voted to cancel.

Marion André issued a personal statement citing bomb threats and obscene phone calls. "He called the attacks against the play 'deceitful' and a form of 'demagoguery and intimidation'. Shaw's central message is that people 'must continually be on guard against their own weaknesses which make them follow where tyrants want them to go. This warning has been deliberately travestied to make it sound insulting and anti-Semitic.' André called the cancellation 'an outrage...an act of coercion...[and] the curtailment of freedom...one cannot block it at home and demand that it be restored elsewhere.'"

Marion André resigned and moved to Toronto; shortly afterwards the Saidye Bronfman Centre shifted the focus of its productions to musicals and light comedy.

It was surely naïve to expect an academic, tea-party response to *The Man in the Glass Booth* from people who have tasted their own death. But in Montreal that particular exquisitely honed sensibility carried enough political clout to force the cancellation of a theatre production.

In 1974 the same sort of pressure obliged the Saidye Bronfman Centre to cancel another event. Shriar and his

committee had decided on *An Evening with Duddy Kravitz* to
open the new season, but as soon as the announcement was
made the phone began to ring and letters began to pour in.
"They sent us statistics," said Shriar. "Did you know there
are twenty-nine characters in Duddy Kravitz who are portrayed as dirty, ugly Jews? The people we heard from were
so angry we had to cancel." And in 1977 when former
Yippie leader Jerry Rubin told an audience that he believed
Arabs had a defensible case in Israel, he was invited "to
leave the country or get his head bashed in." When he asked
for questions, he was attacked. "We ran out, that's what we
did, we just ran out," recalled Shriar.

At the same time, the ingrown character of the Montreal community has created a continuing, historical commitment to Jewish life that is unparalleled elsewhere. Montreal Jews are notably dedicated to Israel and observably
generous in their contributions to the United Jewish
Appeal. And from its original base in Montreal, the Canadian Jewish Congress continues to serve Jews all over Canada.

After the Second World War, Montreal Jews continued to
look towards Ottawa rather than towards Quebec City to
defend their political interests. They were loyal Canadians
above all and they identified with the national interests of
the country. Important questions such as immigration were
decided federally. Indeed, nothing that could affect Jews
on a day-to-day basis seemed to happen in the Quebec
Assembly; there was no such thing as a provincial Ministry
of Education until 1964, and permits to operate businesses
were a municipal affair. Quebec politics were clearly for the
French. It was enough to have one Jewish Liberal in the
Assembly to represent them.

So in 1966 the Jewish community happily helped elect
Dr. Victor Goldbloom to the Quebec legislature. Goldbloom was Jewish, bilingual, and cultivated, and he inspired
confidence among the French as well as among the Jews

and the Anglo-Saxons. In 1968 Montreal Jews were delighted when Goldbloom negotiated provincial recognition for the network of private Jewish day schools and public funding was finally provided on a percentage basis. In 1970 they were even more delighted when he became the first Jew appointed to a Quebec Cabinet post as Minister of State attached to the educational and health departments, then in 1973, Minister for Municipal Affairs and ultimately responsible for the 1976 Olympic Games. Behind the scenes, the Bronfmans, the Steinbergs, the Pascals, and other leaders of the community had established important connections to the Liberal Party, and they got along well with Liberal leader Robert Bourassa. So, with their public welfare in Victor Goldbloom's capable hands, the Jewish community relaxed. Cheerfully (and disastrously) they continued to ignore the evolution of politics in Quebec.

Crisis struck in 1974. Bill 22 was introduced into the Quebec Assembly by their old friends, the Liberals — and the years of easy living came abruptly to an end.

Nobody outside the French community liked Bill 22, but in the bill itself there was nothing that was specifically aimed at Jews. New immigrants of all stripes had to demonstrate a degree of proficiency in English in order to be admitted to English-language schools, and there were quotas set on the number of English-language places available. But financial support to Jewish day schools was not affected and the outstanding growth of these same schools made it certain that any immigrant child who was not accepted in the English-language system would be educated by the Jewish community itself.

Still, the assault on the freedom of choice that Anglos (including Jews) had enjoyed came as a shock. In the Jewish community, growing nationalism among the French Québécois had been largely discounted. Now the community was taken unprepared. Reaction was sudden and emotional. The survivor element likened the legislation to Germany in the 1930s and a wave of fear swept through the Jewish districts of the west end.

An intense laser beam of anxiety focused on Victor Goldbloom, whom the Jews considered their representative in the Liberal Cabinet. And now, for the first time, many people did not like what he was doing.

Everything about Victor Goldbloom speaks of caution, moderation, and careful attention. He looks like the kind of man who might go to bed in his three-piece, pin-striped suit with the white shirt and the red tie patterned with tiny, discreet white squares. He wears his short, greying hair brushed back neatly over his ears. He is, as he acknowledges, not given to confrontation and dramatics.

There is a quiet understatement about Goldbloom that suggests hard work and bone-honest integrity. That quality shines out of his eyes and is audible in his every word. But honesty was no refuge in the face of Bill 22. As a Cabinet minister in the Bourassa government, Goldbloom's thankless job was to explain the new language laws to both Jews and Anglo-Saxons in his riding of D'Arcy McGee — people who saw the Bill as a threat to their constitutional rights and civil liberties. The voters of D'Arcy McGee thought they had elected someone who would carry their point of view to Quebec, but Goldbloom was a member of a Cabinet that had voted for legislation that appeared to discriminate against anglophones!

The Jewish community mobilized. At meeting after meeting they asked Goldbloom why he didn't react loudly and firmly to the proposed legislation. They asked him why he didn't resign from the Cabinet in protest. At every meeting Goldbloom sat stiffly on the stage, the only defender of the Bill. He always had the same reply, delivered in somewhat formal, low-key tones. To resign from the Cabinet might have been a dramatic gesture, but it would not have resulted in any change. The Cabinet would have gone on discussing the Bill, but without the voice of moderation and restraint he brought to bear.

"Cabinet solidarity prevented me from saying what I thought at the time, but my real feelings were different," he would say later. "I was opposed to the restrictive elements of Bill 22. I believed that parents should choose the language of education of their children and that's why I later supported Raymond Garneau and not Claude Ryan for the leadership of the Liberal Party. But as far as the Cabinet is concerned, it is an all-or-nothing thing. You are in or you are out. If I had decided to move out, as people asked me to do, I would have become an instant hero, but also the instant symbol for the inability of French and English to live together."

Bill 22 polarized the Jewish community of Montreal, as the political question of Jewish schooling had polarized it a half-century earlier. On the one flank was Goldbloom, supported by the Canadian Jewish Congress and some community leaders who were becoming aware of the direction the tide was taking in Quebec and who were anxious to keep the lines of communication open between the Jews and the Liberal government. On the other side sat most other members of the community. They thought that Goldbloom was an opportunist who wouldn't give up his power in the Cabinet and who knew nothing about his responsibilities as an elected leader with a constituency to represent. They called him a sell-out and a traitor. "Goldbloom didn't represent Jewish grass-roots feeling and neither did the Canadian Jewish Congress. He became a parade horse for the French," said Max Polok, a Montreal lawyer who was at one time thinking of challenging Goldbloom for the Liberal nomination. "Goldbloom did a snow job on the Jews," said Sam Shriar. "He was trying to play it both ways and everyone felt deserted by him."

But the loudest, shrillest note in the cacophony of voices raised against Goldbloom and the language laws came from a local, controlled-circulation advertising paper called *The Suburban*, which is dropped on the doorsteps of forty thousand households in the high-Jewish-population areas of Côte St. Luc, Côte des Neiges, Hampstead, Snowdon, and

Westmount. "Goldbloom [is] putting in his time until he gets his pension. His attitude is to go along with the government and negotiate. That stinks. We have to scream like hell and expose the whole thing," said Max Wolloch, the publisher of *The Suburban*.

"To equate the French language with the English language is like equating iron and gold. English is an international language. China is entering the twenty-first century on the back of the English language and here they're trying to tell us French is more important than English. They can get their culture in French, if they want, but don't tamper with business. Business is rough enough as it is. . . . I am not optimistic. The separatists are mentally deranged. Educated maniacs, I call them."

The Jewish community was much too excited about Bill 22 to notice that the Parti Québécois was gaining, significantly, in popularity. People refused to believe that Quebecers would throw out the Liberals who had brought such prosperity to the province. But the Bourassa government was in serious trouble in Quebec. One week before the November 1976 provincial election, a poll showed that forty-one per cent of Quebec voters considered economic management the main issue of the campaign and another twenty per cent were most concerned about "honesty in government". Bourassa had won the elections of 1970 and 1973 by proclaiming himself a defender of federalism, but only seven per cent of those polled in 1976 chose to recognize that the Parti Québécois's main goal was political independence.

The Jewish community had been outraged by Bill 22, but the Parti Québécois was another story altogether. It was a frightening and unknown proposition. Separation? Guards at the border of Ontario and Quebec? If the Liberals lost the election, the Jewish leaders, and through them the Jewish community, would lose their contacts, their leverage with the government. But Bill 22 had threatened even Victor Goldbloom's re-election. Two weeks before election day he was publicly booed by an audience of Jews at the Place des Arts.

Charles Bronfman was pressed into service to save Goldbloom and promote the Bourassa Liberals. A rally was planned for November 10, 1976, in the auditorium of the Allied Jewish Community Services building on Boulevard Côte Ste. Catherine. When AJCS director Manny Batshaw protested that a service institution should not be used as a partisan political stage, he was dismissed with a Bronfman brush-off. "This is war," said Bronfman. "To hell with rules and regulations."

A letter endorsing Goldbloom, bearing fifty-six signatures, was circulated through the Jewish community, but all Bronfman's efforts were not enough. An opinion poll taken just days before the election suggested that Goldbloom might lose his seat in D'Arcy McGee (considered the safest Liberal seat in the country). Voters would abstain or vote Union Nationale.

The meeting was postponed until November 14, the day before the election. Charles Bronfman was the keynote speaker and he hinted at how a newly subdued Bourassa would be more responsive to the Jewish community.

> Don't vote with your heads — your heads tell you that Bourassa's a bum. But he hasn't done such a bad job and we can do a lot of things — those of us who aren't elected — we can do a lot of things....
>
> If we turn our backs on the Liberals...we are committing suicide. It would be worse than a disaster; it would be criminal — putting spears and daggers into our own backs. The election *is* the referendum...a referendum on whether we live or die....Because they are a bunch of bastards who are trying to kill us.

Then Bronfman threatened to move Seagram's out of Quebec.

On November 15, 1976, the Parti Québécois won the

election. A mortified Charles Bronfman publicly withdrew
his remarks, then disappeared to Jonquière for a crash
course in French.

He left the Jews of Montreal reeling in dismay at his
overt display of influence-mongering, but the official
organs of the community lost no time in sending quick
congratulations to the new government. The Canadian
Jewish Congress sent a carefully worded telegram to Premier Lévesque clarifying its status as a non-political organization and asking for a meeting with the Premier to conduct
the usual "tour d'horizon" of mutual interests. The letter
pointedly reminded the new government of a long history
of Jewish good-citizenship. The Board of Jewish Ministers
sent an equally direct message. "Aware of your dedication
to the humanitarian principles of liberty, equality and the
brotherhood of man, and also of your commitment to the
rights of all men to pursue their religious and cultural ideals
and identities in an atmosphere of genuine freedom, we
look forward to your promise to 'make Quebec more than
ever the home of all Quebecers.'"

Victor Goldbloom was re-elected (with a substantially
reduced majority), but for him the victory of the Parti
Québécois came as something of a relief. He was no longer a
Cabinet minister at the heart of government. The Jews of
Montreal were still angry, but there was little Goldbloom
could do now, and they knew it.

Worried leaders of Congress and the AJCS met to discuss the new situation. They were anxious about the fact
that they had no access to the Parti Québécois and no
representatives in the civil service or the government
ministries. The Jewish community needed information and
advice on what moves to make.

So, in September 1977 a two-year project called the
Jewish Community Research Institute opened its doors for
business under the directorship of Michael Yarosky, a social
worker who had been employed by the Jewish community
most of the time since 1966. Yarosky's job was, essentially,

to meet people and develop a network of relationships for the Jewish community. He met Cabinet ministers and executive assistants to Cabinet ministers, key civil servants, and Opposition members who used to be Cabinet ministers and hoped they would be again. Yarosky did not pick fights; he was as smooth as liquid honey.

The response was good, but it soon became obvious that the Parti Québécois knew as little about the Jews as the Jews knew about it. The French Québécois understood very well, they said, why Anglo-Protestants would fight for the English language, but they could not understand the attachment of Jews to English, or why the Jewish community had adopted English and not French in the first place. They had little if any appreciation of the ongoing relationship between Quebec Jews and the rest of North American Jewry. But what did become most clear to Yarosky was that the new government was making specific demands on Quebec Jews. After two centuries of mutually exclusive isolation, the government was asking them to participate in the life of Quebec. And to do it in French.

Yarosky carried the message to the Montreal Jewish community, but they weren't listening. Most people felt frightened and besieged by what was being called the "francization" of Quebec society. Bill 101, which the Parti Québécois introduced in 1977, made the Liberal Bill 22 look like a kindergarten manifesto. Funds to Jewish day schools were now tied to the number of hours taught in the French language, and since they already taught Hebrew, Yiddish, and English, Jewish educators felt badly strained. The new language laws also affected advertising and business relationships. Jews were the most bilingual of all minority groups in Quebec, but most of them worked for Jewish enterprises and used French infrequently, if ever. Their residential enclaves were border-to-border English-speaking, shutting out the reality of a Quebec in which eighty per cent of the population was French. But most of all the Jews felt leaderless and powerless. Accusations of

Québécois-style Nazism flared and spread like brush fires throughout the community. Jewish money followed Anglo-Protestant money out of the province. People moved away—to Toronto, to Winnipeg, to the United States. By November 1978 forty-three per cent of anglophone high-school and college graduates of the class of '77 had left the province, compared with only five per cent of French-speaking graduates. Between 1971 and 1980 an estimated ten thousand Jews left Quebec. Of a presumed five thousand or so who left after the victory of the Parti Québécois in 1976, the vast majority were students, at the time of high-school or university graduation. "We assume that they will not be back," said Jack Kantrowitz, executive director for the Quebec region of the Canadian Jewish Congress.

The real problem was, and is, the old one of Jewish identity. Unlike the school crisis of the 1920s, the crisis of the 1970s did not revolve around the preservation of Jewish culture through the Yiddish language. Yiddish had virtually disappeared as a widely used language. Now English was seen as the repository of North American Jewish culture. In the minds of many, to speak in English was one defining characteristic of being Jewish. To contemplate becoming a truly bilingual community, they argued, was tantamount to assimilation.

No one quite trusted the Parti Québécois, either. The new government was not anti-Semitic, but other elements in Quebec society were looking ugly. In 1976 Yvon Charbonneau, then head of the union of Quebec's French Catholic teachers, returned from a conference in Libya and suggested that all children in the Quebec Catholic school system be taught the relationship between "zionism and racism".* In March 1978 the pro-independence monthly *Ici Québec* called international Zionism "the cancer of humanity". To his credit, Premier Lévesque swiftly denounced the article as "reeking of prejudice".

*It is interesting to note that in 1980 Mr. Charbonneau was head of *Le Mouvement Québécois Pour Combattre Le Racisme* (The Quebec Movement To Combat Racism).

The basic problem was xenophobia. What was a Québécois? Could you ever be one if your name was Cohen or Rosenberg? In January 1979 Premier Lévesque spoke continually of "you" and "we" while addressing a crowd of fifteen hundred Montreal Jews until someone yelled "We're not foreigners" from the back of the hall.

Still another wrinkle emerged in the struggle of the Jewish community against the inexorable francization of Quebec. The fifteen thousand French-speaking Moroccan Jews were becoming more outspoken and more militant. Their original immigration had been complicated by the double-edged fact that they were Sephardic Jews (originally Spanish), while the established community was of Ashkenazic (originally German) origin, and, traditionally, the two cultures had been at odds. Western preoccupations with power, money, and business were foreign to North Africans who had lived quietly for centuries in traditional Arab communities. Differences were compounded by considerations of social class. "What does a middle-class person want with an immigrant from any country, whether Morocco or Poland?" asked Jean-Claude Lasry, a psychologist who arrived in Montreal from Morocco in 1957. "From our point of view, the only relationship was with the Jewish agencies, and of course, no one really loves the person who gives him a handout. There really was no relationship."

The established community tried to assimilate the newcomers by educating their children in English, and the French-speaking Sephardim went along with this for a while. But the rise of French-Canadian nationalism in Quebec had unexpected repercussions. The French Québécois could, and did, accuse the established Jewish community of attempting to smother the language and culture of its francophone members, just as "anglophones" had tried to keep them down for the last two hundred years.

The francophone Jews did not have a history of rejection and isolation from the French-Canadian majority, but they had often felt like second-class citizens in the Jewish community—in Canada, in Israel, and in other places where they lived with Ashkenazic Jews. As such they identified emotionally with the anger of the French Québécois. They spoke the same language and felt closer to French-language culture than they did to the English-language culture of the established Jewish community. They began to "defect" in great numbers. By the mid-1970s, fifty per cent of francophone Jews were intermarrying with French Canadians as well as French Catholics from France. (The intermarriage rate in the Montreal Ashkenazic community is twelve per cent.) Many, particularly the young, sympathized with and voted for the Parti Québécois. They established their own synagogue and their own school. But still they continued to feel rejected by the anglophone Jewish community. "I hurt because I belong to a community that isn't prized or accepted or desired," said Jean-Claude Lasry. "For example, in May 1978 we had a big community event to celebrate the thirtieth anniversary of Israel and all the children at the Jewish day schools were invited to parade that night. But someone, somehow, forgot the six hundred children at the École Maïmonides. Eighteen thousand tickets were prepared for the celebration that day, but only four hundred were distributed to the francophone community. We are at least fifteen per cent of the Jewish population and we got four hundred tickets."

The resentment was, and is, mutual. By his very presence, the francophone Jew "proves" that it is possible to live in Montreal, speak French—indeed *be* French—and still be a Jew. And that news is precisely what the members of the anglophone community do not wish to hear. Their "Jewishness" is bound up with the network of Jewish communities in Canada and the United States where the Yiddish language and the particularities of Yiddish culture have, over the generations, been stirred into a North American soup, then seasoned, tasted, and simmered until a new hybrid culture of North American Jewry emerged. And the language of that culture is English.

To change languages is intellectually and emotionally enriching, but it is also a painful experience, as every immigrant knows. To change languages is to lose that part of one's identity that is created in the continuum of intimate shrugs, gestures, elliptical understandings, and minute nuances that are integral to one's first language. The Yiddish-speaking Jews knew that. That is why they fought the "uptown" assimilationists with such passion. The francophone Jews knew that. That is why they are so bitter at their perceived enforced integration into the established anglophone Jewish community. The French Québécois knew that. They felt the bitterness twist in their gut generation after generation as they were obliged to speak English to get ahead in the very province where they and their ancestors had been born.

Montreal Jews have not been asked to assimilate, to give up either the English language or the Jewish culture wrapped within it. They have been asked to become fully bilingual in order to live in a Quebec that will not travel back in time, given the existence of the Parti Québécois and the fact of the 1980 referendum. But sadness and frustration in the community have deepened. The leadership has gone underground and is generally perceived to be sitting on packed suitcases. Funding for the Jewish Research Institute was cut off in the summer of 1979 by the same leaders of the Jewish community who were tired of listening to Michael Yarosky's unpopular reports from Quebec City. Some say that the Institute was simply incorporated into the Canadian Jewish Congress, which is technically true, but it is also true that its important functions of liaison with Quebec City have stopped. When Yarosky gave a hard-hitting speech in Toronto, in August 1979, faulting the Jewish community on its attitudes and repeating his oft-made assurance that Montreal Jews could once again have a vibrant community if they were willing to reverse their isolationist traditions, only the Quebec francophone press reported his remarks in any detail. Indeed, in Quebec City, the loose-tongued tirades of *The Suburban* are now thought to be the voice of the Jewish community.

In October 1979 Victor Goldbloom resigned from the National Assembly and from politics. He had been out of favour with Claude Ryan ever since he supported Raymond Garneau at the leadership convention, and he clearly had no future in the Liberal Party. And as far as the majority of the Jewish community was concerned, he was not their representative. His views were unpopular. Like Yarosky, Goldbloom believes the Jews must adjust to the reality of a French Quebec.

Although the voices calling for accommodation with the Parti Québécois government and revolutionary change within the Jewish community are generating about the same resonance as a whisper at a rock concert, there are a few people who are listening carefully. They are the francophone Jews, of course, and those anglophone Jews who are willing to adapt to the new reality. Those who cannot adapt will continue their exodus from the province — the young, who are leaving with their parents' blessings, the relatively young with small children, and the wealthy. Middle-aged people who cannot face starting life again elsewhere will stay. So will the twenty per cent of the Montreal Jewish population that lives below the poverty level. For them, there is no choice.

My educated guess is that every day more and more people are coming to the conclusion that many of the excesses that appeared after the victory of the Parti Québécois are receding. The Jewish position is not imperilled by anti-Semitism. Jewish institutions are as well treated as any others and appointments to the bench, to certain commissions, and to advisory boards include Jews. What I fear is xenophobia, Québec for the Québécois. Who are the Québécois? If the Québécois are those who were born of French-Canadian parents, then all is lost for everybody else....

—*Saul Hayes, late Honorary President, Canadian Jewish Congress*

This notion of "feeling good about Quebec" is something that needs to be worked on not only by the government of Quebec which has shown too little... interest in how the minorities of Quebec feel, but also by the leadership of the...Jewish community, who need to be much more visibly preoccupied with helping to continue to make the Jewish community of Quebec as exciting tomorrow as it was in the past....

But I am not optimistic about the future of the Jewish community of Quebec, by virtue of its comportment. I think increasing numbers will leave....There will be a new class of people who will make it—the francophone Jews. Unless you are able to speak perfectly in French and defend yourself in your business, you are going to be totally marginal in this society.

—*Michael Yarosky, former Director General, Jewish Research Institute*

The Jewish community is dying slowly. The voices of leadership were silenced on November 15, 1976, when the Parti Québécois took power. They're hoping Ryan will be for them, an idea Ryan has never fostered. If he is, then they will surface again. In the meantime, they've got their tickets to Toronto in their pockets and they've already moved much of their money out. They're just waiting.

—*David Rome, lecturer at Concordia University*

When we have crossed this frightening period of transition and those who are going to go have gone, there will still be a Jewish community here with religious institutions and health and welfare institutions and all the services that a community needs. I believe that this community will not only survive, but will become, once again, as has been repeated so many times in the diaspora, a vibrant, distinct element within a larger society. But the services will be provided in a French context and the community will be increasingly French-speaking.

— *Victor Goldbloom, former Liberal* MNA

There's a pointed little story circulating in Montreal these days that suggests Goldbloom may be right. A minister, a priest, and a rabbi have learned that a flood is about to engulf the earth. "Let us pray to God to save us," calls out the minister, lifting his eyes to heaven. "Let us pray for a happier life in the hereafter," cries the priest, dropping to his knees. But the rabbi just shakes his head gravely. "Gentlemen," he says, "we have got twenty-four hours to learn to breathe underwater."

PART TWO

Toronto:
The Jewish Left

*The world was as now — people were burning
books and murdering. But then, on the dark
horizon, there was a light. The Soviet Union and
the communist movement were that light.*

Sam Lipshitz

CHAPTER EIGHT

The Beckoning Light

THE JEWISH RADICAL LEFT in Canada had a short life-span of fifty years. It was born during the 1906 revolution, in Russia, and transported to Canada by thousands of newly radicalized young immigrants; and it suffered a death blow exactly five decades later, on February 25, 1956, the day Nikita Khrushchev addressed a secret session of the Twentieth Congress of the Communist Party of the Soviet Union. In that speech, Khrushchev put an end to—or, rather, finally confirmed—the terrible doubts that had torn at the hearts of Jewish true believers for two of those five decades. At last they knew what had happened to David Bergelson and Itsik Feffer and twenty-two other internationally known Jewish writers of the Soviet Union, to the members of the Jewish Anti-Fascist Committee, and to the leaders of the nationalist Biro-Bidjan movement who had been promised an autonomous Jewish republic on the blessed soil of Mother Russia herself.

All those people—many of whom had spoken on public platforms right here in Canada about the joys of being Jewish under the new Soviet regime—all those people were dead. They had been murdered by Stalin, by his police chief Lavrenti Beria, and by Beria's "gang" of monsters, as the new Communist leaders liked to call them.

A life's dream was shattered by that knowledge, principles of belief and action utterly destroyed. The old-time

119

Canadian Jewish leftists were already middle-aged or older and many of them were professional revolutionaries who had never earned a living outside of Party work. But there was no doubting that what they had heard from Khrushchev was true, and this time, for many, the reflex mental hop, skip, and jump to a new explanatory Party line was not forthcoming.

That day, that week, and in the months that followed, hundreds of Canadian Jewish Communists left the Party forever. Their exodus thoroughly destroyed what had been a widespread sympathy for the radical left in the Jewish community and so ruptured the Communist Party that it has virtually never recovered.

Before this century, Toronto Jews were practically indistinguishable from their Anglo-Saxon counterparts. There had been Jewish families living in Toronto since the mid-nineteenth century. They had arrived from England or from Germany via the United States, where they had learned English and North American ways. They were educated, anglophone, and anglophile in their predilections.

Toronto Jews were an accepted part of Tory Toronto, a minor religious variation on a common anglophile theme. As such, the more well-to-do among them were accepted in the highest circles of Toronto society; indeed, one of their rabbis, Solomon Jacobs, moved with careless ease among the upper-class Loyalists.

In Toronto as in Montreal, however, the massive waves of immigration from eastern Europe after the pogroms of 1881 would change forever the contours of Canadian Jewish life. Soon the majority would no longer dream of Empire en route to the synagogue, or think longingly of returning "home" to the sceptred isle. The Jews from the east were a different breed—as different from their anglophile co-religionists as Sicilians are from Englishmen. The eastern Europeans were a people, an ethnic group bound together by the Yiddish language—rich, emotional, earthy, funny, and sardonic in its cadences—the language of the marketplace if not of God (God spoke only in Hebrew). These Jews were a people bound to each other by centuries of oppression at the hands of kings and Cossacks and czars. They had shared a common existence in the tiny towns and muddy villages of their homelands; they had shared the ancient rituals of Orthodox religious practice and had yearned together for the end of exile and the coming of the Messiah. Some who had turned their backs on religion shared a high-minded and idealistic belief in the coming of a secular messiah—a proletarian revolution that would be no less than a rebirth of the entire world, an explosion into everlasting justice and equality in which, for the first time, Jews would share.

So they escaped to Canada, believers in God and believers in politics. In Toronto they settled around the Ward, a few congested blocks bordered by Dundas Street on the north, Queen Street on the south, Yonge Street on the east, and University Avenue on the west. "Construction was dense by Toronto standards, most of the buildings dating from the 1850s and 1860s being stuccoed frame cottages of one or two stories. Rear cottages were a common feature. The streets, characteristic of developments of this sort, were numerous, close together and punctuated by alleys and laneways bearing names such as Foster Place, Price's Lane and Cuttle Place," wrote Stephen Speisman in *The Jews of Toronto*.

"Already at the middle of the nineteenth century the area was considered a slum.... Almost a third of the houses...had no drainage; waste and slop were merely thrown into the yards.... About 10 per cent of the dwellings had no water."

Sanitation was an urgent problem in the Ward. Becky Lapedes moved to Elm Street with her family in 1904, on their arrival from Russia. "We lived in a cellar and the sidewalks were made of boards," she recalled. "And we did not have inside toilets. There was a little house behind our house with a board and with two holes in it. Underneath was a box. A few times a week they'd come and take the boxes away and put a fresh box in."

Within this ethnic ghetto lived poverty-stricken buttonhole-makers, collar-and-cuff sewers, fur-cutters, and machine operators — recent immigrants who provided the burgeoning clothing industry with an unlimited supply of cheap labour. After hours, like all immigrants, they patched together a new version of the life they had left behind. Everywhere sprang up "landsmanschaft" societies, literally lodges or clubs of people from the same town. Men of Kielce, of Warsaw, of Lodz, of Ivansk, of Radom, of Shidlow, of Slipia, of Apt — the list read like an atlas of central Poland.

The landsmanschaft societies were central to the psychological well-being of the community. They provided their members with a refuge, a soothing balm for frazzled nerves, and a few hours where one could be sure that no grating English consonants would ever penetrate the air. At meetings one could catch up on the latest news from the old shtetl, sigh over or laugh at a common remembrance. A collection might be taken to send money home to repair the synagogue or to help the relative of a member make the voyage across the sea.

But the most important practical purpose of the societies was to continue the age-old tradition of Jewish self-help. Jews had always needed to look after their own, and it was natural to continue that practice in Canada. So the landsmanschaft societies became a miniature social-security system. They helped members who were unemployed or sick and paid death benefits to widows. But most importantly, they promised their members a proper burial among Jews. Each society bought a plot of land in a Jewish cemetery and every man and woman knew that although they had crossed the world and borne children in a strange land, they could still spend eternity with those who had also known the ancient marketplace and the muddy roads of home.

Outside the landsmanschaft societies, the old hostilities between the Orthodox and the secular continued to flare. The Orthodox (who were the majority in the Toronto community) worried about this raw country called Canada and what it would do to their children. Sometimes they worried so hard that they packed up their families after a year or so and returned home.

The Orthodox fathers were often exceedingly upright and moral and they are remembered by their children with a love born of respect. Sometimes they are remembered with respect only, for the devout man may have had little time for such frivolities as playing with his children. The prosaic tasks of daily life, which included hugging children, blowing noses, and wiping tears, were often left to his wife, whose job it was to look after everyone's mundane life on this earth.

The Orthodox fathers felt no crisis over their Jewish identity. The hours of their days were accounted for and carefully structured according to the commandments of Jewish law. Compromise was clearly impossible; God's laws were not subject to amendment. Like their more secular neighbours, the Orthodox immigrants worked in the needle trades, or as peddlers selling whatever they could to whomever would buy. Often they were laughed at by Anglo-Saxon children who were partly scared, partly fascinated, by the man in the black coat and long beard who led his old nag through the streets of downtown Toronto pulling a wagon full of junk. But at home the peddler was a man of pride and the undisputed head of his household.

Their children went to school and learned to speak English with an unaccented fluency that would elude their parents. For the children, however, the hours of the day were not accounted for according to the dictates of prayer and duty, and in spite of their parents' horrified objections

many of them responded openly to the ideas of the socialists
who were all around them in the community. Families were
split as parents reached out to bind their children with the
long thread of tradition that stretched into a dim past and
linked them with their ancestors. That a child — *their* child
— might break this thread was a frightening prospect, and
heart-breaking when it happened.

In the long run, the Orthodox parents could do nothing, although to give them their due they certainly tried.
Perhaps no one tried harder than the father of Joe
Salsberg. Young Salsberg would become the best-known
and best-loved Jewish communist in Canada and one of the
most successful communists in the country (he sat on the
Toronto City Council, then represented the Party in the
Ontario Legislature from 1943 until 1955). But he was
raised in an ultra-Orthodox family, and in 1918, when he
took his first independent step and decided to join the
youth group of the left-wing Labour Zionists, his father was
devastated.

"My father and one of his friends who used to eat the
Sabbath meal with us tried to convince me that I should
correct my ways and that socialism cannot work," recalled
Salsberg. "It was contrary to human nature, they said. But I
proved it was in tune with human nature. So Mr. Disen-
house, this fine old gentleman, said, 'So you want to distrib-
ute everything equally? Okay. Every woman will want a fur
coat. How will you do it? There isn't enough fur to go
around.' I was stumped for a minute but I finally came up
with an answer. I said, 'We will tell them they will have cloth
coats, but every woman will have fur collars and a fur muff.
That way we will have enough fur to divide it equally.'"

The elder Salsberg was unimpressed with his son's burgeoning logic and began to conceal the Yiddish books Joe
brought home. They were literature — the works of Sholom
Aleichem — but to the devout Salsberg secular reading was a
waste of time. Finally, he asked Rabbi Yehuda Leib
Graubart, the chief rabbi of Polish Jewry in Toronto, to
speak to his son.

Rabbi Graubart sent a messenger for young Salsberg and requested that he come to his home on Cecil Street. "All right," he said to the wilful red-haired boy before him, "You want socialism? Fine. But do it the way the *prophets* wanted to do it. Think of *Amos*. Why do you need prophets from the gentile world? Who is this Marx anyhow?"

When the pleading and the exhortations failed, the elder Salsberg asked his son to leave home. It was a Friday night. He and his friends, men who cared about young Joe, his religious life, and his future, had gone to the Labour Lyceum on Spadina Avenue and St. Andrew Street where the young Labour Zionists met. They peeked through the wooden shutters and there they saw sights that shocked them to the core. Boys and girls were actually sitting together, and his Joe was standing, reading aloud from a book. Pained and shaken, the good man went home to wait, and when Joe arrived he told him in a trembling voice that he would have to leave. The younger children in the family were being affected by the conflict.

The following Sunday Joe put together a few belongings and prepared to leave. But his mother fainted with grief. In the ensuing chaos an aunt came running over from her home on Elm Street. "What are you doing to your *mother*?" she shrieked at him. "She is *sick*, in *bed*!"

It was agreed that young Joe, not quite sixteen, would remain at home. It was also agreed that he would continue with the Labour Zionists.

"My father suffered and I suffered because he did," Salsberg would say later. "He influenced my life more than I ever acknowledged to him, in his dedication to principle, in his dedication to ethics. He would always say, 'A Jew does not do a thing like that. It is in conflict with Jewish ethics.' Later on when I became a communist he suffered again, but he accepted it because, as he told me on more than one occasion, 'You believe in what you are doing. I know you do.'"

The drama in the family of the man who would become the leading spokesman of the Jewish radical left was not exceptional in the Jewish immigrant world. Around the corner from the Salsbergs, on Lippincott Street, the desperate father of a young Trotskyist went through his son's clothing late one night, and when he found Gorky's book *The Mother*, about a woman who finds meaning in life through her son's revolutionary activities, he telephoned the police. Toronto's finest must certainly have scratched their heads over such strange goings-on.

The secularization of the immigrant community continued despite the suffering of an older, more devout generation. Before the era came to an end, the beckoning light of social justice and political revolution would attract some of the finest minds among the young.

The battle between the generations did not begin in Toronto—or in Montreal, Winnipeg, or New York, for that matter. The breakdown of the rigid orthodoxies had happened in the ghettos and shtetls of Russia and Poland in the middle of the nineteenth century when rebellious sons and daughters rode bicycles down the main streets of Lubin and Minsk on the Sabbath to infuriate their fathers, and later attended secret study groups in small rooms where large portraits of Karl Marx glared sternly over the proceedings.

Still, the conflict in the New World was greater and more overt. For the first time, the young immigrants were actually free to engage in political activity. Furthermore, the exploitative social and economic conditions in Canada during the first decades of this century appeared to provide living proof of the oppression of the working class.

The young Jewish radicals believed that they stood at the crossroads of history and that the longed-for revolution in Russia would bring justice and equality to everyone, including the Jews. Underpinning their belief that they were the generation destined to change the course of Jewish history was the unbroken thread of messianism which pervaded Jewish thought. The true Messiah hadn't arrived and they'd grown tired of the waiting and the fatalism of the eternally Orthodox. But although they might forcibly throw over the religious practices and ideas of their past, the young radicals never rid themselves of the belief, implicit in the idea of a messiah, that all of history might culminate in one apocalyptic moment. In the minds of the anti-religious young, the idea of a living messiah who would come to save them was neatly transferred to a yearned-for cataclysmic event. For the leftists, that event would be a communist revolution; for the Jewish nationalists (who had been electrified in 1896 by Theodor Herzl's transformation of the ancient yearning for Zion into a political force), it was the birth of a Jewish state in Palestine.

In both its secular and its religious form, messianism was more than mere belief. It was a bright beacon that flickered seductively in the distance, keeping hope alive through long nights of oppression. For the radicals, the metamorphosis of the Messiah into a dream of lasting political change was a powerful idea, and reason enough to engage the passion of an entire lifetime.

CHAPTER NINE

Spadina

THE CANADIAN ECONOMY WAS BOOMING and expanding between 1900 and 1914. Factories sprang up in the cities and immigrants disembarking from boats were met by manufacturers and their agents, who hired them on the spot and led them away to a first day's work and, they fervently hoped, a pay cheque. In the needle trades, they couldn't always be sure.

Industrial profits were high throughout Canada, but working conditions were abominable. Hours were long, wages were low, there were frequent accidents on the job, and layoffs could and did happen at the whim of a boss.

Between 1900 and 1914, rents in Canada increased by a full thirty-six per cent, but working people were less and less able to pay. Real wages had actually declined, probably because of the entry of women and children into the new world of industry. Women were paid less and exploited more; children often worked for nothing on the pretext that they were "learners". When they had finished their unpaid apprenticeship they were often fired and new "learners" were hired in their place.

Working conditions were universally bad throughout the country, but in the Jewish needle trades of Spadina Avenue they were no less than appalling. Memories are long, and over half a century later the dirty words of the trade—the "black bundle" (cloth that was carried home and worked on through the night) and the "sweatshop" — still slide bitterly off the tongues of old-timers. Wages in the needle trades were lower than elsewhere because most of the work was done at home, out of sight of any official inspection and control. Hours were longer because tight competition in the ready-to-wear market and high public demand for cheap, well-made clothing meant that there was a growing demand by manufacturers for more work at the same wage.

The clothing industry had entered Canada from the United States in the late 1870s, under Anglo-Saxon control, and it was soon notorious for its sweatshops — dirty, unventilated cubbyholes where too many people worked long hours. The Jewish immigrants who began arriving in the 1880s were naturals for the new industry. Economic life in Europe was organized around small-scale industry. Every little Jewish town had its master tailor and his apprentices.

It was basic supply and demand, in its crudest, most straightforward form. The Jews were tailors when there was a need for tailors in Canada. The sewing machine had been invented not long before and the ready-to-wear industry was beginning to explode on to the market. There was work for everyone.

There was room, as well, for dreams and ambitions in the new industry. All one needed to become a businessman was a factory loft on, say, John Street, or a room in the basement of an old building on Spadina. Basic equipment was basic indeed: a couple of used sewing machines and a press-iron did the job. And that's how they started, all of them, including Dunkelman, founder of Tip Top Tailors, and the Posluns family, who now control the manufacturing and retailing empire called Dylex,* with headquarters in Toronto. They started with little more than hope and raw nerve.

Coming from the same town as, or being a landsman of,

*In 1979 combined sales for Dylex were $371,000,000 .

the boss might mean that a man or woman could find a job
fairly easily. It also meant that one might get away with not
working on the Sabbath (though not always). That was an
important consideration, and often literally bound religious Jews to the garment industry.

Sabbath exemption or not, the immigrant labourer and
his boss worked long, hard hours, and by 1914 the garment
industry — both its employers and its employees — was dominated by Jews. Under Jewish ownership the industry
leaped into the front ranks of the Canadian economy, so
that by 1932 there were 461 women's-wear manufacturers
in Canada, most of them in Toronto and Montreal. With
$45.5 million worth of production, the industry ranked
thirteenth in the country's top forty. The next year it had
moved into eleventh place. But wages were still so paltry
that fifty per cent of all workers had to be subsidized by
charities.

The Jewish immigrants inherited the sweatshops, but
conditions did not improve under their control — at least
not until the unions grew strong enough and their members outraged enough to force an end to the most obnox-
ious practices. Actually, it was hard to point the finger of
blame at anyone in particular. The hated sweatshop, for
example, was the end result of a nefarious chain of production that worked the following way: the boss manufacturer
picked his designs, usually in New York City, then hired a
cutter to cut the cloth. Then he opened bids to contractors
who would undertake different production jobs on the
cloth. Some did buttonholes; some did the sewing. The
contractor who bid the lowest got the job.

The contractor, however, was frequently only a
middle-man who sub-contracted the bulk of the work to
someone else. Since he had got the job in the first place by
offering the lowest bid of all, the contractor was forced to
pay his employee even less in order to make a profit. The
sub-contractee would, in turn, enlist the aid of others in
order to complete the work. He'd hire a newly arrived

greenhorn right off the boat or, as was often the case, his own family. Sometimes these people would get paid, sometimes not.

At the end of the scale, entire families including children of eight years and under worked seventy-five and eighty hours a week. In 1898, when carpenters in Toronto earned $3 a day, male needle-trade workers frequently earned as little as $2 a week. Some women were paid seventy-five cents a week.

The horrors of the needle trades did not pass unnoticed by the general population; indeed, one of the first pieces of research on living and working conditions in the Jewish immigrant community was produced by the young Mackenzie King. King was a student at the University of Toronto in September 1897 when he published his series on sweatshops for the Toronto *Mail and Empire*, and his study seems to have initiated a lifelong interest in labour problems.

King estimated that only three per cent of clothing manufacture was carried out in factories. The rest was produced in sweatshops — in lofts, basements, and homes. He was appalled by what he saw and described with some depth of feeling a visit to a woman who worked at home with her two daughters. The older girl, who was sixteen, was working seventy-five hours a week for a wage of $2. She had been working steadily since she was six years old. The other girl was nine and already had her own sewing machine. The family was destitute, yet each member had to supply her own sewing thread, and the number of hours any person worked was limited only by physical endurance.

"What a day I have had and how I have witnessed the oppression of man over his fellows. What a story of Hell," King confided to his diary.

The Toronto equivalent of a New York tenement was a cottage slum house, perhaps on Richmond Street. Every inch of space might be absorbed by the business of sewing men's trousers. Or the shop might be found in a basement room on Spadina where gas lamps burned sixteen and seventeen hours a day, poisoning the air; where toilet facilities were filthy and workers ate their lunch at their machines; where men pressed up to four hundred coats a week with twenty-five-pound gas irons until they could work no longer. Tuberculosis was rampant in the immigrant community, so much so that a "Jewish" sanatorium called the Mount Sinai was built in the Quebec Laurentians near Ste. Agathe des Monts. If the foreman didn't like you or your work you were out on the street, unemployed. If you were caught soliciting for the union you would also be out, but this time you'd likely be blacklisted as well — in Toronto, then in Montreal and Winnipeg, too. Word travelled fast and blacklisting was a fate to be feared.

The worst exploitation came with the piece-work that was carted home — the infamous black bundles. Piece-work was what allowed the "speed-ups" (more work done in the same amount of time for the same money). And when a woman brought her piece-work labour to the foreman, he might still find fault (or pretend to) and refuse to pay her. There was nothing she could do. The foreman was king and any kind of coercion, including sexual coercion, could be enforced. If a woman objected, there was always someone else to fill her shoes.

The Mackenzie King articles in the *Mail and Empire* created a degree of outrage in the larger community and by 1900 at least two full-scale inquiries had been launched. But there was little if any improvement in the trade. In 1901 the minute-book of the Montreal Trades and Labour Council spoke of the "scandalous conditions" at Workman's Clothing Factory in that city, and by 1910 the T. Eaton Company, which was one of the largest employers of Jews, had a reputation as one of the worst offenders (in 1912, seventy-five per cent of Jews in the needle trades in Toronto worked for Eaton's). Hours in the Eaton's shops were so long that "the power was never turned off." Employees ate their dinner in five minutes and put in the rest of the meal hour at their machines.

The years dragged on and still little changed. More than two decades later, the 1934 Royal Commission on Price Spreads reported that the garment industry was marked by "a state of general disorganization". Only slightly more than half the companies that had existed in 1926 had survived until 1933, and almost all the failures were jobber-contractors. Employees were still working up to fifteen hours a day.

Jewish Labour

One battle is won
But the fight's just begun
And the Union flag's unfurled.
United we are strong
Let us march towards the dawn
Of a brave new worker's world.

Oh Union of the Garment Workers
To You we ever will be true
We'll build and we'll fight
And we'll rise in our might
With the ILGWU.

North, South, East and West
All the workers oppressed
Join the Union ranks today.
Our banners are bright
As they float red and white
Where our Union leads the way.

— *The Anthem of the International Ladies Garment Workers Union (ILGWU)*

To those who came to Canada already fired with hopes for universal social justice and a new order, sweating in the Spadina shops only "proved" Marxist theories of class exploitation. It seemed clear enough that on Spadina

Avenue class considerations overrode those of ethnic or national solidarity. For most immigrants, conditions in the garment trades provided a basic and blunt introduction to the need for socialism. Now, perhaps for the first time, the enemy was a fellow Jew—the boss.

In the first decades of this century, belief in socialism (pronounced "tzotzialism", with love and gusto) made many converts in the congested streets of the immigrant quarter. Such socialists found a home in an organization called the Workmen's Circle. In the Labour Lyceum building at the corner of Spadina and St. Andrew Street they read the *Jewish Daily Forward* (a newspaper written and edited in New York and distributed in Toronto by Dorothy Dworkin*) and ran lectures, classes, and a summer camp for their children. But tensions grew within the Workmen's Circle. For the more radically minded, the Russian Revolution of 1917 was the historical turning point. What had been a mere dream had become reality. For the first time in history, capitalism had been overthrown by the oppressed.

As the leftists became increasingly rigid and Moscow-oriented in their thinking, the conflict between them and the moderate socialists of the Workmen's Circle grew more intense. The moderates rejected the ideas of the International on grounds that workers were not organized, not united, and not class-conscious, no matter how much one might wish they were. The "dictatorship of the proletariat" was a dangerous idea that never would be "democratic".

*Dorothy and Harry Dworkin ran Dworkin's Steamship Company on Dundas Street. Each week they collected money from people saving to bring a member of the family from Europe, and in 1919 they spent a year in and around Warsaw trying to help would-be immigrants to Canada. Together they were instrumental in developing the Labour Lyceum, the home of the Workmen's Circle.

Harry Dworkin was committed to the Jewish labour movement and every Friday he would collect his daughter Honey from school and take her with him to the Don Jail, where he would bail out strikers. When Dworkin was killed in a car accident on Friday, January 13, 1928, while still in his early forties, thousands of people marched along Spadina in his funeral procession.

And who would this proletariat holding power be? Just another ruling class.

The split came in 1926. The moderates of the "right", as they were called, stayed where they were in the Workmen's Circle. The "left" revolutionaries (who now thought of themselves as communists, for the most part) founded a new organization called the Labour League.*

The Jewish labour movement (which profoundly influenced the Canadian labour movement as a whole) sprouted directly from the terrible conditions in the needle trades. Between 1900 and 1914, the unions provoked 158 strikes involving forty thousand garment workers. Most were unsuccessful or only minimally successful and, not surprisingly perhaps, the most bitter strike of all took place at Eaton's, in 1912. The battle lasted a long three months and turned into one of the dirtiest confrontations seen to date. Eaton's had been nicknamed "the Jewish uncle", since it provided work to so many people, but when the strike was called, John Craig Eaton was infuriated by the "ingratitude" of his workers. Strike-breakers were hired in England, the United States, and the rest of Canada and the union retaliated by setting up twenty-four-hour picket lines. Eaton's used troops to break the lines and the union organized goon squads.

"I was just a child, but I was taken to hear people on a platform talking about the strike and I marched in a parade wearing a sign that said, 'Don't patronize the Eaton Company,'" recalled Becky Lapedes. "I also remember seeing my sister's husband—my brother-in-law—standing on a soap-box at Chestnut and Dundas streets. He was talking about the strike and he gave an example of how the workers were treated. He told the story of a man who was terribly

*The Labour League was renamed the United Jewish People's Order (UJPO) in 1945, but it remained the cultural home for the masses of Jewish communists until the Khrushchev revelations of 1956 and the subsequent crisis in the Jewish left.

thirsty. The man asked a farmer for a drink and the farmer led him to a pump where there was a washtub. 'Pump a tub of water, then take a drink,' the farmer said. My brother-in-law compared that to the capitalists. If they paid you what your work was worth, they wouldn't make as much profit. So they give you just enough to live on, so you won't die."

Feeling in the Jewish community ran high—the Eaton strike was an important test of union strength—and groceries, clothing, and gifts of money were collected for the strikers and their families. But the larger Toronto community favoured the company, and when Jews tried to hold a public collection, their activity was declared illegal by the municipality.

All in all, it was a rough and violent three months, and when it was over—and the union had lost—the Jewish community was in despair. But the Eaton's strike changed the face of Jewish involvement in the needle trades more than any other event. Since more Jews worked at Eaton's than anywhere else, the strike exposed more people to the labour movement and radicalized them as well. On the other hand, some decided this was the time to pull out and risk setting up in business for themselves. Many failed; some succeeded. For the successful, a new boatload of immigrants at the war's end in 1918 brought a fresh supply of cheap labour.

Not infrequently complications arose because the boss, the contractor, and the workers in the shop were all Jews with a shared history and point of view. Sometimes they were members of the same landsmanschaft society. During the bitter strike at the Mark Workman factory in Montreal in 1900, the battle carried over to the synagogue. A new building had been erected and Workman, who was president of the congregation, was to inaugurate it. Early on opening day the strikers gathered at the synagogue and occupied all the seats. Workman was forced to deliver his ceremonial opening address to a sea of hostile, angry faces.

The boss was usually someone's relative, which aggravated matters but didn't prevent workers from picketing his home. Fist fights broke out in family parlours and bitter rifts divided brothers and sisters from each other. Feisty Max Federman (who at seventy-nine is still head of the Fur and Leather Workers Union) was locked in an ongoing struggle with his manufacturer brother-in-law, Eli Herman, of Herman Furs in Toronto.

Conflicts of loyalty also created personal suffering. One young man was brought to Canada by his uncle, who took him into his shop. In time the shop was organized and the boy joined the union, but only after much soul-searching, for he loved his uncle and was truly grateful to him. When the union went out on strike, the boy agonized, but in the end he walked out with his co-workers. That was the end of his job and the end of his relationship with his uncle. Occasionally, however, apparent adversaries understood each other better than one might have imagined. In a small, gabled house on Beverley Street, two brothers shared a bedroom. One of them owned a millinery shop; the other brother worked for him and was the shop chairman for the union. Inevitably the union called a strike. On the morning of the strike, the owner brother woke the union brother. "Hurry and get up," he said. "You have to watch the picket line. I'm the boss. I can sleep in."

Even winning a strike didn't always guarantee results. A possibly apocryphal story from the period tells of a settlement in which the union won an increase of $1.84 a week for its members. But when the first pay envelope arrived, there was only a dollar more in it.

"Why?" asked the union manager, sincerely puzzled.

"I should bother with change?" retorted the boss.

The first significant so-called Jewish union was the International Ladies Garment Workers Union (ILGWU), which was organized in 1900 at a conference in New York. Eleven delegates were present at that meeting and there was $30 in the treasury. For nine years the union struggled through disastrous strikes, problems with the radical Wobblies (Industrial Workers of the World), and a falling-off of membership — until November 1909 when they initiated a spectacular strike that lasted thirteen months and involved 20,000 New York City shirtwaist-makers — mostly exploited, militant young women.

The heroine of that strike, wrote Irving Howe, was "a frail teen-aged girl named Clara Lemlich, who had been picketing at the Leiserson plant day after day. [At a meeting of workers at Cooper Union] she burst into a flow of passionate Yiddish which would remain engraved in thousands of memories. 'I am a working girl, one of those striking against intolerable conditions. I am tired of listening to speakers who talk in generalities. What we are here for is to decide whether or not to strike. I offer a resolution that a general strike be declared — now.' A contagion of excitement swept the meeting, people screaming, stamping feet, waving hankerchiefs. . . . Shaken by this outburst [the chairman] cried out: 'Do you mean it in good faith? Will you take the old Jewish oath?' Thousands of hands went up: 'If I turn traitor to the cause I now pledge, may this hand wither from the arm I raise!'"

The New York connection — it was more like an umbilical cord — fed facts and rumours from the Jewish immigrant metropolis to smaller urban centres all over the continent, and when the news of the great shirtwaist strike reached Toronto excitement coursed through the streets. The entire community was caught up by the courage of the young women in New York. The following year the struggle of the New York Cloakmakers' Union seized their imagination once again. In both cases meetings were held on street corners, and collections were taken up in the landsmanschaft societies and in the multitude of Jewish organizations.

In 1909, fourteen cloakmakers, led by Yudel Cohen and Abraham Kirzner (described as "recent Russian emigrés imbued with the revolutionary spirit that climaxed in the 1905 revolution"), met in the Zionist Hall on Simcoe Street and formed the Toronto Union of Cloakmakers. The initiation fee was 25 cents and the weekly dues were 10 cents. In 1911 they decided to join the ILGWU.

The young Toronto local flexed its muscles and promptly called a strike against a factory owned by the Robert Simpson Company. To everyone's joy and (no doubt) surprise, they won, although they went on to lose a number of other strikes. But when in September 1911 the New York Cloakmakers won important demands, including a fifty-four-hour week and wage increases, there was a surge among workers on Spadina to join the ILGWU.

The signs of future strife were already present, however. Leftist workers were opposed to the ILGWU because it was affiliated with the American Federation of Labor (AFL). They objected strenuously to the attitudes of AFL president Sam Gompers. Gompers was not a socialist. He promoted pure "business" unionism and refused to talk of class warfare and the other evils of capitalism. Sam Gompers was an ugly, pragmatic class collaborator. He consorted with the enemy.

The Yiddish leftists of the Toronto Workmen's Circle, and later the Labour League, were not about to give up their respective theories, their social activism, and their dogma for something as prosaic, as practical, as downright boring as Gompers-style unionism. It lacked what they needed—a passion fiery enough to satisfy the messianic soul. But the majority of workers were sceptical about abstract theories. They opted to join the ILGWU—and the Jewish union movement was born in Toronto.

Until 1935, when collective bargaining was finally established, the Canadian labour movement, and in particular the needle-trade unions, were in a shambles. Union activity was reason enough for a firing, and workers were easily intimidated. Such attitudes were not unique to the garment

industry, moreover. Business was the darling of government and public alike, and the idea of unionism was toler-
ated, even by a sympathizer like Mackenzie King, only in
the form of relatively powerless company unions or coun-
cils which had primarily an advisory function. Constant
strikes born of frustration and bitterness disrupted the
economy, especially the needle trades, and company goons
and municipal police were routinely used to break them up.
The unions used equally pernicious tactics to intimidate
their members, such as threats of beatings for those who
didn't join the union or wouldn't take part in a walk-out.

The first major action of the ILGWU in Toronto — the
infamous Eaton's strike of 1912 — was a disaster from the
point of view of the union. Other disasters followed in other
places, and by the 1920s union membership had fallen to an
all-time low right across Canada. The bitter aftertaste of the
1919 Winnipeg Strike had soured public sympathies, and
both the public and the federal government saw "subver-
sives" behind every lamp-post.

The tide turned in favour of the unions in 1933, the
year of the last general strike of the Toronto Cloakmakers
Union. Although no collective agreement resulted from the
strike, Sam Kraisman, head of the ILGWU local, claimed a
victory (unions never liked to admit a loss). But some of the
manufacturers were getting fed up with the strikes and
moving out of Toronto. Among them was Superior Cloak,
owned by the Posluns family. Superior moved to the town
of Guelph and set up under the name of Popular Cloak.

"[Posluns] had no love for the people of Guelph. They
just wanted cheap labour and concessions from the local
government [with whom] they had made an anti-union
deal," recalled Harry Clarmont, who was a radical Trotskyist and fought on the picket line.

The resultant strike was an angry one. Locked-out
workers drove the fifty-eight miles from Toronto in trucks
and slept on floors so they'd be ready for the picket line the
following morning. The line itself was the usual free-for-all,

with the ILGWU, the communists, and the Trotskyists all fighting the bosses and each other. A weapon was anything you could get your hands on. Chairs were torn apart and the legs used as clubs.

The strike in Guelph lasted about ten weeks, but it was so successful in interrupting production that Superior Cloak was forced to return to Toronto. The Depression had pushed public opinion so far to the left by the mid-1930s that the union was backed by such prominent politicians as Arthur Roebuck, then Attorney General of Ontario, and David Croll, Ontario's Minister of Labour. Roebuck had given specific instructions to the police not to bother the trucks carrying strikers to the picket line in Guelph.

Collective bargaining came to the Cloakmakers on January 9, 1935, in the form of an agreement between four locals of the ILGWU and the fifty-eight manufacturers of the Toronto Manufacturers Association. The forty-hour week was introduced, a minimum wage was established, and wages were increased. It was agreed to end sweatshop work and, most importantly, to set up procedures to enable the cloakmaking industry to regulate itself.

The agreement between the ILGWU and the Toronto Cloak Manufacturers Association was a ground-breaking event in Canadian labour relations. The following year the Ontario government passed the Industrial Standards Act of Ontario, which legalized the very hours and wages the ILGWU and the manufacturers had agreed upon. Without question the impetus for that legislation had come from Jewish labour and the needle trades.

The garment industry was a family affair writ large. It was also a one-generational affair. Jewish factory workers swore that their sons and daughters would never know the shops of Spadina. If they were lucky enough to earn $10 a week they spent $3 on rent, $2 on food, paid 50 cents to the union, deposited a few dollars with the steamship company towards the ticket that would eventually bring a parent, sister, uncle, or cousin to Canada, then put the rest into an education fund for the children. The children. In their lives, they prayed, the Canadian dream would ripen and explode into sweetness. And the key to the dream was education.

Newly emerged from the stale air of the shtetl and the ghetto, the Jewish immigrants were hungry for ideas. Left-wing ideas made sense in light of their daily experience in the shops, but in the evenings almost any speaker and any subject could lure them to a never-ending series of lectures. The "speakers" (referred to with awe and reverence because they appeared to be knowledgeable about some-thing) fanned out from New York City—the Mecca of North American immigrant Jewish culture—and hit the high spots along the Canadian lecture circuit—Montreal (of course), Toronto, Winnipeg, Vancouver, and some-times the small Jewish farm communities of the Prairies.

But evenings were also the time to attend Yiddish theatre at the Standard, on Spadina at Dundas Street, where audience participation was known to reach heights hitherto unimagined in WASP, Tory Toronto. The plays themselves were often about the hazards of family life. Actresses playing mothers cried loudly over profligate sons and daughters (who would eventually see the error of their ways), while real mothers in the audience wept noisily and fathers yelled rebukes at the stage. It was a homey atmos-phere. Melodramatic moments in the action were regularly interrupted by the crunch of teeth bearing down through juicy apples or the sharp cracking of newly shattered peanut shells.

The Yiddish theatre was not shy about translating and interpreting great classics of world literature. In Winnipeg, during the first decade of this century, the Jewish Operatic Company performed two pieces called *The Jewish Hamlet* and *The Jewish King Lear*. *Lear* was a favourite, of course, having as its theme the suffering of too-loving parents at the hands of unfeeling, ungrateful children. The Jewish version of *Hamlet* (advertised as *Hamlet, Translated and Improved*) was rewritten to include a chanting of the Kaddish, the Jewish prayer for the dead. Act IV was described in the Winnipeg program as "the great scene of the Jewish cemetery [where the] sad wedding of Vigder (Hamlet) and his dead bride, Esther (Ophelia) [took place] according to the Jewish religion."

It may not have been Shakespeare, but it felt cosy and comfortable. So did the long hours of talk at the United Bakery restaurant on Spadina, where you could get cheese blintzes the way Mama used to make them, or play dominoes, or sometimes do a little quiet bookmaking in a back room. So did Feder's Brown Derby on the Lakeshore, where there was more food, more talk, and the excitement of a game or two of chance.

There was more to life on Spadina than the sewing machine.

CHAPTER TEN

The World of the Jewish Communists

MOST CANADIANS FEARED LEFT-WING IDEAS before the 1930s, but Ontarians were particularly conservative. Their United Empire Loyalist forefathers had come to Canada to avoid one revolution and no one was going to find *them* supporting a new version of wild-eyed radicalism. In Quebec, French-Canadian Catholics opposed Marxism on religious grounds. And in the West, raw memories from the 1919 Winnipeg General Strike persisted for years and produced Section 98 of the Criminal Code, some of the most restrictive legislation ever put to paper in this country.*

Undaunted by this distinctly unfriendly atmosphere, twenty-two young communists secretly organized the Canadian Communist Party in May 1921, under the direct supervision of a representative sent from Moscow. Suitably pseudonymed, the delegates travelled singly to a farmhouse near Guelph, Ontario, where they pledged loyalty to the Comintern and agreed "to prepare the working class for the destruction of the bourgeois state", a task that included the sabotage of the AFL bureaucracy in the trade-union movement.

Not long afterwards, a left-wing Jewish man and woman had their first child, and to celebrate they threw a party in their home on Palmerston Avenue in Toronto.

*Section 98 made it illegal to advocate any change in government through the use of force.

144

During the festivities, some of the men went upstairs to the third-floor attic to talk. They spoke excitedly of the new Canadian branch of the Communist Party — just a few years had passed since the revolution in the old country and now the breathtaking new ideas were spreading so fast. Right then and there they decided to organize a Jewish section in the Canadian Party. Thrilled by the significance of what they had just done, they returned to the celebration downstairs. "Who will join?" they asked. Almost everyone cried out their allegiance. Then they toasted the new child and the revolution of freedom which would soon overtake the world.

In November 1937 the *Globe and Mail* editorialized that although not all Jews were communists, most communists were Jews. A former Party official estimates, however, that in 1929, membership in the Canadian Communist Party stood at about two thousand, of whom ninety-five per cent belonged to three language groups: Finnish (fifty per cent), Ukrainian (twenty-five per cent), and Jewish (twenty per cent). The remaining five per cent were those ubiquitous "others". In the 1930s and 1940s, when the fascist threat loomed ominously both inside and outside Canada, Jews grew deeply attached to the Communist Party's official United Front against fascism. Jewish membership in the Party grew substantially during this period, but it never represented more than a fraction of the Jewish population.

Numbers speak a fuller story. In the 1940s, the Communist Party claimed to have about a thousand card-carrying members in Toronto, of whom three hundred, or approximately thirty per cent, were Jews. The Jewish population of Toronto then numbered about fifty thousand. According to Sam Lipshitz, who was head of the Party's Jewish section, about fifteen hundred more people would probably have considered themselves communist sympathizers.

In Montreal, Jewish membership in the Quebec branch

of the Party during the 1940s formed a higher percentage of the total membership, as high as seventy per cent, according to Harry Binder, who was head of the Quebec wing at the time. The reasons for the proportionately greater involvement of Quebec Jews are clear in view of the circumstances. Communism had never appealed to French Canadians, primarily on religious grounds, so they were absent from left-wing politics in general. The "Anglos" of Quebec were, at the time, a wealthy business establishment that was hardly likely to embrace such ideas as the dictatorship of the proletariat. That left the Jews—whose interest was further aroused by the rise of Adrien Arcand and the overt nature of fascism in Quebec. In the final analysis, however, out of a population of seventy thousand (mostly in Montreal) in the 1940s, only one thousand were members of the Party. Another thousand might have thought of themselves as communists.

Although they may have been few in actual numbers, the world of the Jewish communists was a very special place. Many people worked for the Party during the day and socialized only with their communist friends in the evening. They sent their children to special schools (after the regular day in the public-school system), where they were taught the proper "line" on Russia and Jewish history. In the summer, these same children were dispatched to vacation camps where the process continued.

The adults sang in their own choir (the renowned Jewish Folk Choir which was directed by Emil Gartner), formed their own brass band, had their own modern dance company, and produced their own theatre, which was usually about their particular proletarian experience. One successful production in the early 1950s was called *No Time to Cry*. It was advertised in a paper called *The Needle Worker* (put together by the "Needle Trades Clubs" of the Party) as "A PLAY ABOUT YOU!... the true story about the lives of the needle worker trade workers". The play told the story of "Al Zippen, a young operator on cloaks, about his life in the shop, and at home, [and] his friends (many of whom are old-timers in the trade). It tells about what happens between him and his wife Julia when Al is laid off work." The paper went on to explain that "Needle trade workers were active in helping to write this play...[and that] some of the scenes are set in: the market [Kensington], corner Spadina and Camden; inside the cloak shop; the union beer hall; Al's home; the union manager's office etc." The UJPO even had its own Yiddish-language newspaper, which started in 1924 as *Der Kamf* (*The Struggle*), metamorphosed along the way to *Der Veg* (*The Way*), and, when *Der Veg* was banned in 1940 as a communist publication, finally emerged under the innocuous title of *Der Vochenblatt* (*The Canadian Jewish Weekly*).

The locale for these cultural activities was the Labour League, whose members had broken from the Workmen's Circle in 1926. The Labour League was a universe limited by specific boundaries but with much intellectual, cultural, and emotional richness to offer. All of life could be, and often was, encompassed by the movement's warm embrace, and Jewish radical leftists felt no need to venture outside its womb of comfort and predictability.

Once people had entered this world and had committed themselves to its beliefs, few wanted to leave. Some already-politicized immigrants from eastern Europe arrived looking for a Yiddish, left-wing community of the sort they had left behind. Others became revolutionaries because they were unable to erase the terrible memories of persecution and pogroms from their minds. Morris Bederman, who was president of the Labour League/UJPO (same organization, renamed in 1945) until 1959, could never forget his childhood experience in Poland, coming home one night and seeing Jews being chased like dogs from one house to another. Or the day he left for Canada at the age of twelve. Two older brothers saw him off on the train, but they had to wear handkerchiefs over their beards so they wouldn't be recognized as Jews. "That made an unforgettable impression on me," Bederman recalled, a lifetime later. "There just had to be a better way for us."

Joshua Gershman, editor of the *Vochenblatt*, had watched the Bolsheviks rout the feared pogromists from his village in the Ukraine and abruptly switched from the Orthodox Yeshiva school into the revolutionary movement before joining his father in Canada in 1921.

Some literally grew up in the communist movement. Al Blugerman was born in Toronto in 1920 to Russian émigré parents who were deeply involved in the left-wing world. Their home, like so many in the immigrant Jewish community, became the stage for an ongoing debate. Only the characters on the set changed — new immigrants arrived in town, transients looking for work passed through, as did labour organizers and visiting "lecturers" from New York. They all sipped hot lemon tea from glasses in the Blugerman front room. But the subject of discussion never changed: what was happening in the garment unions; what was happening at the factory; what was happening in the Labour League or the Workmen's Circle. As a young child Blugerman hung around and listened to the adults, and when he got older his parents took him along to various meetings, lectures, and concerts. What he heard most clearly was the edge of passion and the yearning stretched thin behind the voices of the strangers whose words filled the days of his childhood. Not surprisingly, Blugerman grew up to become a full-time professional worker with the Labour League/UJPO.

For anyone interested in reading leftist theory there was plenty of literature available. There were also lectures and Marxist study groups sponsored by the Young Communist League where theories of democratic centralism and the dictatorship of the proletariat were explained and debated and where young minds might be kindled by the flame of rhetoric. On the other hand, some young immigrants went to study classes just because they were hungry for knowledge — any knowledge — and got converted to Marxism as an incidental benefit.

By the time she was thirteen years old, Becky Lapedes was being taken to lectures by her older, radicalized sister; but the biggest influence came when she was sixteen and working in a shop on the Avenue. There she made a friend — a young girl her own age — who introduced her to the Russian intelligentsia among the immigrant community. These were radicals of Jewish origin who had fled Russia after the failed 1905 revolution, and they proclaimed their emotional and intellectual commitment to the revolution (as well as their intellectual superiority) by speaking only in the Russian language. Young Becky was introduced to books that shaped her thinking. She read Gorky and Turgenev in English translations and Upton Sinclair and Sinclair Lewis. "I read only progressive books," she recalled. "There was always the hero who was arrested and tortured. I used to think, that's what I would do."

In 1921 she watched a street-corner debate on Spadina between Jimmy Blugerman (Al Blugerman's father), speaking for the Bolsheviks, and Sam Esser, speaking for the less radical Mensheviks. The arguments she heard that day convinced her that the Bolshevik option was the right one. "I understood that the social democrats wanted to go step by step, by reform, gradually, until we got socialism. They didn't want to take anything over. But as I interpreted it, Blugerman said, 'Of course there's no question of revolution here in Toronto, but if things really get bad the workers would have to take over completely or they'd just be destroyed. Only if the workers become the boss will we be able to accomplish something.'"

So she became a communist. It seemed just and right.

To be a communist, however, was no flighty affair. You committed yourself to a course of action in your union and a code of behaviour in your life. When Manya Lipshitz married her husband Sam, they were called on charges before a Young Communist League executive for having dared to indulge in a rather traditional Jewish wedding. Manya pleaded that her brother had arranged it all and that they had done it for the sake of her old mother, but the discipliners were not impressed. She apologized, but Sam Lipshitz had the last word. "Comrades," he said, "I admit I made a mistake and I promise never to do it again."*

The Jewish section of the Party was structured somewhat like the Party itself. At the bottom of the pyramid were the rank and file. They were the members of the Labour League/UJPO which had branches in Montreal, Winnipeg, Hamilton, Calgary, Windsor, and Vancouver.

Although not all members of the United Jewish People's Order (UJPO) were signed-up members of the Communist Party, the organization was controlled by the Party. Only communist candidates were welcome to address UJPO members during election campaigns and money would be collected for their support and to finance the *Vochenblatt*. The UJPO supported communist-instigated strikes and, in the 1930s, anti-fascist demonstrations. But nowhere was it written that the UJPO was connected to the Communist Party. "If you asked any of the leaders—including myself—whether the organization supported the Party, they would have said no," acknowledged former president Morris Bederman. As a result, the UJPO was a handy front for the Party when it was declared illegal and was forced to go underground.

The members of the UJPO were like a large, extended family that spent most of its time together. The women were as committed as the men, but their activities were often separate and apart. They created the Jewish Working Women's League in the early 1920s and they demonstrated in and marched for issues that were thought to be in the domain of "women's interests". They organized a meat strike against the Jewish meat retailers who had raised their prices from fifteen cents to eighteen cents a pound; they held a mass meeting in the Labour Lyceum and succeeded in bringing down the price of meat; they became part of the

*He kept his word. Sam and Manya Lipshitz recently celebrated their fiftieth wedding anniversary.

Housewives Association to protest a hike in the price of milk from fifteen cents to seventeen cents a quart, and were successful there as well. "When our men broke away from the Workmen's Circle and formed the Labour League, the Jewish Working Women's League was afraid to join them," said Becky Lapedes. "We were afraid of becoming a Ladies' Auxiliary. But that didn't happen. We were equal branches, though, of course, the men needed the benefits more than the women."

The police didn't beat up the women demonstrators, but they didn't hesitate to pick them up in their wagons and keep them in Toronto's Don Jail. "In the late 1920s and the early 1930s we were picked up often," recalled Lapedes, her bright eyes belying her eighty-two years. "We were so young, so full of enthusiasm; we would sing in the police wagon—'Solidarity Forever...The Union Makes Us Strong'—and there was nothing the police could do about it."

The adults of the Labour League/UJPO were concerned about their children's education, and they called the private school they created the Morris Winchevsky School after the New York Yiddish labour poet who "wrote declamatory odes on behalf of justice and socialism". Winchevsky was the ideal hero for the educators of the UJPO. He was a *littérateur* with a social conscience and he shared their predilection for what might be called romantic transcendentalism. Through song and dance and poetry and drama one might be lifted to a new plateau of understanding and a more passionate commitment to a better world.

The Morris Winchevsky School was located at the corner of Brunswick Avenue and College Street upstairs from a bowling alley. Quarters may have been small and lacking in a certain elegance, but, oblivious to obstacles, the school sailed ahead teaching Jewish history from its own peculiar angle. At the Morris Winchevsky School, Passover was not a religious holiday but a revolutionary event in the lives of the ancient Jews of Egypt. The story of Bar Kochba

exemplified the struggle against oppression and was also
seen as a revolutionary happening that sprang from an
uprising of the people. After the Second World War special
emphasis was placed on the uprising in the Warsaw Ghetto.
"We learned of the struggle for liberty, the struggle for
freedom of speech, the struggle for equal rights," said Al
Blugerman. "The question of religion wasn't demeaned. It
just wasn't put forward."

Although the Jewish left claimed to be dedicated to
perfect equality, it also gave full-blown expression to the
strong, velvet-gloved, ancient, patriarchal traditions of
Judaism. If the ancestral prophets like Amos were the
Fathers of Israel, so the men of the UJPO and the school and
the Jewish labour movment were the "Fathers" of the
women and children in the movement. Without question,
they were the new Hebrew prophets of a better world.

Nowhere does this become more evident than in a Yiddish poem written in 1949 by a thirteen-year-old boy called
Jerry Bain. Today Bain is a professor of medicine, an
endocrinologist, and a director of the Reproductive Biol-
ogy Unit in Toronto's Mount Sinai Hospital. Then, he was a
student at the Morris Winchevsky School.

My Teacher *
(IN HONOUR OF HARRY GUARALNICK,
PRINCIPAL OF THE MORRIS
WINCHEVSKY SCHOOL)

My teacher is a man like no other
For young and old
He's like a father.
He wants us to grow
Tall and strong
To fight for freedom
To progress along....

*Translated by Jerry Bain, July 1979; edited by the author.

My teacher teaches us
To read and write
About the Jews
And their long, hard fight. . . .

Sometimes he yells to control the class
Because he wants us to learn more
But these moments quickly pass
And he is not truly sore. . . .

He teaches us
Unknown things
And the unknown
Within us sings.
In addition to teaching he writes as well
He's a labour leader beloved by all.
In our land of Canada
He's a faithful fighter
And wants us to complete the "shule"
Better and brighter.
He wants us to grow and to come
To really know peace and freedom.

During the summer vacation when the children weren't
in school, the UJPO operated summer camps where the
process of left-wing education continued. Camp Naivelt
(New World) just a few miles outside Toronto housed the
adults in a series of small cottages and the children (called
Red Campers) in tents. It was the UJPO family moved to the
country for the summer. Joe Salsberg appeared frequently
to give talks or merely to socialize with his friends; campers
wrote plays with heroic, revolutionary themes and performed them for the assembled group. Occasionally, campers from the equivalent left-wing Ukrainian camp came
over to perform Kozatska dancing in a spirit of internationalism; camp songs were anti-racist ("Jim Crow

Blues"), the Russian Internationale, and freedom songs of all origins, including the rousing "Freiheit".

School in the winter, camp in the summer, clubs on Sundays, meetings, choir practice, sports training, and, of course, political activity. The world of the UJPO was sufficient unto itself.

One level above the UJPO on the pyramid of the communist movement was the executive for Jewish affairs, the Jewish National Committee. The job of this committee, which was headed by Sam Lipshitz, was to tailor and interpret Party policy to so-called Jewish interests. This was the Party line from Moscow two degrees removed from source—first interpreted by the national Communist Party for Canadian consumption, then reinterpreted for the Jews.

The Jewish communists had all the answers. "The Party Program gives fundamental answers...to all the problems facing Jewish people. Socialism solves all the problems of the Jewish working masses," announced a report to the Jewish Conference held in Toronto in the early 1950s. "There never is nor will there be any matter [which affects Jews] on which we should not take a position."

First and foremost, the Party attacked Zionism, that "reactionary, bourgeois-nationalist movement [that is] hostile to the working class and always in the vanguard of the struggle against socialism." When the Cold War began in the late 1940s and 1950s, attacks were stepped up. Zionism was condemned as part of the "camp of war" (i.e. anti-Soviet) and an agent of the U.S. State Department in Europe and in Israel. Its leaders in Canada were gouging capitalists who wanted to betray Canada to the interests of U.S. imperialists (in this respect, Samuel Bronfman was singled out more often than anyone else). Zionists were accused of having contributed to the breakdown of democracy in Europe and of having made Hitler's job a lot easier.

Beyond attacking Zionism, the Jewish National Committee actually had very little of particular Jewish interest to communicate. In line with Party policy, the Committee hoped to recruit new Party members from within the mass organization of the UJPO (they were fairly unsuccessful, as they admitted to each other in 1953 and again in 1955), and to do this they needed to promote the study of Marx and Lenin with special emphasis on what the masters had said about the Jews. They also encouraged the intellectual and cultural activities of the UJPO and Camp Naivelt, on condition that the content of the programs was ideologically sound. The Jewish Committee hoped, of course, that the considerable cultural flowering of the UJPO would be national (i.e. Jewish-ethnic) in *form* and socialist in *content*. Frustratingly for Lipshitz and the other leaders, the reverse was often the case.

The Jewish Committee also instructed all Party members in their duty to win over Jews wherever they were found, which meant infiltrating existing non-political organizations; in the early 1950s the youth clubs of the YMHA, Hillel — a Jewish club at the University of Toronto — and the Jewish boys' university fraternities were specifically targeted.

But the Committee's avowed "key weapon" in the propaganda war was assigned to the *Vochenblatt*, the Yiddish-language Party newspaper. The *Vochenblatt* published weekly from 1926 until 1979, faithfully defending the Party line over such rough terrain as the Prague Trials in 1952, the so-called Doctors' Plot in 1953, and other events that appeared to signal an ominous, full-blooded revival of anti-Semitism in Mother Russia. Under the editorial direction of Joshua Gershman, the *Vochenblatt* survived the storms, steering a zigzag course around shoals of discontent. It survived even the final shudder of dread in 1956 when the Twentieth Congress revealed the truth about the Stalinist terror and the liquidation of Jews. Through it all, Gershman remained stolidly loyal to communism, while around him Jewish comrades left the Party and the UJPO and the left-wing movement forever.

Through the good times and the bad times, the main line of attack and defence on the Jewish Question fell to Sam Lipshitz. Lipshitz is a complex man. At seventy, the adjectives most often used to describe him are "brilliant", "decent", and "charming". But when he was younger and head of the Jewish Committee, there were fewer who thought of him as "charming". Then he was known as "brilliant" and "ruthless".

Certainly no one defended the Party line more aggressively than Sam Lipshitz. When objections and fears over what was happening to Jews in Russia were raised, Lipshitz could slice through the questioner and leave him or her a speechless blob on the floor. Who could argue with his facts? The proof of their absolute truth was that Stalin had proclaimed them.

Lipshitz was born in Poland in 1910 and came to Canada at seventeen, just after he had graduated from high school. Conscription into the Polish army lay ahead. That, in addition to his parents' belief that there was no future for Jews in Poland, sealed the decision to send him to an aunt in Montreal.

Lipshitz had been raised in an atmosphere of Yiddish culture and he soon sought refuge from the strange new world of Montreal in a club that attracted the lonely and the homesick. The Jewish Cultural Club of Montreal offered young immigrants a place to read Yiddish literature and talk of home. But this was 1927, when political divisions in the secular community were felt everywhere. In the Jewish Cultural Club were several young communists, who were Yiddish culturalists themselves, no doubt, but who were also recruiting for the Party. Lipshitz was attracted to radical politics by an intellectual young woman called Manya Cantor, who would later become his wife.

"What attracted me most in our conversations about Russia was that Yiddish culture was positively flourishing there," Lipshitz recalled. "There was a network of Yiddish schools, there had been a tremendous growth of Yiddish literature, there were scientific institutes and Jewish courts. I was deeply moved by all that. I felt that something new had arisen in the world — complete equality for Jews."

In 1928 he joined the Young Communist League, but his loyalty was soon tested. The following year, what amounted to an Arab pogrom took place in Palestine. Sixty Jews were killed in the skirmish, but Moscow considered the rebellion a justified revolt against British imperialism. As a Young Communist, Lipshitz naturally agreed.

He was working at the Jewish Public Library, and when his views became known, the director called him into his office. "Look here, young man," he said, not unkindly. "You cannot be a functionary in a Jewish institution and maintain that the murder of Jews was a revolutionary act. It is up to you to decide where you stand." Lipshitz sided with the Party, left his job, and moved to Toronto.

By 1932 he was a full-time Party functionary and editor of *Der Kamf*. After the rise of Hitler in 1933 he became secretary of the new anti-fascist committee in Toronto which, it was hoped, would help convert many more Jews to communism. Lipshitz sat on the Central Committee of the Party from 1943 until 1956 and headed the Jewish section for more than two decades. Finally, in 1957, he left the Communist Party — painfully and forever.

One step higher than Lipshitz on the Party pyramid was Joe Salsberg, undoubtedly the most visible and publicly influential Jewish communist in the history of the Party. Salsberg was loved by the Yiddish masses because he had never forgotten his Yiddish roots. His easy, joking manner drew people to him like flies to honey and made him an ideal politician for the Party.

To the gentile world he was simply J.B., the head of Communist Party trade-union activities and a member of the Ontario Legislature. But to his Jewish comrades and contemporaries, he was known as Salsberg, pronounced "Zaltsbairg", in a full-throated Yiddish tribute. Even today voices rise slightly as admirers pronounce his name.

Salsberg had joined the youth group of the Labour Zionists in 1917, but by 1924 the organization split further into "left" and "right" factions. Salsberg went with the "left" branch and in 1926 took the next easy step into communism.

Like so many idealists, he joined not in spite of but because of his Jewish heritage. "It was a very promising period and everyone was impressed," he would say years later. "Anti-Semitism had been declared a crime in Russia and the Yiddish language was given official recognition. Yiddish writers from all over Europe were leaving their homes and going to the Soviet Union because Yiddish literature was being encouraged there."

But the deciding factor for Salsberg was the failure of the 1926 general strike in Britain. It looked to him as though the socialists were headed for defeat in the trade-union field. Perhaps the communists had a better way.

By 1926 Salsberg was already Canadian vice-president of the Cap and Hatters International Union, so when he joined the Party a little agreement took place. The affiliation would remain secret for a while, so as not to affect his role in the union and jeopardize the important Party work he could accomplish from the inside. Amazingly, the secret held for two years, but in 1928 the truth leaked out and Salsberg was expelled from the union leadership in Chicago where he had been working. He returned to Canada, where he became head of the Workers Unity League, the Canadian centre for the communist-led unions and a powerful, aggressive force in the organizing of the garment industry, mining, fisheries, and steel and auto works in Canada. By 1930 he was a trade-union spokesman for the Party. By 1936 he was national head of the trade-union section.

Salsberg's trade-union activities for the Party were complicated by the fact that Moscow had changed its labour policies. In 1921 Moscow had decreed that the work of communists all over the world was to take over the unions. The strategy was called "boring from within", and the tactic was to join the union and usurp the leadership by convincing workers that success was not possible in a capitalist system and that only revolution and the dictatorship of the proletariat would free them from exploitation.

Within the unions, the struggle between "left" (the communists) and "right" (the socialists) became intense. Meetings of the Joint Board of Unions were a fiasco. The leadership of the Board (which was "right") would come with recommendations and the communists would oppose every one of them and denounce the leaders as well. The leaders would fine the communists or expel them; there were fist fights on picket lines. In a word, the unions disintegrated into a chaotic mess, and after a few years the "boring from within" strategy was seen to be a failure.

So in 1929 the Communist International in Moscow changed its tack. Now communists were to leave the established AFL unions and form parallel "revolutionary" unions of their own. In Canada, the Workers Unity League (under Salsberg) was to parallel the Canadian Congress of Labour (CCL).

Communist organizers signed up workers for their unions with an energy the business-oriented AFL could only marvel at and eventually fear. Like all true believers they *cared* more intensely than anyone else and were willing to put more into the struggle. They exhorted, cajoled, and ridiculed the opposition—then signed up more workers. Their papers, the *Tribune* and the Yiddish-language *Der Kamf*, rolled off printing presses that operated day and night.

Now union began to battle union in internecine warfare. Forgotten were the *real* bourgeois capitalists, forgotten were the majority of workers who were apolitical and middle class in their ambitions, forgotten were the Orthodox Jews. For the communists, the only enemy worth fighting was the socialists; for the socialists, the only enemy worth fighting was the communists.

The battle between the "left" and the "right" took place every Saturday in Queen's Park. Salsberg would be there delivering a ringing speech to his public when the socialists (his AFL rivals) would arrive. A fight would inevitably break out. The Trotskyists would also be there, fighting both the socialists and the communists. Then the Special Section of the Metropolitan Toronto Police also known as the Red Squad would arrive. Chief Draper would send his mounted horsemen — Draper's Dragoons, they were called — into the crowd.

"The police would charge and everyone would run, then they'd catch whomever they could and beat them up," recalled Becky Lapedes who had become one of the most active women in the Jewish section of the Communist Party. "Five or six policemen would jump one man. But they never succeeded in stopping us. We'd get beat up on Saturday and we'd call a meeting for the next Saturday."

Needless to say, Chief Draper was hated by the young radicals and they loved to taunt him by singing a song they'd made up to the tune of "John Brown's Body":

We'll hang Chief Draper
On the sour apple tree
We'll hang Chief Draper
On the sour apple tree
We'll hang Chief Draper
On the sour apple tree
When the Revolution comes.

The period of dual or parallel unions ended as abruptly as had the previous policy of "boring from within". Hitler took over as Chancellor of Germany in 1933. By 1935 reports from that country were grim and a new call trumpeted forth from Moscow ordering communists to end the union skirmishes and to join with their former foes in a

The author's great-grandparents and three of their children in Tarnapol, Galicia, around 1900 (Courtesy of the Newman family)

The strain on the face of this immigrant tells a story of hardship, circa 1910. (James Collection—City of Toronto Archives)

A Jewish family at the rear of their house on Centre Avenue in the heart of the Ward, circa 1912 (City of Toronto Archives)

Workers in a Toronto textile factory, 1907. Women were sometimes paid less than one dollar for an eighty-hour week. Children worked for nothing as "learners". (James Collection — City of Toronto Archives)

Members of the International Ladies Garment Workers Union in 1912 (International Ladies Garment Workers Union, Toronto)

Jimmy Blugerman. His home, like many others, was the scene of a never-ending discussion of socialism and unionism and the condition of Jewish factory-workers. (Multicultural History Society of Ontario)

The strike committee was the nerve centre of the union organization. (Multicultural History Society of Ontario)

Becky Lapedes (right) as a young child in Toronto, standing beside her mother. Becky decided on the communist option after listening to Jimmy Blugerman defend the revolutionary left in a streetcorner debate. (Courtesy of Becky Lapedes)

Workers of the World...Labour Temple Activists in Winnipeg, circa 1926. Joshua Gershman is seated third from left. (Multicultural History Society of Ontario)

Labour League Camp at Rouge Hill, Ontario, circa 1927. The sign reads "Red Camper Colony". (Multicultural History Society of Ontario)

J. B. Salsberg (right) and Max Dolgoy in Winnipeg, 1929. Salsberg became the best-known Jewish communist in Canada. (Multicultural History Society of Ontario)

Joshua Gershman, editor of the *Vochenblatt*, at work in his Toronto office. (Multicultural History Society of Ontario)

May Day parade, Queen Street, Toronto, 1935 (Multicultural History Society of Ontario)

Communist Party leader, Tim Buck, and Becky Buhay in 1948 (Multicultural History Society of Ontario)

For twenty years Sam Carr was the acknowledged brains of the Communist Party in Canada. During the Gouzenko trials in the late 1940s, he was convicted of falsifying a passport and was sentenced to Kingston Penitentiary. (Multicultural History Society of Ontario)

Folk dancing and performing were part of the varied activities organized by the United Jewish People's Order, a radical, left-wing cultural organization. (Multicultural History Society of Ontario)

Sam Lipshitz headed the Jewish section of the Communist Party in Canada until, disillusioned, he left the movement in 1957. When Lipshitz and his wife, Manya Cantor, married, they were disciplined for having dared to have a traditional Jewish wedding. (Photo courtesy of Sam Lipshitz)

united front against fascism. The Workers Unity League was instructed to disband and union members were told to reintegrate into the international AFL unions.

The new directives from Moscow meant that for the union movement a most difficult era had come to an end. It was surely no accident that in that same year, 1935, the ILGWU was at last strong enough to establish the first collective bargaining unit with the Cloakmakers Manufacturers Association.

One significant carry-over from the haranguing and fighting that characterized Spadina during the period of dual unions took place in the small, scrappy Fur and Leather Workers Union. There a unique situation existed.

By 1937 the communist faction had won control of the top administrative positions in the Fur Workers Union (AFL) in the United States. The new U.S. leader was Ben Gold, a charismatic, flamboyant man whom Irving Howe described in *World of Our Fathers* as a "flaming rabble-rouser". "There was no one quite like him," wrote Howe. "When he spoke a stream of fire came pouring out of him...as a rush, a flood of rage....Anyone familiar with east European Jewish history would not have found it difficult to imagine Gold as a disciple of the would-be Messiah, Jacob Frank, predicting an end to days and an escape from mundane torments...."

Gold was a hero to the Yiddish fur workers of New York City and his small, militant union became the toughest and most violent of any in the garment trades. The union's first act under his leadership was to withdraw from the AFL and affiliate with the more militant CIO. Soon the fight between "left" and "right" fur workers on the streets of New York became gang warfare.

In all of Canada and the United States, only Local 40 in Toronto dared defy Ben Gold and remain affiliated with the AFL. Its manager was Maxie Federman, who was, and is, a feisty, funny, combative man who has spent his entire life fighting hard for his union members (as even his former enemies ruefully admit). Although he's approaching eighty, Federman is still head of the Toronto Fur and Leather Workers, and one of the things he enjoys most is to sit in his office on Cecil Street, in the old Spadina district, and look out the window and across the road to the offices of his erstwhile enemies, the Communist Party of Canada. Federman is amused by such neighbourliness and the memory of having fought Ben Gold for twenty years — and *won* — makes him lean back and smile with deep satisfaction. "Where is Gold now?" he asks rhetorically with undisguised pleasure spreading across his face. Since Gold is in his eighties and retired somewhere in Florida, the inevitable comparison is clearly to Federman's advantage.

In the 1930s Ben Gold was a powerful, effective man with a huge ego and Federman's very existence bothered him. Who *was* this local "gangster" from Toronto who dared challenge the entire International?

Gold came to Toronto to find out; in doing so, he split the union and immediately the enemy camps lined up for battle. On the side of the AFL were Federman and Harry Simon, an organizer for the AFL, who later became regional director of organization for the CLC. On the side of the International, the Toronto leaders were Myer Klig (a vice-president of the International under Gold), Pearl Wedro, and Leo Robins.

The fighting between the two fur-workers unions raged throughout 1938 and 1939 as the gang warfare of the Lower East Side moved to Spadina Avenue. Blackjacks, clubs — all weapons short of guns were in order. Patrols euphemistically called "committees" were sent out by both sides to raid and to brawl. One Friday Federman had two doctors working full time in the basement offices of his headquarters at 346 Spadina, bandaging the wounded. "My people were excellent fighters," he recalled with pride. "When the others came out of their shops, we'd be waiting for them on the street."

The battle was waged in print as well as on the street. The International printed one handbill a day calling Federman a gangster, a thief, and a racketeer. "DOWN WITH FEDERMAN GANGSTERISM IN THE TRADE UNION MOVEMENT!!!" screamed a typical black headline. Federman retaliated by writing and printing *three* handbills a day. He used exactly the same language, though sometimes he dreamed up his own extravaganzas. "FUR WORKERS: SMASH THE IRON HEEL RULE OF THE COMMUNIST CLIQUE...RID THE LABOR MOVEMENT OF THE COMMUNIST DECEIVERS, GANGSTERS, AND RACKETEERS!" trumpeted one message. Pearl Wedro was called a "Stalinist fish wife." Robins was something called a "Communist-Fascist" and a "Floor Boy".

Late one night, according to Federman, an old friend who happened to be a member of the Communist Party knocked on his door. "Listen, Maxie," whispered the friend. "I've just come from a meeting. They've decided to kill you. Get a gun. Watch yourself."

"I went to Chief Draper at the police station and got a gun permit," said Federman. "He assigned me police protection and he also showed me how to use the gun—right there in the office."

Federman never had to use his gun but he claims he took no chances. During a fourteen-day trip to New York in 1939 he hired two guards and slept in fourteen different hotels.*

The International Fur Workers finally succeeded in getting rid of Federman (though only temporarily) by accusing him of stealing $2,000 from the unemployment

*Federman's claim that he was a marked man is categorically denied by J. B. Salsberg, by Sam Lipshitz, and by others. All claim that Federman is a dedicated union leader but that he has been known to exaggerate. His story about Chief Draper is impossible to verify, as there are no records of the incident. However, according to Sergeant Rombeau, who has been on the Metropolitan Toronto Police Force since the late 1940s, "If you're talking about Chief Draper and the way things were then, I'd say the story is quite plausible."

fund of the union. The money had been withdrawn, but Federman swore it was used for union business. He was tried by the Toronto Trades Council in 1938 and expelled, but he appealed to the Provincial Court of Ontario and was officially cleared of wrongdoing.

"I didn't think so at the time, but I now believe Federman was framed," said Sam Lipshitz. "He may have used the funds to make donations to his Party—the left Poale Zion—after all, he couldn't go to the union executive, which was communist, for money for the Poale Zion. But I don't think he ever used union funds to enrich himself. The fact was that the Toronto local was the only local outside the influence of the Communist Party and they wanted Federman removed. And it was also a fact that the Toronto Trades Council was heavily influenced by the communists at that time."

Federman says he was framed and that was the reason he fought so hard for so long. "I was determined to fight them," he said. "They had published so much about me all over the United States and Canada, that I was a gangster and an embezzler. I wanted to clear my name and I did. It was war."

The outbreak of a bigger war in 1939 ended the violent fighting between rival fur workers in the streets of Toronto, but hostilities continued (as did the split union) until 1955, when Ben Gold was forced to resign during the McCarthy era. The communist-controlled International had become vulnerable and it sought refuge from red-baiting by affiliating with the Amalgamated Meat Cutters and Butcher Workmen (AFL) under the leadership of Abe Fineglass. Maxie Federman was hailed as a hero and welcomed with open arms; and the saga of the "left" and the "right" in the Fur Workers Union finally came to an end.

One of the many thorns in the side of Maxie Federman was everyone's friend—Joe Salsberg, the communist. Salsberg dominated Spadina by sheer force of personality, the way

Ben Gold had dominated the Lower East Side of New York. Indeed, Salsberg seemed to be omnipresent. At 5 p.m. he might be seen at an indoor meeting urging workers to join the Party; then someone else would swear on his dead mother's grave that he'd seen him at 5:02 standing at the corner of Spadina and Camden* delivering the same message to the masses. At 5:07 a young woman might lift her eyes from her machine and see Salsberg striding into the factory shop, joking, his red hair signalling energy, and a bushy red stubble — grown in a futile attempt to make his round, cherubic face look older — on his chin.

Salsberg's personal popularity was such that on the night of his first provincial election in 1943, a parade started spontaneously at his campaign headquarters at College Street and Brunswick Avenue, in the heart of the old Jewish quarter. Thousands of people marched at midnight burning candles and singing. They paraded along College Street and down Spadina, where hundreds of the Jewish needle-trade workers who lived above the shops shouted congratulations to the first Jewish communist to be elected to the Ontario Legislature.

At one point several hundred marchers broke off from the main parade and moved towards Salsberg's family home on Cecil Street. They called for his parents to come out and clamoured for the old man to speak — the Orthodox father whose rebellious son had become a triumphant communist. The elder Salsberg declined. "My wife will speak for the family," he replied. Mrs. Salsberg accepted the congratulations of the campaign workers. "May you all have such *naches* [satisfaction] from your children," she cried.

During his term of office — from 1943 to 1955 — Salsberg fought hard for anti-discrimination legislation (Jews were being forced out of cottages on the Toronto

---

*Salsberg staked out the corner of Spadina and Camden for his soap-boxing for well over a decade. He was still at it during the provincial election campaign of 1951.

Islands and a sign on one of the city's east-end beaches read: "NO JEWS, NIGGERS OR DOGS") and he was successful in helping to push the Drew government into passing a bill in 1944. Salsberg also played a role in promoting fair-employment legislation in Ontario (Jews were not being hired; indeed, they were being dismissed from their jobs) and in his other capacity as head of the trade-union section for the Communist Party (by then called the Labour Progressive Party) he was instrumental in the development of the CIO unions in Canada

His legendary popularity persisted. During the election campaign of 1951, a "fighting song" was created for him and A. A. Macleod, the other communist member of the Ontario Legislature, to the tune of "John Brown's Body":

We have seen them in their mansions
While we sought a place to stay;
We have caught them profiteering
While they tried to freeze our pay;
We have fought for peace and won it
While they whittle it away,
And it's time to make a stand.

CHORUS
Stand beside Macleod and Salsberg,
Stand beside Macleod and Salsberg,
Stand beside Macleod and Salsberg,
On the way to a People's Land.

When you've worked your shift you're tired
And entitled to a rest,
As our older folks have worked it
And are worthy of the best;
But they feed them worse than convicts
And they're not as warmly dressed,
And it's time to make a stand. (CHORUS)

There are millions in munitions,
Millions more in atom bombs;
When we give the rich our ballots
We are ordering our tombs;
All their promises are piecrust,
Let us work for peace and homes,
And it's time to make a stand. (CHORUS)

Salsberg's political career ended in 1955, when he was defeated by Liberal Allan Grossman. The Cold War had arrived in Canada and the Jewish voters of Spadina were feeling nervous about communism, even though everyone's favourite comrade—Joe Salsberg—was the politician they preferred.

But what finally killed Salsberg was a lot more subtle than politics. Prosperity. Many of his working-class constituents began to move out of Spadina. They moved north, into the suburbs and the middle class. A television aerial perched on each new roof and a new car stood parked in each double driveway, and in this new setting there was little place for Salsberg or his concerns.

By the time he was defeated Salsberg already had grave personal doubts about his Party and the Moscow connection, and when he left communism after the Khrushchev revelations, hundreds of Jews left with him. His departure, and theirs, virtually destroyed the Jewish wing of the Party and the UJPO.

The highest-ranking Jew in the Canadian Communist Party was Sam Carr, whose intelligence and commitment were such that he became national organizer in 1930, just six years after he arrived in Canada as a youth of nineteen. Carr is described variously by his contemporaries as tough, brilliant, and sometimes mean, but no one denies the power he held. In fact, Carr was generally considered to be the real brains of the Party. Tim Buck may have been the leader, but

Carr was always close enough to whisper in his ear.

Unlike the majority of Jewish communists, Carr had no interest in his ethnic heritage. He was a Marxist above all. As a child in the Ukraine he had learned Russian and not Yiddish; his father was a bank clerk, neither religious nor political. "I wasn't very much of a Jew," acknowledged Carr. "I didn't learn to speak Yiddish until later in my life and there were no Zionists in the family. Zionism has a place in the history of the Jews, but it is a regressive theory. It went hand in hand with the religious group who used to repeat, 'Next year in Jerusalem' and all that business....Zionism could not but divert the Jewish worker from the fact that he lived in Russia and had to fight for a better life there.... [Generally speaking] Judaism was a faith, and in my family, we were not religious."

Carr (born Shloime Kogan in 1906) dedicated his life to certain ideals of human justice (as he perceived them) and to the political structure of the Soviet Union as the means to carry them out. Whatever he was called upon to do in this cause, he did. But one incident and one incident alone decided him on this career and for more than sixty years he has carried it emblazoned across his memory like an angry scar. When he was thirteen years old his father was murdered before his eyes. There were fifty-six Jewish adults in Tomachpol, the little Ukrainian town where he lived with his family. One night in 1919, fifty-two of them were killed. Young Kogan and his mother, brothers, and sisters were saved only because the Red Army arrived the following day and, after a rudimentary trial, dispatched the local tormentors to a hasty death. Saved by the Red Army. Saved by Bolshevism. From that day on, Kogan/Carr's loyalty would never waver.

After the pogrom the family moved to Romania (then Bessarabia), where Kogan became involved with the underground communist movement. His involvement became more and more intense, and by the time he came to Canada in 1924 he was, in his own words, "a committed internationalist". His first moves were to change his name to Cohen and to join the Young Communist League.

The singleness of his commitment to Marxism, his knowledge of Russian, and a striking natural intelligence made Kogan/Cohen an obvious choice for further education at the Moscow Lenin School in the late 1920s. He had had to leave school at the age of twelve, but now he could pursue what he already believed in a more structured way. There was also important practical work, such as the organization of political movements, the management of strikes for political purposes, and espionage, taught at the Lenin School. None of this learning would be lost on this bright student.

In 1928-29 the Canadian Communist Party went through a period of torturous inner dissension that reflected troubles within the Soviet Union itself. The battle lines were drawn between the supporters of Leon Trotsky on one side and the supporters of Joseph Stalin on the other. When the fighting ended and the Stalinists emerged victorious, the Trotskyists, Macdonald and Spector, were expelled, and the future direction of the Canadian Party was set. In this struggle, Carr (he had changed his name again) supported Tim Buck, who supported the Stalinist faction. And when the dust of battle settled, Carr was found sitting at Buck's right hand.

As national organizer, Carr had a controlling finger on all Party activities. He travelled constantly, talking to large and small crowds of people, and overseeing Party recruiting, organization, and trade-union work. In 1931 he was arrested under Section 98 of the Criminal Code, charged with preaching the overthrow of the government through violence, and sentenced to ten years in Kingston Penitentiary as one of the famous "group of eight" that included Tim Buck himself.

Many Canadians, including non-communists, were outraged by Section 98 and the existence of "political prisoners", and 425,000 signatures were collected on a petition circulated by the Canadian Labour Defence League demanding their release. The pressure was successful, and in 1934 the eight men were freed. They returned to Toronto as heroes, to the biggest political meeting ever held in Canada. Seventeen thousand people crowded into Maple Leaf Gardens to hear Tim Buck speak and to see the others, including Carr, seated in their places of honour on the platform. Eight thousand others listened from outside the Gardens — including Joe Salsberg (late, as usual), who sent a telegram.

Carr resumed his activities and in 1935 he organized the famous "On-to-Ottawa" march of the unemployed. He also co-ordinated the Party's important drive for unemployment insurance (after the Second World War, this was legislated by the Liberal government of Mackenzie King as part of a package of welfare reforms intended to co-opt the left-leaning sectors of the electorate). As part of the Party's United Front Against Fascism, Carr helped put together the Mackenzie-Papineau Battalion of Canadian volunteers to the Spanish Civil War. And he also wrote propaganda for the party paper, *The Clarion*, which he continued from his hideout in Philadelphia after the Party was declared illegal under the War Measures Act in 1940. The Communist Party was opposed to the war (until Russia entered on the side of the Allies) and Carr's prose reflected that opposition:

> The Canadian people need leadership in the struggle against the war which is daily butchering millions, among them some of the best sons of Canada. The Canadian people need leadership in this struggle against the endeavours of the ruling class to impose wage cuts, longer hours, and lower standards of living in the name of "common sacrifice". The Canadian people need leadership in their determined struggle to safeguard their democratic rights. Though once again outlawed, our Party will furnish the leadership the peo-

ple need. It will hold in honour the revolutionary Banner of Leninism and lead the people of Canada on the road to the decisive battles for a new socialist Canada.

In September 1942 (after Russia had entered the fray and the "imperialist war" had become a "just war"), Carr and sixteen other leaders of the Party surrendered to the RCMP in Toronto. They promised not to participate in any Communist Party activities and were duly released.

When the news about some of Carr's less visible activities first became public, it hardly came as a surprise that he had been invited by the Russians to become part of information-gathering activities that had operated in Canada since the 1920s. Carr's crucial role as principal recruiter of Soviet spies was revealed by the 1946 Royal Commission on Espionage, set up after a young cipher clerk at the Soviet Embassy, Igor Gouzenko, defected to Canada, bringing with him documents and the names of people involved in the spy ring.

The director of the espionage operation was Colonel Grant Zapotin, the Soviet military attaché in Ottawa. Sam Carr and Fred Rose, the federal MP for Cartier riding in Montreal, were his senior liaison agents.

The espionage system itself was as bizarre and improbable as second-rate fiction. Leading agents had cover names, but so did assistants, places, and things. Canada was called *Lesovia*, the Soviet Embassy was *Metro*, the NKVD (Russian secret political police) was called *The Neighbour*, and passports were *shoes*. The Canadian Communist Party was called *The Corporation* and members of the Party were *Corporants* or *Corporators*; a hiding place was a *dubok*; a legal front for illegal activities was a *roof*, and the espionage organization itself was called *Gisel*.

Colonel Zapotin's instructions to his agents were explicit:

—[I] beg you to instruct each man separately about conspiracy in (his) work.

— all materials are to be signed with [your] nickname.

— meetings [with contacts] must not take place indoors, but on the street...separately with each person and once a month.

— materials received from them must be given to me the same day....

— wives must not know you work with and meet their husbands.

— warn them [the contacts] to be careful.

Zapotin's standard closing to his messages was, "After reading, burn."

According to the Royal Commission on Espionage, the Russians were looking for "technical information regarding devices to be used in the post-war defences of Canada, the United Kingdom and the United States; information to assess the economic and military potential of Canada; information regarding the location of Canadian defence industries; information about certain telephone land lines and tapping devices; documents that could be used by agents planted in Canada; and information as to how such agents could enter and acquire a base of operations." But their priority was uranium, and the workings of the atomic bomb.

Colonel Zapotin was so successful on so many fronts that in August 1945 he was awarded the Order of the Red Banner and the Order of the Red Star by Moscow. This recognition came as sorely needed relief to Zapotin, who was under heavy pressure from the Party. "Now I have nothing to be afraid not to go to Moscow," he said to Major Rogov, the assistant attaché who was known by the code name of "Brent".

When Gouzenko defected, Carr (whose code name was "Frank") went to a Party congress in Cuba and never returned. He hid in the United States until 1949, when he made the fatal mistake of telephoning an acquaintance whose phone was tapped. He was arrested in New York and returned to Canada, where he was tried on charges of attempting to procure a false Canadian passport for a Soviet undercover agent then living in Los Angeles under the name Witczak. The prosecution asked for a penalty of two years, but the judge shocked civil libertarians and many in the legal profession by sentencing Carr to six years in Kingston.

> I wasn't charged with espionage, they had no evidence on that. I was National Organizer of the Party and it was obvious they were going after the Party. So I was charged with rendering a false document. [The whole thing] was a travesty. Dr. [John] Soboleff, who was a friend of mine, he signed for a passport for someone. That someone, apparently, was involved in certain things, and when the RCMP came to him and asked him about it — it was in the press that this man was in trouble — Soboleff panicked and tore his files up. When the RCMP said "Did you sign? We have your signature," he said "Yes." They said, "Why?" And Soboleff said, "Because Sam Carr asked me." So I was charged with promoting a false passport. The whole case was blown up out of all proportion because it was part of the beginnings of the Cold War. In court Soboleff stood there with sweat pouring off his face and said I had asked him to sign that document. Son of a gun...he died of leukemia eight months later and I was sent to jail for six years.

Carr continues to proclaim his innocence. The following instructions, however, were included in his dossier in the Soviet Embassy and handed over by Igor Gouzenko:

Assigned personally 16.8.45
1. To write a report on the technique of making up passports and other documents, indicating precisely

who on your side (Frank's) is engaged in this activity.
2. What documents can be made and can be received
through you?

The man who actually transmitted Canadian atomic information to Russia was Fred Rose (born Rosenberg), the only
communist MP to sit in Ottawa. Rose represented the Montreal riding of Cartier (the seat of Liberal Sam Jacobs until
his death in 1938) and had been elected there twice — in
1943 and again in 1945 — with large majorities.

A highly respected Canadian chemist called Raymond
Boyer had developed an explosive called RDX. Boyer told
Rose about RDX and Rose, in the words of Sam Carr, "gave it
to the Russians".

"They charged him disregarding the fact that espionage presupposes enemy interest," said Carr. "Actually the
Canadians should have given the Russians RDX. But that's
the kind of allies they were; they were holding out right in
the middle of the war. The Canadians made speeches and
the Russians died by the hundreds of thousands. . . ."

The Gouzenko trials created a scandal and the reaction
of the Communist Party was predictable. The revelations
had come at the high point of the Party's influence and
respectability. Tim Buck responded by turning sharply on
Carr and Rose, denouncing both men and denying all
knowledge of espionage. Some years later Buck told an
interviewer that he had called Rose to account. "What's
going on here, Fred?" Buck claimed to have asked. Rose
denied everything. "Come on, Freddie, come clean," Buck
apparently retorted.

Although the rank-and-file members of the Communist Party were probably as unaware of espionage as the
public at large, it is unimaginable that the activities of members as high-ranking as Carr and Rose could have been
carried out independently of the Party leader. But Carr
isn't bitter about Buck. "It was only a question of politics,"

he said many years later. "I didn't feel betrayed, but I did think it was a mistake. Who was going to believe we were acting independently? It just put egg on their faces."

The effects of Rose's conviction ricocheted through the Jewish community of Montreal, and through Cartier riding in particular. "Who would believe that Fred Rose would be stupid enough to allow himself to get into that position?" asked Harry Binder, chief organizer of the Quebec Party from 1946 until 1955. "It was so upsetting. I went to the Russian Embassy myself and asked if they could supply witnesses to prove this was all a frame-up, but they wouldn't let me in. And we were never able to explain it to the people who had elected Fred Rose. When I arrived in Montreal there were close to 3,000 members of the Party. When I left there were 1,200."

The people of Cartier riding, which included Mordecai Richler's famous St. Urbain Street, were humiliated by the unflattering publicity their district received. Richler touched on the scandal in his novel *The Street*.

One black, thundering day there was an article about our street in *Time* magazine. For several years we had been electing communists to represent us at Ottawa and in the provincial legislature. Our M.P. was arrested. An atomic spy. *Time*, investigating the man's background in depth, described St. Urbain, our St. Urbain, as the Hell's Kitchen of Montreal. It brought up old election scandals and strikes and went into the housing question and concluded that this was the climate in which communism flourished....

The offending magazine was passed from hand to hand.

"What's 'squalor'?"

"*Shmutz*."

"We're dirty? In my house you could eat off the floor."

"... This write-up's crazy. An insult..."

After his release from Kingston in 1951, Rose returned to Montreal for a few months; but a normal life was impossible for him in that city. Former friends shunned him as though he had leprosy, and his family had been deeply hurt. In 1952 the Polish government offered him a job on the English section of a glossy propaganda magazine called *Poland*. Rose moved to Warsaw, and soon after his departure the Canadian government passed legislation stating that any naturalized citizen who returns to his country of origin and lives there for two consecutive years without returning to Canada loses his Canadian citizenship (Rose was born in Poland). Reached by telephone in Warsaw in June 1980, Rose refused to comment on any of his activities except to say that he had "never even considered" a return to Canada.

Sam Carr was released from Kingston Penitentiary in 1953, but his relationship with the Communist Party was never the same. He was never again a functionary or even a card-carrying member, though ironically, given the fact that he "wasn't very much of a Jew", he did become the leader of the United Jewish People's Order after 1960. He found work in a jewellery shop in Toronto and, at the time of writing, is still there. But he remains a free-lance Marxist, privately criticizing the now tiny Communist Party for its policies, though still personally committed to the ideals of Marx. And he still defends the espionage activities of the 1940s with the defence used by true believers of the day. "Academically speaking, it was espionage, but I don't feel that Fred did anything wrong. We were allies of Russia during the war, after all, and we were fighting and bleeding on the same side. Fred's act was an act of conscience."

And Carr has no personal regrets. "What impelled me after my father was killed and I saw the rottenness of the society set me in a certain relationship to my fellow man. That has remained all my life and is still true. I believe what I believed when I was thirteen years old, that man should not exploit man. . . ."

The Gouzenko trials corresponded with the beginnings of the Cold War and anti-Soviet feeling in Canada. In the world of Jewish communism, they were the first stones to fall in what would soon become an avalanche.

CHAPTER ELEVEN

The Downhill Plunge

FROM 1934 UNTIL THE END OF THE DECADE, support for communism grew with each passing week. It started, of course, with the Depression. The harangues of the Communist Party began to make a lot of sense, especially its push for unemployment insurance. Stomachs were empty and children were inadequately fed and clothed, and now, as never before, the challenges of the radical left reached into the hearts of ordinary Canadians.

The Party was acquiring new influence. Communists hated R. B. Bennett—loudly and relentlessly—for having established what they liked to call "slave camps" to get unemployed youth off the streets and, undoubtedly, away from the siren call of their own propaganda. When Bennett was defeated in 1935 the Party claimed a victory. Furthermore, many people believed that the communist leaders had been unjustly persecuted by Section 98 of the Criminal Code (which was hastily repealed by the incoming Liberal government in 1935), and saw them as maligned martyrs; and former doubters, those who had observed the chaos of dual communist and AFL unions and their ugly street battles with a jaundiced, disapproving eye, were won over by the latest Communist Party policy piped in from Moscow in 1935. The radical left was now ordered to join forces with yesterday's enemy, the reformist left (CCF), in a "united front against fascism" in Germany. The era of co-operation

178

had begun. In 1934 there were 5,500 card-carrying communists in Canada. By early 1939 there were 16,000, backed by thousands more sympathizers and believers.

The United Front Against Fascism had a fairly wide appeal throughout Canada, but nowhere more so than in the Jewish community. Fascism in Quebec had convinced the establishment-oriented Canadian Jewish Congress that a low profile was the best profile and their efforts at bringing in Jewish refugees from Nazi Germany were channelled through the three Jewish MPs in Ottawa. The communists, on the other hand, appealed to that sector of the community that thought Congress should be making a lot more noise about the fascist threat. The communists organized rallies and marches and petitioned the government to take action. Jews were appreciative and they joined the Party by the hundreds.

But the honeymoon did not last long. Things started to go wrong between the Party and its Jewish followers in 1939, and, except for a brief revival of support during the 1940s, the relationship never recovered.

The first blow to strike the Jewish communists came in 1939 from an abrupt shift in Soviet policy. Without warning the enemy became a friend. Hitler, who yesterday was the scourge of the earth, a dragon fiend who played cards with a deck of Jews, was today an ally and a comrade. Russia had signed a non-aggression treaty with Germany. The United Front Against Fascism was a farce and thousands of Jews who had tied their hope to communism felt betrayed.

As usual, the Party had an explanation, but this time the suddenness of the policy change was startling even for the old-time true believers. Harry Binder, for example, had asked to be relieved of his duties as a Party organizer so he could join the army to fight against Hitler. As a good communist he had been advocating all-out mobilization of the Canadian people for the war effort. On the day the news came through that the Party was now *opposed* to the war with Germany, Binder was in Ottawa, in uniform and ready to go. "I had a lot of trouble accepting this and I lay awake nights thinking about it," he said later. "But finally I rationalized it to myself and got busy with Party work — publishing leaflets denouncing the Canadian war effort and calling the war against Hitler a phony war."

In 1940 Binder, his brother, and a colleague were arrested and made to stand trial under the War Measures Act. The other men were acquitted but interned; Binder, however, was convicted and sent to Kingston. As a result of his conviction the Communist Party was declared illegal, and leaders and functionaries were forced to go underground. Under these difficult conditions the work continued, but by now many Jews had withdrawn their support. Cosying up to Hitler was just too much.

When Hitler attacked Russia in 1941 the "phony war" was suddenly transformed into a "just war". Binder was released from jail and in 1942 other Party leaders surfaced (they included Salsberg, Lipshitz, and Carr), having guessed, correctly, that they would not likely be considered enemies of the state much longer. And as it happened, no one supported the Allied cause with more patriotism and passion than the communists. They even asked their union members not to strike.

Their new position on the war made them very popular, and the communists now reached out for greater respectability by reconvening and renaming themselves the Labour Progressive Party (LPP). Same people, same place, new name. The "new" party also acquired several unlikely allies, including the federal Liberal Party, for one, which was glad to accept their support of the war effort. Another strange bedfellow was Mitch Hepburn, the Liberal leader in Ontario, who had an ongoing feud with Mackenzie King over the conscription issue. Hepburn wanted King to take a strong stand in favour of conscription, but King was waffling in an attempt to appease Quebec, which was opposed. Hepburn approved of the communists because they were now unequivocal in their support of anything that would help win the war.

Hepburn used the communists to put added pressure on the federal Liberals. The communists used their "friendship" with Hepburn to bolster their new status as a respectable, mainstream political party. This strategy worked, to a limited degree. In 1943 J. B. Salsberg was elected to the Ontario Legislature and Fred Rose was elected as a federal MP. Within the Jewish community, also in 1943, the communist-led UJPO was finally admitted as a member of the Canadian Jewish Congress with the full support of the leadership (Samuel Bronfman was president). Salsberg and Lipshitz were even elected to the executive.

But a new blow to Canadian communists came with the 1946 Gouzenko trials and the betrayal of the primarily Jewish voters of Cartier, who found themselves represented in Parliament by a convicted spy. The support lost in Cartier was Jewish support and it never returned to the Party.

The unfriendly atmosphere of the Cold War made communist sympathizers everywhere squeamish about having their names publicly identified with the Party, but in this regard Jews were perhaps slightly less affected than others. For one thing Jews of all persuasions were grateful to the Soviet Union for having saved thousands of refugees who had escaped into Russia during the war. Second, and most important, negotiations were taking place over the establishment of Israel in 1947 and the Soviet Union had initially taken a pro-Israel stance. As a result, communists who were ideologically and unrelentingly opposed to Zionism now appeared to be pro-Israel. On the other side, Russia's position on Israel naturally predisposed "right-wing" Zionists to look upon the Communist Party with new tolerance.

None the less, in the atmosphere of the Cold War the status of communism was still only slightly higher in the Jewish community than it was in the community at large. It was getting harder for communists to receive a polite hearing, or even, some claimed, to rent a hall for a UJPO musical evening. Soon the Canadian Jewish Congress began to have

doubts about its communist members (particularly the
Labour Zionist delegates, who were always ready to revive
feuds with their old enemies). As early as 1947 unofficial
quotas had been established on the number of communists
who could serve on any given Congress committee. "They
were a thorn in the side," recalled Ben Kayfetz, who is
presently executive director of the Joint Community Relations division of Congress. "I can't remember the issues, but
it's probably significant that I can't *forget* the dissension the
communists caused. They wanted Congress to do this and
that and they *never* gave up. Eventually our landsmanschaft
or societies division had to be dissolved because of the
problems they created."

In 1951 Congress voted to expel the UJPO. In 1979, the
UJPO was still actively (and futilely) seeking reinstatement.

The "Waterloo" for many Jews in the Party was the Prague
Trials in 1952. The trials centred on Rudolf Slansky, the
man who had been the general secretary of the Communist
Party of Czechoslovakia. Slansky was a Jew, and in 1952 he
and fifteen others were charged with being spies and
Zionist agents and plotting the destruction of the communist regime in Czechoslovakia.

What struck people about the trials was the tone of—
was it possible?—anti-Semitism in the prosecution. "Why
do you speak with an accent?" defendants of Yiddish-
language origin were asked. "Because you are a homeless
cosmopolitan, that's why. What's your name? Oh. What was
it *before*? You changed it because you are a bourgeois-
nationalist Zionist. . . ."

In answer to the charge that the trials were disturbingly
anti-Semitic in tone, the Jewish communists had only one
answer: Impossible. It was written right into the Russian
constitution that anti-Semitism was a punishable crime. Stalin himself had said it was a dangerous survival of cannibalism. Since this was so, it followed that there could be no
anti-Semitism in a people's democracy. Impossible.

One day a troubled sympathizer asked Sam Lipshitz how Slansky and his colleagues, who had been true and stalwart Party members all their adult lives, could suddenly become enemies of the people.

"Don't you know?" replied Lipshitz. "Rudolph Margolius has a brother who's a Zionist."

"So what?" countered the sympathizer. "He hasn't seen his brother since he was fifteen years old. Is he responsible for his brother's politics?"

"Yes," replied Lipshitz. "He's the product of a bourgeois-nationalist background."

"I was shocked that a man's brother's politics could be used against him," recalled the sympathizer. "And I was even more shocked that Lipshitz — whom I respected then and still respect enormously today — would condone it."

Slansky was put to death, but there was still more to come. On the heels of the Prague Trials came the so-called Doctors' Plot in the Soviet Union. Most of the doctors were Jewish and they were all accused of being Zionist agents. Once again the Jewish branch of the party defended the Party line.

The doubts and the rumours about the treatment of Jews under communism had originally begun in January 1948 when Shloime Michoels — the head of the Yiddish State Theatre and the man who had called on the Jews of the world in an international broadcast to support the war against Hitler — died. The official explanation was that he was killed in an accident, but rumours of a more deliberate sort of demise persisted. (Michoels was well known in the Toronto community. He had visited the city in 1943 as a guest of the Canadian Jewish Congress, along with Itzik Feffer, another Soviet Jewish writer.) Several years later, before the time of the Prague Trials and the Doctors' Plot, Feffer and twenty-three other internationally celebrated writers also disappeared. Rumour held that they had been shot, or, at the very least, interned. Next, the Yiddish cultural institutions of the U.S.S.R. stopped replying to correspondence from their communist counterparts elsewhere in the world. The Soviet Jewish Anti-Fascist Committee also seemed to have vanished.

The official explanation was that Soviet Jews were so advanced along the road to international socialism that their "national" interests were no longer relevant. The phase of Yiddish culture had disappeared because the participants were such good communists that they no longer needed such structures. Needless to say, Sam Lipshitz and the Party leaders adopted the explanation. As always, the bottom line was the Russian constitution. There could be no anti-Semitism in paradise. It was written — by Lenin himself.

But Jewish communists continued to drift away from the Party, and no amount of rhetoric, explaining, or table-pounding could bring them back.

The Dilemma of J. B. Salsberg

Of the four high-ranking Jews in the Party,* only Joe Salsberg repeatedly questioned the goings-on in the Soviet Union. He had first-hand knowledge no one else was privy to. By the mid-1930s Salsberg was aware that the promise of Biro-Bidjan seemed to have withered into nothing. Biro-Bidjan was a remote, unpopulated area on the eastern border of the Soviet Union that had been designated by the authorities as an autonomous Jewish area. Jews were told it was rich in mineral resources, forests, rivers, fisheries, and agricultural land. Biro-Bidjan was seen as a chance to escape the enforced shtetl and ghetto existence that had typified the czarist regime. Jews as agriculturalists would be but one more example of the new synthesis of Jewish life and socialism. Biro-Bidjan was also, of course, a shrewd attempt to co-opt the Zionist opposition, and left-wing Jews

*Carr, Salsberg, Lipshitz, and Gershman.

did indeed speak of "next year in Biro-Bidjan" in the same tones of messianic fervour that Zionists used when speaking of Jerusalem.

The idea of Biro-Bidjan had caught the imagination of radical Jews in Canada and the United States. A new group, the Yiddish Colonization Organization (YCOR), was formed, rousing speeches were made, money was raised, farm machinery was bought, and delegations of agricultural experts were sent to the Soviet Union. But by 1937 something had clearly gone wrong. Connections between the headquarters of YCOR in New York and Biro-Bidjan were severed. Letters went unanswered and the leadership seemed to have disappeared.

Joe Salsberg decided privately that he needed answers. In 1937 he raised the possibility of impropriety in the Soviet Union with Tim Buck, who "pooh-poohed the whole idea". But he did not raise his concerns outside the Party or even on the executive of the Central Committee.

As head of the Party's trade-union section, Salsberg found it easy to arrange a trip to the Soviet Union in July 1939, but his real reason for making the trip was to find out what had happened to Biro-Bidjan. Only two people knew of his intentions: his wife, Dora Wilinsky, a social worker and a non-communist, and Joshua Gershman. Gershman accompanied Salsberg to Union Station at the start of his trip. "He was as worried as I was," recalled Salsberg. "I told him, 'Look, Gershman, I want you to know that my main purpose is to go to Moscow and through the Communist International and Dimitroff* find out what has happened. Don't tell anyone.' And he didn't."

Salsberg met Dimitroff, and the two men communicated with ease — Dimitroff in German, Salsberg in Yiddish. In answer to his questions, Dimitroff told Salsberg he did not know what had happened to Biro-Bidjan, but agreed to set up a joint commission of Jewish communist

*George Dimitroff was head of the Communist International (Comintern) from 1935 to 1943.

leadership in Canada and the United States and Russia to study the question under the chairmanship of Earl Browder, leader of the Communist Party in the United States.

The investigation committee was created and it did report a few months later, but its conclusions were unacceptable to Salsberg. "The report was woolly and nebulous. When they had to stand on their feet and state their concerns, they buckled," he would say later.

War fell over Europe and Salsberg shelved the report, before even sending it to Dimitroff;* but when the fighting ended in 1945 Salsberg felt hopeful again. Russia had fought valiantly and had helped rescue Jews; the wartime alliance between Churchill, Roosevelt, and Stalin seemed to point towards continued friendly relations; a special Jewish Anti-Fascist Committee was established in Moscow. . . . But communications snapped once again and a dense fog soon settled over the two and a half million Jews of the Soviet Union.

Now Salsberg found himself on the horns of a personal dilemma. What, if anything, ought he say publicly about his doubts? "I, too, believed the Soviet Union could do no wrong," he wrote in 1956. "Perhaps I should have spoken out, but there was plenty of criticism of the U.S.S.R. I decided to pursue investigations quietly through the Party and the Comintern."

By 1979 he had not changed his view. "I couldn't come out and cry publicly without destroying [my] own credibility. When I came back in 1939, the majority of the Political Bureau did not want me to take [the matter] up."

For that silence, many have not forgiven him. Salsberg had plenty of evidence to suggest that terrible things might be happening.

From 1948 Salsberg rationalized his private anxiety by simply refusing to defend the Soviet Union on the Jewish question. He would continue to sit in the Ontario Legisla-

*The Browder report was never published, Salsberg still has it "in a drawer somewhere".

ture and would carry on his trade-union work as usual, he told Party leaders, but the Jewish issue would be out of bounds.

This decision caused consternation in the Party and in the UJPO. Tim Buck cajoled him endlessly to have faith, and the Jewish rank and file pestered him continuously to allay their growing fears. It must have been hard to find excuses. One day he would say he had an important legislative committee meeting. The next day he'd be going out of town on trade-union business.

The pressures were relentless and hard to bear, and on at least one occasion Salsberg agreed to half-measures he later regretted. At the time of the Prague Trials he agreed to be present on a platform with Hewlett Johnson, the Red Dean of Canterbury. This public meeting had been organized by the Communist Party, and the speakers that night all attacked Slansky and defended the Trials. Salsberg thought he would protect himself by reading from a prepared text, but his speech was later edited by one of the Party papers to make him sound more sympathetic to the events than he had intended.

In 1954 the Party executive expelled Salsberg from its ranks for refusing to defend the Soviet Union against charges of anti-Semitism and for insisting that the Party demand an explanation for what was happening to Soviet Jews. The official Party line about Salsberg was that he was misguided, if not dangerously ill. In a 1953 report on the Jewish wing of the Party, Sam Lipshitz wrote, "I hope that Comrade Tim will in his address deal...with the steps that the National Executive has taken to assist Comrade Salsberg in overcoming some of his ideological weaknesses and wrong views that he is holding as well as some mistakes that he has committed, particularly in relation to the Soviet Union's solution of the Jewish question. I am sure Comrade Buck will also inform us as to what progress Comrade Salsberg has made in this direction."

In 1955 Salsberg lost his seat in the Ontario Legislature.

Now, with little more to lose, he returned to the Soviet Union for the first time since 1939. There he was told that the Jewish Anti-Fascist Committee had been disbanded because it had developed "bourgeois-nationalist tendencies" and that secret Zionist circles existed in the country. He was also told that the Jewish writers had been shot, and he learned about some of the other crimes committed during the Stalin era that were to be revealed by Khrushchev the following year.

Salsberg returned to Canada and told the Party mandarins what he had learned. "Tim [Buck] appealed to me," he said later. "He asked me not to talk about what I had learned. He said he was going to the Twentieth Congress of the Communist Party and would take up the question." Salsberg agreed and, once again, said nothing outside the inner circles of the Party. Once again he remained loyal to Party discipline.

But his own mind was made up. "After the trip in 1955 I could see nothing but a total split from the movement. The fact that as of 1948 I couldn't even get my colleagues, my closest co-workers, to agree that I should go there and discuss the question strengthened my feeling that this was terribly, terribly wrong." But he didn't leave until after the explosive revelations of the following year. Again he rationalized. "As far as I was concerned, the break should come at a time when the largest numbers of people would be convinced to leave. And that is exactly what happened."

Although his failings were real, Joe Salsberg questioned events more critically than any other member of the Canadian Communist Party—in spite of the fact that he had a lot more to lose than most. His career was very public, unlike that of most Party functionaries, and his considerable successes as an important force in the Canadian trade-union movement and as a politician were tied, inextricably, to his involvement with the Communist Party. To criticize the Soviet Union openly would have been to kiss this happy career goodbye, and no one, least of all the man himself, would ever dream of suggesting that Salsberg didn't like being a politician. He adored the grandstanding, he appreciated the platform his position gave him for his Party's ideas, he revelled in his personal popularity, and he loved to feel he was a leader of men. "My election carried with it the heart and soul of thousands of people. You don't just walk out like that. You fight things out on the inside," he rationalized then, and again many years later.

Salsberg remains a paradox to those who know him well. On one level he is everything his disciples over the past fifty years have believed him to be. He is devoted to the Jewish people and to secular Jewish life, including the preservation of the Yiddish language. He is a strong defender of his beliefs (which are now pro-Israel). He was unquestionably an important figure in the development of the Canadian trade-union movement. He is still everyone's "best friend", and at seventy-seven the blue eyes are still prepared to twinkle on cue, to illuminate the dull landscape of another man or woman's life for a passing moment. He is deeply loyal and even sentimental in his devotion to his family. Salsberg was and is all these things to the masses, as he still calls them. They loved him then, and some of them still love him now.

But not everyone agreed with Salsberg's actions when the Party was in crisis, and more than two decades later there are still those who resent his leaving the movement with a passion that has scarcely diminished with time.

"If there was a Jewish God in the Communist Party, it was Salsberg," said Dr. Jerry Bain, who was twenty-one when the break-up occurred. "Whatever he said was Truth. If he looked out the window and said, 'What do you know, Lake Ontario has dried up,' we would look out and say, 'What do you know, Lake Ontario has dried up.' That's why it hurt so much when he betrayed us. He made a lot of noise when he left. And he did betray us."

Some of those who left with Salsberg also continued to hold doubts about him in their hearts. Salsberg never did convince them that they had not been misled and betrayed for almost twenty years by the most beloved and trusted Jewish leader of them all.

1956

By the time the Doctors' Plot burst on the scene the credulity of many Canadian Jews had already been stretched to the breaking-point; but by the mid-1950s there was still no indisputable evidence of wrong-doing in the Soviet Union. In 1956 that evidence was provided by Moscow itself. At the Twentieth Congress of the Communist Party, Stalin's successor, Nikita Khrushchev, pulled out a silver stiletto and punctured the balloon. He dethroned the god-figure of the post-Lenin period and proceeded to expose Stalin as a suspicious, all-powerful, and barely human tyrant who had spent a shocking amount of time "liquidating" so-called "enemies of the people". The twenty-four Jewish writers had indeed been executed, as had the leaders of the Biro-Bidjan project and the members of the Jewish Anti-Fascist Committee. As for the Doctors' Plot, it was a fabrication from start to finish.

News of the Khrushchev speech threw Canadian Party leaders into a tizzy and for a full month they met every night to discuss the crisis. Then Tim Buck unveiled the pièce de résistance of the new Party line. The Soviet Communist Party (CPSU) was to be wholeheartedly commended for its courageous act of self-criticism. Buck went on to recommend that the Canadian Party continue to trust the CPSU in its efforts to right injustice. Our job, he suggested, is to get on with the struggle for socialism in Canada.

"Those who speculate that exposure of the evils that flourished during Stalin's leadership is a sign of weakness are badly mistaken; it is conclusive evidence of strength and unshakeable confidence. Public exposure and condemnation of the evils is part of the action to eradicate them...," he wrote in the Party paper, *The Canadian Tribune*. Leslie

Morris, then national organizer of the Party, also tried to steady the rocking boat. "Some are asking what guarantees are there [that] it will not happen again? The guarantee lies...in the very nature of socialism, in the fact that the U.S.S.R. is a classless society.... The necessary and justified stress upon the wrong methods of leadership gradually developed by and around Stalin must not cause us to lose sight of the fact that from the beginning, the general Leninist line and work of the CPSU were correct...," he wrote in the same issue of the *Canadian Tribune*. And commenting on the murder of the Jewish writers, Party member Norman Freed wrote: "...Socialism, the system which abolishes exploitation of man by man, at the same time abolishes all forms of discrimination. If such practises occur, as they did, they result basically from the left-overs of capitalism and are perpetrated by enemies of socialism...."

But Jews in the Party and in the UJPO were shattered by the news and began to ship out of the movement like rats deserting a sinking ship. The *Vochenblatt* tried to stem the tide, relying as ever on theories and principles of the Soviet constitution to deny actual events.

"It is possible to state with a full measure of certainty that injustices [against Jews] are being rapidly corrected," wrote Gershman.

> This is not to say that anti-semitism was a deliberate policy pursued by the government of the U.S.S.R. The fact that these grave errors are being admitted is a glowing tribute to the strength and basic health of socialist democracy....
>
> The Jewish people will always appreciate that the Soviet Union was the first country to outlaw anti-semitism.... And let us recall the words of Molotov in March 1954: "The old Czarist regime could not exist without...anti-semitism....The October Revolution put an end to this harmful policy....The friendship between all peoples of our great country is growing more powerful every day...."

But this time *Vochenblatt* readers were openly con-
temptuous. Two weeks later the paper printed this
decidedly rebellious letter from a Montreal reader:

> I refuse to accept your glib statements blaming every-
> thing on to the Beria gang (who else was in it?) and the
> cult of the individual. Surely you cannot condone the
> silence of the present Soviet leadership when these
> murders were committed.... I cannot agree that this
> was not anti-semitism. Just imagine the United States
> killing off the cream of American Jewish cultural
> life.... What would the *Vochenblatt* call it then?

As a gesture of good will, the Party reinstated Joe
Salsberg on the executive — after all, they had originally
expelled him for raising questions about what was now
proven fact. But the conflict and tensions among the leaders did not abate. The name-calling and labelling they had
formerly reserved for their erstwhile enemies — the CCF,
the AFL unions, the Bennett government, the Tories, the
American State Department, the CIA, Zionists, and all perceived enemies of the Soviet Union — were now unwrapped
and dusted off for internal use. Still the arch-defender of
the Soviet Union, Buck urged his supporters to "defeat the
right deviationists, the opportunists and the liqui-
dationists." The other side, led by a now thoroughly disillusioned Salsberg, accused the Buck faction of being "dog-
matic" and "left-sectarian". Soon they crossed the road to
avoid meeting.

By August 1956 things had become so chaotic among
the leaders and the rank and file that Buck, Salsberg, and
two others went to Moscow to see for themselves whether
wrongs against the Jews were being corrected. Salsberg met
with Khrushchev, who said some decidedly un-Marxist
things. "Wherever a Jew sinks his anchor, there immediately springs up a synagogue," confided Khrushchev to a
shocked Salsberg. Then he warned ominously, "Do not

allow yourself to be saddled by the bourgeoisie and the Zionists."

Back in Canada rebellion within Party ranks soon grew so fierce that Buck and Salsberg were dispatched to Montreal to try and answer questions about their visit to Moscow. But Buck's personal pro-Soviet position had hardened, and although he had initially condemned the "cult of the personality", he now began to question the right of Party members to raise sensitive issues. Salsberg disagreed openly, Buck was accused of muzzling free discussion, and the meeting broke down in chaos. In October 1956 provincial leader Gui Caron left the Party, followed by three members of the national committee who lived in Montreal and hundreds of rank-and-file Party and UJPO members.

Now the factions within the national Party manoeuvred into position for the decisive battle. On one side were Buck, Stanley Ryerson (considered the Party's outstanding theoretician), and Leslie Morris (who became leader of the Party in 1962 after the resignation of Buck). This element was supported by most members in western Canada, particularly the Ukrainians and the Poles. On the other side were Salsberg, Stewart Smith,* Edna Ryerson (Stanley's sister-in-law), and Norman Penner. They were supported by eastern members in the main—from Montreal and Toronto—and certainly by the majority of Jews, including Sam Lipshitz and Harry Binder.

The latter "revisionist" group opposed the idea of "democratic centralism" with its narrowing pyramid of power, and wanted less authority vested in Tim Buck. The Ryerson-Buck faction accused them (with some justification) of attempting to destroy the structure of a Lenin-style Party in Canada.

The debate and the meetings and the recriminations and the on-going exodus from Party ranks continued during the next months, and in April 1957, at the sixth

*Smith had been a Toronto controller and was at one time Ontario leader of the LPP.

National Party Convention, the Salsberg reformist faction
was voted out of office.

Three weeks later four leaders left the Communist
Party. Three of them were Jews. On May 16, 1957, Joe
Salsberg, Harry Binder, Sam Lipshitz, and Stewart Smith
published a statement in the Toronto *Globe and Mail*.

> The LPP is unwilling to make a break with the deeply-
> rooted sectarianism and Stalinist methods of working
> and thinking.... We will not approve nor associate our-
> selves with policies which are in conflict with the present
> and future interests of the Canadian working people
> and with the cause of socialism in this country....

Their resignation was followed by that of Edna Ryerson, Norman Penner, A. A. Macleod (a former Ontario
MPP), and Steve Endicott, a youth leader in the Party. In
their wake, hundreds upon hundreds of Jews in Toronto,
Montreal, Winnipeg, and elsewhere turned their backs on
the dream that had darkened their lives.

UJPO

The defections of Salsberg and Lipshitz created chaos in
the United Jewish People's Order. Only the leadership
were Communist Party members, but for thirty years the
UJPO had faithfully promoted communist causes, campaigned for their candidates, and served as a front organization wherever it seemed necessary.

"When people [became aware of] the truth about Stalin
they were terribly upset and some refused to believe.
Because whoever we are, we like to feel our life wasn't
wasted," said Al Hershkovitz. "I got into the movement
when I was a kid, spent the best years of my life in the
movement and it's traumatic — I may sound dramatic — but
it's traumatic to realize that all you have done is, to a large
degree, wasted...."

Hershkovitz left the Party after an interesting exchange with a fellow comrade. "Don't worry," said the comrade, "the situation is now in a state of flux. Everything will blow over soon and the Party will regain its position. We'll be back to where things were." Hershkovitz agreed, but for him that was reason to leave, not to stay.

Some stayed behind, hoping the UJPO might redirect itself and become less dependent on the Party. President Morris Bederman felt that way. Salsberg and Lipshitz told him he was naïve—that the Party would never let go—but Bederman persisted and prepared a document that was read and actually adopted at the 1957 annual UJPO conference. The issue was, of course, control of the organization.

Bederman was unprepared for the struggle that then took place. The UJPO split into two camps, one led by Bederman himself, Al Blugerman, and Sam Lipshitz, the other led by Sam Carr and Joshua Gershman. The Communist Party faction moved in the machine to stop the independence manoeuvre and for the next three years the UJPO was an ideological battleground where clashes sometimes erupted into physical violence. Members who supported Bederman were branded "social fascists", and the work of the organization ground to a halt as Party members discussed and debated and proposed counter-motions at every level of business on the executive and on the committees.

By December 1959 the pro-Party faction had won and national president Bederman was unable to get elected to the executive. "We got to the stage where we were so unhappy we didn't want to fight," recalled Bederman. "Our supporters stayed away from meetings. They were disillusioned. They had no ideology. But the Party people, *they* had socialism, the Canadian Party and the Soviet Union to fight for. And they had to defeat the enemy—us."

In the early months of 1960 the defeated members of the Bederman faction left the UJPO, taking about thirty per cent of the membership with them.

Becky Lapedes stayed. "Lipshitz and Bederman didn't

have to leave," she said. "Even if there is a dark corner in the Soviet Union, I don't think we should forsake it. They do the same things we do. I knew and I could acknowledge that painful things happened in the Soviet Union, but I refused to be an enemy of the Soviet Union then and I hope I will never be in the future. I have given my whole life to this movement."

Some people stayed with the UJPO because they still believed in the ideology of the Communist Party. Some stayed because they were now middle-aged and had given their all to this organization which had seeped into every nook and cranny of their existence. Without it they'd be lost. Others remained for very personal reasons. Their wives or husbands were buried in the UJPO plots and, when their time came, they wanted to be laid to rest together.

Whatever happened to . . . ?

For Salsberg and Lipshitz, a long winter of the soul set in. Lifelong relationships were frozen. Party publications — the *Tribune* and the *Vochenblatt* — vilified them as renegades and friends of fascists. But as Lipshitz freely admits, "None of this was surprising. We had done the same to others."

One day Lipshitz met a former comrade and a good friend on the street.

"Sorry you left," said the man.

Lipshitz nodded his thanks, and the friend pulled out a bazaar ticket for a draw the Party was running.

"Sorry," said Lipshitz, "it's not the money. I just can't support the Party any more."

"I always knew you were a sonofabitch," said the man, turning on his heel.

When Salsberg's wife, Dora, died in 1959, only one Party member came to her funeral.

The established Jewish community (represented by the Canadian Jewish Congress) also wanted nothing to do with the repentants. They neither trusted the converts nor believed in the conversion, and when Sam Lipshitz asked whether Congress would sponsor a speaking tour in which he would tell all about the Communist Party, he was turned away. Almost fourteen years passed before suspicions began to fade — but they did, bit by bit, and by the end of the 1970s Salsberg, Lipshitz, and Harry Binder all occupied important positions on various boards and committees of Congress.

Naturally enough, their "rehabilitation" did not endear them to their former comrades. Sam Carr's bitterness belied the passage of more than two decades.

> Salsberg would never have left the Party if he hadn't been defeated in the election of 1955. He's a superficial man who never was a Marxist. All he needs is a platform.
>
> So now he's a red-baiter. Really, you have to wonder at anybody who can so easily cross the Rubicon, so to speak, after so many years in the movement.

In truth, to leave the Party was a trauma unequalled by anything else in the lives of the men and women who endured it. For the first time people who had relied on stock responses and a world view prefabricated for them in every detail were forced to seek answers within themselves.

LIPSHITZ

> When I left it was a very shocking experience and very sad. For thirty years I was a skilled worker. I had worked for the Party at minimal wage, but it didn't matter. We went through hell and exciting moments together, the war, Hitlerism and the loss of friends, but we felt we were a part of the future, of a world family. When I was in a leading position in the Party I once went to Italy. I knew no one in Italy so I went to the Central Committee. There I had comrades. This was

my family. The same thing in England, Romania, Poland. We were fascinated by the movement. The world was as now—people were burning books and murdering. But then, on the dark horizon, there was a light. The Soviet Union and the communist movement were that light.

But I regret nothing. I belonged to the Communist Party out of conviction and if I said now I was sorry, I wouldn't be honest. Even though I sometimes had doubts, I felt the Party must be right. I didn't know all the facts, but the Party was imbued by the ideals of Marxism-Leninism which appeared to me to be the most just guide in life. When I became convinced otherwise, there was no way out but to leave. I kept thinking about what an American friend who had been accused of being a Communist by McCarthy, but who never was a Communist, had said to me. He said, "Sam, the problem I've had with communism is that I happen to like the color gray."

When we issued our public statement I also wrote a letter to the Central Committee with my formal resignation. I will never forget. I stood before the mailbox. I held the letter in my hands and I felt a terrible pain in my heart.

SALSBERG

It was a break, a wrenching experience. It called for a reshifting of all the bases on which you stand, personally and socially. But I think I was less disturbed than some of the others. I was prepared ideologically and emotionally for the break.

I am not bitter. I wasn't a baby. I wasn't misled. I moved from the Jewish socialist sphere to what I thought was the best at the time—theoretically and organizationally. My conscience is not disturbed, except for a feeling that I didn't appreciate that the Marxist-

Leninist line that Lenin promulgated could not but lead
to the final demise of every element of democracy in the
Party or in the country where that Party comes to
power. That should have been foreseen. But then, I was
not the only person not to foresee it.

Many ex-communists entered the dirty capitalist world of
business—including a disproportionately large number
who went into advertising. That was not an unnatural
choice. Their job in the Party had been to spread communist ideology. One step sideways led them to advertising,
the propaganda of capitalism. Sam Lipshitz became a modest success as a linotype operator and as editor of a Yiddish-
English newsletter sent around the world to survivors of
Radom, his birthplace in Poland, whose Jewish population
was practically wiped out in German concentration camps.
In 1964 he established a typesetting firm from which he
retired in 1975. Joe Salsberg went into the insurance business after he left the Party and politics, and set himself the
task of speaking out publicly against communism. "I was
determined not to accept any salaried job that would have
tied my mouth," he said. "I wanted to undermine the Party
as much as I could. I felt we owed a debt to the people we
influenced for so long. Thousands trusted us and followed
us. We owed it to those people to make sure they would not
enter or re-enter that maze." Morris Bederman went into
the printing business and became a rich man. So did Harry
Binder, now a jeweller.

  With the exception of Salsberg and Lipshitz, who were
proud public communists and are now proud ex-
communists, most do not talk much about their past. One
man (in advertising) who is still a communist sympathizer
put it this way: "I have not suppressed my background, but
I haven't worn it on my sleeve either. There are guys in big
business in this country who think all the guys in the NDP
should be lined up and shot, for Chrissakes! The NDP! They
consider any involvement in the left as a threat to their class.

Marx didn't invent the class struggle. It goes on and on."

Some Jewish defectors from the Party shifted their allegiance to the CCF/NDP, although few actually joined. They had had enough of political activism — and perhaps they would not have been welcome. Instead, they formed the New Fraternal Jewish Association, a secular, pro-NDP, pro-Israel club. But over the years membership has dropped off and now only a few old-timers (including Salsberg and Lipshitz) are active.

As the Soviet Union bound them to each other in the past, now they are bound together by the existence of Israel — although, they hasten to state, they are not political Zionists. The object of the passion has shifted, but the passion still remains.

Joe Salsberg is seventy-eight years old now, but sharp and shining and warm and intense. Alone in his Toronto apartment he lovingly tends huge tubs of geraniums. And sometimes at night he carefully singes orange and grapefruit peels on the burner of his electric range. Then he shuts his eyes and dreams he is in an orange grove in Israel.

GERSHMAN

Some left the Party because they cared a lot about their heritage; some stayed because they cared very little. One man both stayed and cared. The combination did not work well.

Like a lot of other people, Gershman had begun to worry about what was happening to Soviet Jews after 1948. His own family still lived there. An emotional man, he would arrive at Salsberg's home literally crying with worry. "They're killing them, they're killing my family!"

But Gershman was also editor of the *Vochenblatt* and therefore a director of Jewish propaganda. So he continued to defend the Soviet Union in his writings in spite of his personal terrors.

At meetings of the Central Committee in the early

1950s Gershman spoke against the issues Salsberg raised. "One time when we were discussing the Jewish question Gershman stood up and said, 'I, too, had doubts but now I see clearly,'" Salsberg recalled. "Afterwards I said, 'Gershman, you either cry or you make speeches. You can't do both.'"

Salsberg and Gershman did not speak again after that confrontation, and when Salsberg left the Party in 1957 the *Vochenblatt* rang with denunciations of the deserters.

But Gershman showed up at Dora Wilinsky Salsberg's funeral. There the two men whose lives had been locked together for so many years clasped each other and wept.

Gershman remained in the Party, rationalizing that he would "remain inside, no matter what, and fight," but things got worse and worse for him as anti-Semitism in the Soviet Union became more brazenly obvious. He tried a balancing act on the tightrope of his conscience by publishing a critical article in the *Vochenblatt* one week, followed by a strong pro-Party piece the next week. But that didn't work, either.

In 1977 the Central Committee of the Communist Party officially censured Gershman for his attacks on the Soviet Union and for his support of Eurocommunism.* Gershman went to Russia, spent a month there seeing for himself, and then returned to tell his comrades that nothing had caused him to change his mind and that he would not withdraw his criticisms.

In May 1977 Gershman was forced out of the Communist Party. He was seventy-four years old and he had devoted fifty-four of those years to the movement.

*Gershman later claimed never to have said anything at all about Eurocommunism.

CHAPTER TWELVE

The Second Generation

THE TINY UNIVERSE OF THE UJPO, with its school, its camp, and its sports, music, and theatre clubs, centred on the second generation, the Canadian-born children of the immigrants. But if the "Fathers" of the Jewish radical left had seriously hoped to produce a new wave of believers to whom they could throw the torch of revolution, they failed miserably. The sons and daughters of the movement resolutely did not follow in their parents' footsteps.

Their reasons were not mysterious. The world of the UJPO was isolated from Canadian life, and its teachings were rigid and sectarian. Any adolescent emerging from the idolatries of childhood into the beginnings of independent thought would be quick to observe that the political and social values communicated at, say, Harbord Collegiate, from 9 a.m. to 3 p.m., Monday through Friday, were in no way similar to the values that were promoted after hours at the Morris Winchevsky School or in the summer programs at Camp Naivelt. It was no fun to be isolated or mocked by one's peers or, worse still (during the Cold War years), angrily scorned by as intimidating a person as an adult teacher. Victor Solnicki, now a lawyer and film producer, recalled his Grade Ten class at Harbord Collegiate in the early 1950s. The subject was trade-union history, something he had already been taught a great deal about.

"I said something about improving the life of the working classes, but the teacher stopped me and started yelling that he would not have any of this communist drivel in his classroom. I was fourteen years old and I cannot imagine what he was afraid of from me. It hurt and it was a stupid thing to do."

"We didn't know anything about the experiences of other Jewish kids who were going to Hebrew school and attending synagogue with their parents," recalled Al Blugerman. "We thought of those kids as leading a strange life, much inferior to our own, of course. Obviously, when you go to public school you get to know other children and I played with all sorts of kids at Clinton Street Public School. But there was always a screen between us. Even at camp the rivalries persisted. In the early years Yungvelt, the Workmen's Circle camp, was only a few miles from Naivelt. We played volleyball together and for a while we sat in the same dining room. We were all children of the left — the communist left and the socialist left — but our parents were at war on the Spadina picket lines and that meant we drew the line at friendship. It was clearly a case of 'us' and 'them'."

"We grew up feeling sympathy for the underdog and we were against racial prejudice, but none of us believed that life was better in Russia," said Solnicki. "We also noticed that nobody seemed to be in a hurry to go there or to change Canada into Russia. It was pretty schizophrenic. I wanted a CCM bicycle and Fleer's bubble gum and one thing I did know was that nothing in Russia had *that* kind of pizazz. It also wasn't terrific to be told that everything around you doesn't work and in Russia it's better. It set you up against your own society and the kids didn't buy it at all."

The schizophrenia extended into the community of elders, the classic divide between immigrant parents and their children. The parents didn't know in any realistic sense what their kids were up to or what was going on in their minds. Their children were of another time and place. At the same time, the parents were sweeping into the mid-

dle class on a wave of post-war prosperity. The garment
workers of the 1920s and 1930s were going into business
and moving north, away from Spadina. They were also
unmistakably proud when a son became a doctor and made
a good living (few Jewish daughters became doctors in the
1950s). "They weren't materialistic," said Solnicki, "but
they lived in Canada and like all immigrants they wanted
the so-called better life for their children. Maybe they
thought that someone else's kids would sustain the movement and work on Spadina and organize the unions — but
not their own. They were wonderful, warm, and honest
people, but when it came to their personal future and the
future of their kids, they were schizophrenic. I think they
would have been very upset if the revolution had actually
come."

It was true. Most of the children of the Jewish communist leaders did go on to have careers in business and the
professions. While Morris Bederman's son was at the University of Toronto in the early 1950s, the Party decided that
he had had enough education and it was now time he went
to work for it. Although Morris Bederman was national
president of the UJPO and a member of the Communist
Party (as was his wife), both were upset by this request. With
their full support, young Bederman turned the Party down
and went to law school. Sam and Manya Lipshitz's children
changed their name during the Cold War and went on to
become, respectively, a doctor and a university professor of
mathematics. Sam Carr's son is a research physician in the
United States.

It wasn't easy to reconcile better economic status for
themselves and upwardly mobile ambitions for their
children with the dogma of the movement to which they
had dedicated their lives. The children watched their parents struggle, and with the cruel intolerance of youth called
them hypocrites.

A woman in her late forties recalled her father's
dilemma:

My dad was in the movement, yet he was doing very well in business. That was his problem. When he first went from being a factory worker into his own business—he was a jobber on Spadina—he vowed he would only work until he had enough money to pay the bills for that week. Then he'd close the shop—on principle. He did that for a while until one day he said, "What's the point?" So he kept the shop open all week, like a normal merchant. He felt guilty though, because he was doing very well, and when he came home he'd read all his communist papers and go to his meetings. Then he drew the line again. A lot of people were buying buildings and houses, but he refused to be a landlord. After a few years he gave in there, too.

His problem was he didn't really know what to pass on to his kids. I knew he was concerned about money. You have to be if you're in business—that's what it's about. In the store he was very fair and he extended credit—but he wanted his bills paid before the revolution.

I found him inconsistent and it was a source of conflict between us for a long time, but in recent years I have come to understand him better and to accept him.

In spite of its ideological rigidity and isolation and the fact that it failed to produce a new generation of Canadian communists, the UJPO and the Morris Winchevsky School did produce an unusually high number of talented people who have risen to the top of their fields. They have become lawyers, doctors, successful advertising executives, and wealthy business people. They have excelled in the arts as writers, directors, producers, and musicians. Nathan Cohen, probably Canada's best-known theatre critic, was a product of the movement. He started his career in journalism as editor of the mine workers' paper in Nova Scotia, then moved to Toronto to work for the Party journal, *The Canadian Tribune*. From the *Tribune* Cohen moved to the staff of the *Vochenblatt*, and from the *Vochenblatt* he leaped

the ideological chasm to land in the bosom of the establishment press at the (then) *Toronto Daily Star*. Zalmen
Yanofsky (whose father, Avrom, was a cartoonist) formed
the pop music group The Lovin' Spoonful. Film director
Ted Kotcheff went to Camp Naivelt, and so did Jerry
Goodis, who later became Pierre Elliott Trudeau's personal
advertising media consultant.

That the children of the radical left have emerged as
highly successful should come as no real surprise. After all,
the object of study at the Morris Winchevsky School every
day of every week of every year was capitalism. The elders
didn't like capitalism, of course, and to get their point across
they talked about it constantly and analysed it carefully.
Their children learned well.

UJPO children were also taught to think. Where else
were youngsters immersed in an environment where they
were compelled to reason, to debate, to analyse, and to
construct disciplined arguments from the time they learned
to talk?

A youth spent in committee work and club activities
taught them organizing skills that became valuable tools
when they moved into the outside world. They also learned
an appreciation of culture. It was limited and ideologically
slanted, to be sure, but the UJPO often succeeded in instil-
ling a basic love of literature, music, and dance in its
children, and it was not difficult for them to expand their
tastes once they had "graduated" from the movement.

Possibly the most striking example of the leap from the
UJPO into successful capitalism can be found in the person
of Jerry Goodis, fifty-one, advertising executive, founder
of Goodis, Goldberg, recent vice-chairman of the board of
MacLaren Advertising, and now president of a new firm,
personal communications consultant to a prime minister,
and one of a group responsible for Liberal Party advertising beginning in 1972 and continuing into the present.

Yet Goodis has been caught in the conflict between idea

and reality that beset his parents' generation. Goodis still manages to think of himself as part socialist ("I am a capitalist but I still have socialist feelings") in spite of the fact that he moves in a world of dazzlingly high finance.

Jerry Goodis describes himself as non-intellectual ("In any debate with an intellectual, I lose in eighteen seconds"), and his continuing attachment to the left-wing movement of his youth is essentially emotional and sentimental. It has its real base in Goodis's intense admiration for his father, Louis Goodis, who was a well-loved trade-union organizer and a founder of the Labour League. The elder Goodis died forty-three years ago when Jerry was eight years old.

Because his father believed in Russia and the revolution and the tenets of Marx, Goodis believed in them too. And because of his father, he continues to feel personally insulted that the UJPO was rejected by Congress in 1951. That was a long time ago, but Goodis's anger (like that of Sam Carr) challenges the passage of time.

> What kind of democracy was that? To be told by the establishment that you're not good enough? Well, they can go fuck themselves as far as I'm concerned because I *am* good enough. I'm richer than most of them now so I guess it doesn't matter. But now they have the supreme gall to ask me for a lot of money for the UJA. Now I'm okay because I have a lot of money. I will *never* forgive them. What has made me kosher is my bank account. I will not buy myself into their hearts.

How does Goodis convince himself that he is still a socialist? "Life is full of contradictions," he mused. "After all, why should we have a class society when there are people in Cape Breton who don't have enough to eat and I'm sitting here getting overweight and putting half-billion-dollar deals together? Marxism is a good idea that human beings keep screwing up."

And he has at least attempted to resolve the conflict

between his loyalty to his father's ideas and the radically different turn his own life has taken.

> If my father could see me now, he might turn in his grave. But more likely he would have a little smile on his face. He'd say, "It was a nice idea, but now that things have changed, go do what you have to do." Why the hell should I feel guilty? I gave the other ideology a hell of a shot. I gave them my whole youth. It didn't work. Now I have set my hand to something else.

The man who has remained closest to the old style is Dr. Jerry Bain. He and a few other children of the UJPO formed the Secular Jewish Association, an organization that celebrates the religious holidays from a secular viewpoint and runs a Sunday school that culminates with a graduation and an occasional bar mitzvah. But Bain is quick to point out that the new association has no connection with the UJPO. He also bristles slightly and answers in the negative when asked whether the new organization has a political point of view.

The sons and the daughters have dissociated themselves with a vengeance. The UJPO simply failed to spawn a second generation.

CHAPTER THIRTEEN

The End of an Era

THE UJPO IS STILL AROUND—SORT OF. It has three hundred members and their average age is seventy, but it can still rally its forces to produce a fine choir recital and some of its members still summer at Camp Naivelt. Every June, on Father's Day, the whole clan gathers at the camp, and it feels so much like the old days that someone almost always jumps up and makes a rousing, cheerleading sort of speech that ends with, "And let's get a drive going to sign up the young people!"

But these days things tend to get a little strained at Naivelt. Some Russian immigrant Jews have bought cottages, and there they are—living right next door to people who have yearned for Russia all their lives and fought battles for its political system. The two groups eye each other watchfully. The Russians are disdainful of these Canadian Jews who have never been to Russia, will never go to Russia, and do not speak the language. The Canadians are incensed at being confronted—at the summer cottage, no less; on their home territory at Naivelt, no less—with living, breathing proof that the Soviet system has not worked out for the Jews.

It isn't easy.

As for the Communist Party, it has lately served notice of an attempt to revive Jewish interest. In 1977 the Central Committee published the first issue of a *Progressive Jewish*

Newsletter edited by William Ross, a long-standing Party functionary. Isolated from Jewish reality, sectarian in outlook (nothing had changed), the new *Newsletter* read like a message tossed into the sea by an ancient mariner and washed up on the shores of a new world. It purported to enlighten its readers about "Zionist bourgeois-nationalism". It spoke of "Jewish masses" and the slanders of anti-Sovieteers who dare to claim there is anti-Semitism in the Soviet Union. It attacked Joshua Gershman for having allowed an anti-Soviet letter to appear in the *Vochenblatt* without editorial rebuttal,* and in conclusion "proved" that all was well in the Soviet Union — by quoting Lenin and the Russian constitution.

But the Jewish "masses" failed to respond to the siren call of Soviet Marxism. The tiny minority who remembered were jaded or indifferent. The promised messiah had not materialized, and yesterday's dream was interred long ago in a deep, though troubled, sleep.

---

*The *Newsletter* appeared around the same time that Gershman left the Party.

PART THREE

Jewish Farmers in the West

A false impression has become prevalent, more particularly in the urban centres of Canada, that there is no such being as a Jewish farmer. So much is this belief widespread among Jews and non-Jews alike, that when a Jew declares himself to be a a farmer, doubts are expressed as to the possibility of his being a Jew, and if he declares himself to be a Jew it is taken for granted that he is no farmer.

Louis Rosenberg, 1934

The Pioneer

If each event in my life were registered truly as it happened, how many people of this generation would believe? What can I tell my own children? That my dresses were made of denim because the material was strong and had to last? That my shoes were round-toed and strong because they, too, had to last? Nothing was made for beauty. Only for lasting. You carried your shoes to school, if you had shoes. Your foot grew, but your shoes remained the same size. . . .

Life seemed so good. The sky and the whole outdoors as far as I could see was mine to investigate. Population was very sparse. I loved it. The grain, the cattle, the chickens, the sky, the berries in the field, strawberries, raspberries, gooseberries, Saskatoons, choke berries. It was a lovely life. Maybe my children would think it was terrible? How can I tell them about it? About the Bow River and how it meandered crookedly through all the small places? How the berries hung over the river banks and into the water? And how mother would make wine and jelly and jam and how we never went to the store except for sugar and tobacco for father? Would they care? Would my children care?

—unpublished diary, Winnipeg, 1964, by Maggie Wasserman Brownstone, born in the colony of Wapella, North-West Territories (Saskatchewan), 1896.

CHAPTER FOURTEEN

The Politics of Jewish Settlement in the West

BY THE MIDDLE OF THE NINETEENTH CENTURY the Russian czar Nicholas had passed more than six hundred laws directed specifically at the Jews of Russia. He told them where they were allowed to live, what limitations there were on schooling for their children, and just how they could and could not make a living. But worst of all was the law that was whispered with undiminished horror from the mouths of one generation into the ears of the next — the law concerning the military conscription of Jewish children. Boys of eight and nine years were called into the Russian army for twenty-five years' service. Many of them died on forced marches to the army camps; those who survived rarely saw their families again. Small shtetl villages were torn apart as parents tried to hide their children and were betrayed by others who hoped by doing so to prevent a pogrom from destroying the community.

But the remnants of Russian tolerance of Jews (and Jewish tolerance of Russia) collapsed in 1881 with the pogroms at Yelisavetgrad and Kiev. By the end of 1881, 215 Jewish communities had been attacked. The sand had finally drained out of the time-clock for close to five million Jews whose ancestors had been born and had died in eastern Europe. They gathered up their belongings and began an exodus out of Russia that continued until the bullets of

214

August 1914 stopped them in their tracks, pushing steadily across Europe to the points of departure for the new world. There they waited — in the ports of Hamburg, Brody, Bremen, and London — while world organizations writhed in despair over where to send them.

Meetings protesting the pogroms were held in major cities in Europe and the United States, and it was at the London meeting at Mansion House, the residence of the Lord Mayor, that the possibility of connecting Russian Jews with Canada was first raised.

The Mansion House Hall was crowded for hours before the proceedings began at which the Lord Mayor presided flanked by several of his distinguished countrymen. A letter was read before the assemblage from Alfred, Lord Tennyson, who was unable to attend. A resolution was adopted declaring that while "we disclaim any right to interfere in the internal affairs of Russia and desire the preservation of amicable relations with the country, it is our duty to express our opinion that the laws of Russia concerning the Jews tend to degrade her influence." The Earl of Shaftesbury, Cardinal Manning and Canon Farrar spoke in support of the resolution.... The cardinal invoked "the laws of humanity, of nature and of God, which are the foundation of all other laws" and maintained that these gave the Mansion House meeting the right and obligation to protest uncivilized acts of hostility being perpetrated in Russia against Jews. Further, he called attention to the anti-Semitic movement in Germany and expressed the fear that it would set off a great holocaust of animosity and violence throughout the world similar to that in Russia.

This was indeed a unique and historic meeting when Catholic and Protestant leaders gathered to express their abhorrence at the inhumanity directed against the Jews. The resolutions of the occasion were forwarded to

Mr. Gladstone with the hope that the British government would exercise its friendly influence on behalf of the persecuted Jews. Nor was the gathering content with resolutions alone; a relief fund was opened and monies were subscribed by those in attendance.

Present at that meeting on February 1, 1882, was Alexander T. Galt, Canada's first High Commissioner to London and one of the Fathers of Confederation. Galt eagerly joined a newly created working group called the Russo-Jewish Committee and began a series of moves that would, he hoped, result in the emigration of Jews to the new Dominion.

Canada needed immigrants. In 1872 the government had taken over the North-West Territories (with its tiny population of 73,000) from the Hudson's Bay Company and had begun to cast about for ways of attracting settlers to open the land. To date they had had little success — except for small pockets of Mennonite and Icelandic immigration — and it seemed clear to Galt that there was an obvious correlation between the needs of the refugees huddled in the Jews' Temporary Shelter in Whitechapel, London, as well as in other centres, and the population needs of the Canadian North West. Here you had thousands of homeless people with nowhere to go; there you had thousands of square miles of uninhabited land waiting to be settled. The Russian Jews were also said to have had important agricultural experience — a report based more on wishful thinking than on verified fact.

Many of the refugees doubtless believed that being a "farmer" was the quickest and easiest way to be accepted into Canada. Still others were inspired by the *Am Olam* (Eternal People) movement that had sprung up in the Russian shtetls after the pogroms began. The left-thinking idealists of the *Am Olam* believed that Jewish farm co-operatives (which they hoped to establish in America) would "normalize" Jewish life by creating a new economic

base radically removed from petty trade and the middle-
man role that Jews had traditionally been consigned to.
They thought of agriculture as "noble" and they hoped that
a generation of Jewish farmers would put an end to accusations of "non-productive" Jewish labour. They had thought
it all through theoretically, but they had no experience. As
Irving Howe put it, they marched to the trains that would
take them from Russia "with Torah in one hand and *Das
Kapital* in the other".

Alexander Galt wrote to Sir John A. Macdonald, Prime
Minister of Canada, "I am discussing with the Jews...an
exodus from Russia to Canada.... How would you like to
have an influx of 'Ole Clo'?" he asked.

Galt held no particular love for the Jews—his off-hand
reference to the stereotyped peddler, 'Ole Clo', makes that
abundantly clear—but he *was* interested in the possibility of
Jewish financing for Jewish resettlement in Canada. He
wrote again to Macdonald to say he had made contact with
Lord Rothschild. "[The Russian Jews] are a superior class of
people," he added, "partly farmers, but generally trade
people." Most of them were well off, he believed (errone-
ously), although some had been ruined, but Galt was convinced that many of them had enough money to establish
themselves. He was also intrigued by the fact that American
Jews were successfully routing the refugees to the United
States and offered the opinion that "what was good for
them could not be bad for us."

The Prime Minister responded in the same vein. "The
'Ole Clo' move is a good one," he wrote. "A sprinkling of
Jews in the North West would do much good. They would
at once go in for peddling and politics and be of much use in
the New Country as Cheap Jacks and Chapmen." And he
was in complete agreement with Galt about financing.
"After years of ill-concealed hostility of the Rothschilds
against Canada, you have made a great strike by taking up
the 'ole clo' cry, and going in for a Jew immigration into the
Northwest. By following up this subject, and establishing a

Jew colony here...a missing link will be established between Canada and Sidonia."*

Encouragement for Jewish settlement also came from the office of the Governor General, the Marquess of Lorne. He had received a letter from the Icelandic immigration agent in Manitoba suggesting that a block of land be obtained from the Macdonald government to settle the Jewish refugees from Russia. "Such a timely measure for the relief of the Jewish refugees, if happily connected with those now being made in England, would be a lasting credit to this country and a bright memorial of your Lordship's distinguished administration," the agent wrote, sweetening the proposition. The Governor General's secretary forwarded this letter to Macdonald with a covering note from himself:

> A large and influential committee of Jews in England...have taken up the cause of their fellow country-men—and it has occurred to His Excellency that if the committee were approached by the Department of Agriculture they would have no difficulty in raising 5 or 10,000 pounds and sending out, say, 1,000 Jews. They are—the Russian Jews—a very dirty lot but if the English Jew will subscribe liberally and settle his Russian brother why shouldn't the Canadian government get the benefit of the transaction?

Believing that homestead land was awaiting them in Manitoba, 260 Russian Jews set sail for the Dominion of Canada in the spring of 1882. On May 13, just hours before their arrival in Montreal, the executives of several benevolent help groups hastily formed the first Jewish Immigrant Aid Society, launched a fund-raising campaign, and rented three warehouses to provide temporary shelter when the refugees arrived. In late May the Anglo-Jewish Committee

---

*Macdonald had tried and failed to get Rothschild support for CPR construction. Sidon was a Phoenician seaport whose traders were considered immoral by the prophets of the Old Testament.

of Toronto sent a telegram to the Jews of Winnipeg informing them that 247 immigrants had passed through Toronto
that morning and were on their way west. They were, at that
moment, travelling to Sarnia. There they would board the
steamer *Ontario*, which went to Duluth, Minnesota. From
there they would head for Winnipeg.

Winnipeg in the 1880s was exploding with energy. The
building of the railway was a vast business employing hundreds of men, and it had brought a wild boom in land
speculation in its wake. Between 1800 and 1886, ambitious
adventurers poured into the West, changing Winnipeg
from a tiny settlement to a city of twenty thousand. Settlers
arrived on the new CPR line, and instant tar-paper shanties
mushroomed to accommodate them on streets where ox
carts rumbled, spraying mud over wooden plank "sidewalks" and pedestrians alike. The city was raw and electric
with the brittle flash of money changing hands.

Into this boom town stepped 247 Jews from the Russian
shtetls. They were greeted by the Jewish community of
Winnipeg — exactly twenty-three very nervous individuals.
The promised homestead land had not been made available
and the welcome party wondered anxiously what they were
going to do with 247 penniless, bewildered, travel-weary,
culture-shocked refugees from another world.

To begin with they provided a hot, kosher meal and
housed them in an immigration shed at the mouth of the
Assiniboine River. They took a collection among themselves and raised $360. Then they appealed in desperation
to the citizens of Winnipeg, who opened their hearts in an
outpouring of frontier generosity. Businesses donated
mattresses, ticking for pillows, blankets, and cooking uten-
sils; the Bishop of Rupert's Land donated $100 of his own
money; and immediate work was offered on a temporary
basis. The men finished their first meal and went off to
unload two rafts of lumber. Some of the women were hired
for domestic service.

Over the next few weeks the citizens of Winnipeg

watched the new arrivals with open curiosity. The *Manitoba Free Press* and the *Winnipeg Times* tripped over each other reporting on the strange habits of the Jews. On June 3, 1882, both papers rushed to detail the Sabbath services being held in the immigration sheds. Wrote the *Winnipeg Times*: "The Jewish immigrants who recently arrived held divine services...this morning presided over by one of the old Jewish rabbits. Saturday, as is well known, is observed among them as Sunday...." The editor of the *Manitoba Free Press* gloated over his competitor's *faux pas*. "We observe by our esteemed contemporary that the divine service held at the immigration sheds on Saturday was presided over by 'one of the old Jewish rabbits'. This is base calumny. The community of Jews in this city are not in possession of any rabbits, and if they had, it is not likely that they would permit one to preside over such a grave occasion...."

But the honeymoon soon ended as it became clear that the federal government had made no plans at all to aid the refugees. In Toronto the Anglo-Jewish Association hired a lawyer to look into the land-grant situation, but all he was able to learn was that vast tracts of land were being held by colonization companies, the Hudson's Bay Company, and the CPR. Alexander Galt was personally distressed and made his own inquiries—but to no avail.

By June a government immigration agent in Winnipeg was writing to Ottawa suggesting that some of the immigrants were "utterly useless for this country". He was particularly incensed that the Jews would not work on Saturday and recommended that Jewish immigration be stopped altogether. Another agent called them "very inferior ordinary labourers—a trading class", who would be unable to make a living because they didn't know English. By July the *Winnipeg Times* was editorializing that the Jews were lazy, dirty, and useless and ought to be deported. They were refuted by the *Free Press* (as usual), which retorted that the Jews were working at whatever jobs they could find and that the good burghers of Winnipeg ought to understand that

they were having a difficult time. Then in a paroxysm of
Victorian condescension, the paper explained: "It is not
denied that they came here only half civilized; indeed, after
having been, as a people, for ages ground down by their
oppressors, they could hardly be otherwise.... Besides
being ignorant of many things which Canadians think all
the world should know, they are ignorant of the English
language...."

As for the immigrants themselves, they weren't much
happier about their situation than their reluctant hosts. In
June 1882 one of them wrote an open letter to the Russian
Hebrew publication *Hamelitz*:

> I know not in what to dip my pen, in the inkstand before
> me, or in the flow of tears running from the eyes of the
> unfortunates who have come here with me.... One
> hears nothing but weeping and bewailing one's youth
> destined to be wasted and vainly spent in this desert of
> Winnipeg. They have sent us to a wilderness.... We
> wanted to come here in order to honestly earn our
> livelihood in a land where we would not be exposed to
> the mockery and ridicule of our Gentile neighbours
> because of our faith and our looks.... Even such work
> as chopping wood, hewing stone or digging soil is not to
> be found and the cost of living, to boot, is extremely
> high.
>
> One does not see the shadow of a Committee* that
> would come to the aid of the wretched immigrant dur-
> ing the first days of his stay in this country. We shall
> perish from hunger and cold which here reaches 40
> degrees below zero during the winter. What is worse
> still is that there are very few regularly built houses.
> There are only canvas tents in which we too live, for
> only the rich can afford to rent or build a house.
>
> It is evident that under such circumstances no one

*The Russo-Jewish Committee from Mansion House that had sent
them to Canada.

can think of anything of a higher order, such as the reading of a newspaper or a book.... Nor do we have time to do our daily prayers. We come home at night and sleep overtakes us before we have even eaten. We shall all perish here and not have so much as a Jewish burial....

By September the same young man felt happier and decided to correct the impression he had left.

The situation has, thank God, partly improved. We have gradually become inured to our hard labours, whether they be the construction of some new railway lines, the carrying of mortar and cement for the erection of some new buildings, or the laying of sewers in the streets of Winnipeg.... The New York and Winnipeg newspapers have nothing but words of praise for the Jewish refugees in Canada, and compare us favourably with those of our brethren who have gone to the United States. The former, willing to work, endeavour with their own hands to earn their livelihood without relying on the generosity of strangers, while the latter are still idling in the New York sheltering house for immigrants, expecting to be fed and disinclined to work....

Then he described how the tiny group of refugees had celebrated the Holy Days of Rosh Hashanah and Yom Kippur.

... Rosh Hashanah was celebrated in our tents near the railway station some forty miles from Winnipeg. Each of us donated three dollars and we collected the sum of $100, which we have sent to New York ordering a Sefer Torah and a Shofar. We have all stopped from work and gathered in a large tent and poured out our hearts in prayers, before God, during the Day of Atonement.

The Christian inhabitants, who had never seen nor heard the like before, collected in groups without and admiringly said, "Away from the city and from human society, they still remember the God of their ancestors."

Two years passed and still there was no land for the Jews. One very good reason was that they were unable to pay the high speculative costs of the day. They were paupers. They needed homestead land—*free* land—as had been promised. In January 1882 a Jewish delegation from Montreal met with John Henry Pope, the Minister of Agriculture, who agreed to "assist with all his aid". But by June the government had backed away again. "The government has made no arrangements for bringing the Jews to this country other than are made for bringing out other immigrants. The work of settling and providing for them will be carried out principally by the Jewish residents in Canada," the *Manitoba Free Press* reported. The promised homestead land had been allotted, instead, to private colonization companies.

Finally, in 1884, Alexander Galt successfully arranged for land near Moosomin in the North-West Territories, but by this time many of the refugees had jobs in Winnipeg which they were unwilling to give up. The others—twenty-six families—set out for their land which was situated about 225 miles south-west of Winnipeg close to the Manitoba border. They settled on 8,960 acres, each family with $250 worth of equipment and some cattle provided by Galt. They had had no experience of farming, but they were filled with hope—so much so that they called their community New Jerusalem. That name would haunt them over the next five years with a bitter, mocking irony. Their hastily erected shacks could not protect them from the sub-zero temperatures and raging blizzards of their first Saskatchewan winter. In the summer of 1885, frost killed their first crop. In 1886 a drought afflicted the entire area, and that winter the rabbi froze his feet in a blizzard and had to have them

amputated. The Russo-Jewish Committee wanted to be
repaid and there was no money. Still they held on. But
when fire broke out in September 1889, destroying hundreds of tons of hay, and the cause was suspected to be
arson, they gave up. Most returned to Winnipeg and
became peddlers.

All the new colonies in the area had failed during those
years. As Arthur Chiel described it, "Jews, Scotsmen, Englishmen, Germans and Danes were all part of heroic
attempts at colonization which met with dismal disappointment. It was clear that there had been need for expert
advice in farming matters, for extensive general assistance,
and above all, the blessings of nature. In the 1880s none of
these was forthcoming."

In spite of the general distress the colonists suffered,
Alexander Galt felt personally affronted by the failure at
Moosomin. Galt had hoped that a successful Jewish settlement would encourage the Rothschild family to invest in
the Canadian West. And he was angry about the loss of the
money the Russo-Jewish Committee had invested in the
settlement. "From the outset I protested against the experiment as I never thought they would make farmers," he now
wrote bitterly to the secretary of the Commission of Dominion Lands. "The colony at Moosomin is a failure. The Jews
have sold their crops [and] the cattle I gave them and
turned to their natural avocation of peddling...."

In 1888 the colony of Wapella was established (also in
south-eastern Saskatchewan) by a group of Russian and
Bessarabian Jews who had come to Montreal with the hope
of acquiring land. They did not have official financial assistance, but their venture was a success—the first success.
(Ezekiel Bronfman, the patriarch of the Bronfman family,
was one of the early settlers.) But Jewish colonization in
Canada might not have developed much further were it not
for the efforts of a single man—the Baron Maurice de
Hirsch.

Baron Maurice de Hirsch was to immigrant aid in Canada (and in the United States and South America) precisely what Cinderella's benefactor was to her — a dream material-ized, a miracle. The Baron was born in Germany in 1831 and became a large-scale industrialist and financier with an international reputation for philanthropy. During the pog-roms of 1885 he committed vast sums of money to getting Jews out of Russia and to various colonization schemes for their resettlement. But the definitive turning-point in his commitment came in 1897 when his son — a beloved and only son — died. Herman Landau, a British financier, came to Paris to express his sympathies, and at their meeting he suggested that the Baron and his wife "adopt all of Israel as their children." Then he recommended that farm colonies in Canada would be a good place to start.

Baron de Hirsch was interested in Canada, but wary — he had already committed large sums of money for Jewish colonization in Argentina — but he was impressed with the idea of pursuing agricultural colonization in general. In 1890 he set up a fund of 2,400,000 francs (about $480,000) for emigration to the United States, to be administered under the laws of New York State, and in 1891 he estab-lished the Jewish Colonization Association in Paris with capital of 10,000,000 francs, or $2,000,000.

In Canada the Young Men's Hebrew Benevolent Soci-ety, run by Harris Vineberg, Lazarus Cohen, and the other established Jews of Westmount, was struggling to survive as thousands of immigrants and refugees poured into Mont-real. There had been some encouragement to settle Jews on land in the West — a Dominion immigration agent had writ-ten to the Department of Agriculture saying that good homestead land was still available within a ten-mile radius of Regina — but the government seemed unwilling to get involved. Mansion House had bowed out of the picture and the YMHBS had no money. The situation seemed desperate. In 1891 seventeen Russian Jews arrived in Quebec City from Hamburg utterly destitute and helpless and when the immigration agent in Quebec wrote to Ottawa asking for advice, the Minister of Agriculture replied: "The government has no vote from which such assistance can be afforded.... If there are not means at the disposal of the Jewish community to take care of further arrivals of the same class of immigrant it would be wise to cable the parties on the other side to discontinue sending them; otherwise, it would be necessary for the government to invoke the clauses of the Immigration Act to prevent their landing as a necessary step to stop scandal and suffering."*

When the YMHBS heard of the Baron de Hirsch fund, they decided to ask for help. They petitioned the Baron himself, and they were successful. In June 1891 the Baron donated $20,000 for Jewish immigrant relief in Canada. The members of the YMHBS were elated and immediately created the Baron de Hirsch Institute, which provided a hostel for arriving immigrants and housed a school to teach English and orientate children before they entered the regular school system. They also set up a colonization committee to study the possibilities of further land settlement.

The Canadian government also lit up at the news of possible Baron de Hirsch funding and became newly and deeply interested in the question of Jewish colonization. In December 1891 the new Canadian High Commissioner to Britain, Hugh Sutherland, wrote in confidence to Harris Vineberg, president of the Baron de Hirsch Institute:

I have learned in a most confidential way that some rather serious trouble has arisen in the Baron's negotiation in the Argentine Republic.... If negotiations are broken off, I am led to believe I have the first call for Manitoba on an extensive scale.... I am using my best

*Between 1882 and 1889, 7,580 Russian Jews were returned "home" on cattle ships from the United States, and as early as 1874 the YMHBS desperately asked Mansion House to send only people with a bit of money.

endeavour to get the Baron to throw his weight in the direction of Manitoba and have blocked out a scheme which has attracted his eye and the confidence of his agents. . . .

Sutherland then recommended that Vineberg send judiciously chosen newspaper clippings and reports about colonization in the Canadian West to the London Mansion House Committee, in the hope of rebuilding its interest in Jewish land settlement.

Also in December 1891 a petition to the Baron was presented to the mayor of Montreal for endorsement:

We undersigned unfortunately expelled Israelites of Russia do hereby ask your Honour to sign our petition what we give to our celebrated Philanthrop Baron de Hirsch, to buy for us some land and all articles what is necessary for farmers as we are farmers from home, and do understand well farming. Beside this we ask you, as we are sending two Delegates. . . to give them some paper as passport, maybe they will have to stay a couple of weeks in Paris. . . .

Seventy-six signatures were affixed to the petition (all but seventeen in Yiddish), including that of the illustrious Reverend Mendola de Sola, son of Abraham and brother of Clarence. The mayor, James McShane, replied favourably, and delegates Leib Hershkovitch and Benzin Leibovitch set off to see the Baron in Paris.

In January 1892 the director of the Jewish Colonization Association in Paris, Sigmund Sonnenfeld, wrote to Harris Vineberg asking whether he thought another colonization venture might succeed. The JCA and the Baron felt positively disposed to donate money for Jewish colonization in Canada, but they hoped that the Russo-Jewish Committee of Mansion House in London would also contribute. The London Committee, however, was still angry about the

Moosomin failure and refused to co-operate. Eventually the JCA went ahead anyway, and 20,000 francs was provided to establish forty families on the land. They were to be hand-picked for their suitability by the officers of the Baron de Hirsch Institute in Montreal.

The same month, members of the Baron de Hirsch Institute met with Prime Minister John Abbott to talk about the possibility of Jewish colonization in Manitoba. "It was the first time that a group of Jewish leaders had met with a Canadian prime minister on an official mission, and it was a most cordial encounter. . . . The Jewish delegates were satisfied that the Canadian government would do its utmost to further the colonizing effort . . . ," wrote Arthur Chiel in *The Jews In Manitoba*. "The government found it sound policy to have the land selected by the settlers themselves or their accredited agents. . . . "

Harris Vineberg and the colonization committee of the Baron de Hirsch Institute were excited and hopeful. They were convinced that the failure at Moosomin was due to climatic conditions and to the boom in Winnipeg that had drawn settlers off the land. This time they would plan more carefully.

They did their research painstakingly. Homestead land was indeed available — 160 acres to each head of family and to every male over the age of eighteen — and the Canadian government was granting bonuses to settlers west of the Manitoba border — ten dollars to every head of family and five dollars to everyone over the age of twelve. They looked into the cost of the trip west (twelve dollars for adults and six dollars for children over the age of six) and the cost of food for the duration (twenty cents per day per person). They calculated the cost of buying agricultural implements, food, seeds for planting, and cattle, then estimated that five hundred dollars per family would be enough to begin with. They chose their forty families from immigrants waiting in Montreal as carefully as they could. Then they hired two overseers with farming experience to help the colonists get started.

The first official venture had been called New Jerusalem. The second would naturally be named Hirsch.

CHAPTER FIFTEEN

Hirsch

ON APRIL 27, 1892, twenty-seven families and their over-seer, Charles McDiarmid, left Montreal for the North West. In Winnipeg and Regina they were joined by twenty-two more Russian Jews who had been waiting for land, and together the group set out for the town of Oxbow, warmed by a wave of sympathetic press coverage. "God help the poor Jews," clucked the *Canadian Gleaner* as they made their way towards the Souris River. On May 2 they arrived in Oxbow, which consisted primarily of a tiny general store run by Asher Pierce, a Jew who had settled in the region not long before. They stopped and rested, then continued on to their land, which was located several miles east of Estevan.

The *Gleaner*'s tone was prophetic, for things went badly from the start. Provisions were scarce and the work horses arranged for by the Baron de Hirsch Institute in Montreal were useless. One died almost immediately and the others limped along on reluctant last legs.

None of the Russian Jews had ever farmed before ("Some have never seen, let alone handled a plough," Asher Pierce wrote to Montreal) and almost none spoke English. Charles McDiarmid, needless to say, did not speak Yiddish. A few days after their arrival he wrote a despairing letter to Harris Vineberg in Montreal:

All hands arrived here on Monday night and they stayed in the train all night. I have them since in a warehouse here and I am having an awful time with them owing largely to the cramped place....I feel it would have been much better to have kept all the children in Montreal for they are certainly going to see some hardship here. Was those people made to understand anything about what must be done on their Sunday? If they persist on going without a fire or waiting until someone comes to make one, they will certainly freeze....

McDiarmid worked sixteen hours a day to earn his $100 monthly salary. He surveyed land for homesteads and arranged to buy lumber for building. His job was to look after everything on the ten-mile-square area the settlers had come to, from ploughing to buying implements and food. But he had only the cash forwarded to him from Montreal, and when that money was short or late in arriving, as it often was, the new "colonists" went without. By June individual houses had still not been built, owing to delays in getting money to McDiarmid, and people were still living communally. That was working out poorly — and when a rainstorm tore the paper roof off their shack, the grumbling became a roar of discontent.

In desperation ten men and two teams of oxen built four sod houses measuring twelve feet by twenty-four feet inside. Then McDiarmid wrote to Vineberg complaining that the Baron de Hirsch Institute had seriously underestimated costs. He complained about being harassed to the limits of endurance. "[Every day they say] 'I want table to eat on; I want chair, can't sit down; I want lumber to make shelves to put things; I want oxen to plough my farm; I want pick, shovel, spade, rope to make well....'"

Far from the rigours of the North West wilderness, the Montreal officials blamed McDiarmid for the difficulties in the settlement. The colonists were getting along badly and

hoarding scarce implements that belonged to the community. Any *Am Olam* idealists among them must have been
rudely shocked by their desperate failure to generate a
communal spirit.

By the end of June, conditions had begun to improve, at
least on the practical side of the ledger. On June 30 McDiarmid wrote that sixteen ox teams were ploughing, two on a
section and two men to a pair; other men were building a
house; four people were drawing lumber; two were baking
bread; and several were digging wells. But social conditions
were still difficult. In August McDiarmid wrote again to
Montreal asking for instructions. The problems he was
called upon to solve seemed endless. What, for example,
should he do about families that had a little of their own
money? Should they be allowed to pay extra and have better
houses than the rest?

In October the colonists created a council to set up
guidelines for living and working together. They may have
modelled it after a "constitution" created six months earlier
by another Baron de Hirsch farming colony in Philadelphia. There the Russian immigrants pledged themselves to
"peaceful, honourable and friendly intercourse with one
another and to shun all possible gossip, intrigue and quar-
relsome disputation." (They also swore not to indulge in
any game of chance anywhere or any time and to conduct
their weekly meetings in "regular, parliamentary fashion".)

The council did improve the atmosphere at Hirsch, and
by November the colonists had formed a choir and were
planning a "sacred concert" — with McDiarmid and his wife
invited to perform their own "sacred" selections. In December the CPR investigated the "condition and progress" of
Hirsch on behalf of the Jewish Colonization Association in
Paris and reported that the colony was "a decided success".
But the bureaucrats in Montreal remained dissatisfied with
McDiarmid. They felt—probably unfairly—that he was
spending too much money too fast. They put pressure on
him, and in January 1893 McDiarmid resigned.

Later that year Lazarus Cohen visited the colony. Cohen had just been named chairman of the colonization committee of the Baron de Hirsch Institute and he was anxious to see how the colony was working out. It is recorded that he gave the colonists "sage advice" but he must have been deeply shocked by their living conditions. Until 1894 drought parched the land. Crops failed and many left Hirsch, although they were optimistically replaced by others and, after 1894, farming did improve. It took four and a half years, but by the autumn of 1896 the settlement seemed well-established. Every family at Hirsch had a wagon, a sleigh, a plough, a harrow, a horse, a horse-rake, a mowing-machine, and garden tools. Three families had binding-machines and there was one horse-powered thresher for the community. The colony also had a school and a small synagogue.

In 1897 the JCA in Paris sent another assessor, who also came up with a favourable report; and in 1898 a second school opened in the colony. It looked as though the inexperienced shtetl refugees who had never seen a plough were successfully turning the wilderness into agricultural land.

Ten years later Hirsch was still a success and, as such, a public challenge to the myth that Jews were congenitally incapable of farming. "There is no destitution or need of assistance from any source [at Hirsch] and the general health of the colony is good," wrote J. Obed Smith, assistant superintendent of immigration for the federal government in his annual report of 1907. "The gratifying progress made by these Hebrew farmers proves that under reasonable conditions and guided by expert leaders, they are fully as successful as any other class of people in Canada."

Although, for most, a plough was a new implement and an ox was as exotic and strange a creature as a mammoth, Jewish "farmers" continued to enter Canada. Colonization companies advertising in Europe, in German, were attracting Yiddish-language émigrés. Then, of course, there was the five-dollar bonus offered by the Canadian government to transportation companies which brought in immigrants of the "agricultural class". The only test of who was and who was not a farmer was the statement of the transportation company and a perfunctory examination by Canadian immigration officials to see whether incoming immigrants had rough or smooth hands. The same five-dollar bonus accounted for the fact that people who thought they were headed for the United States sometimes—to their utter surprise—found themselves in Canada.

More and more Jewish immigrant "farmers" rolled across the country in CPR cars from Montreal to the North West, and by 1906 ten separate Jewish farm colonies had been established, the majority in Saskatchewan.* Eight of them had been founded without the aid of the Jewish Colonization Association and the Baron de Hirsch Institute. They were struggling along alone.

In 1907 the Canadian Committee of the Jewish Colonization Association was formed and the organization moved in to assist all Jewish farmers in the country with low-interest loans and helpful advice. Their guiding motto was: "To make the Jew a farmer and to keep the farmer a Jew." By 1917 there were three thousand Jews farming in Canada. Dugouts had been replaced by mud houses, then by log cabins, then by homes built from lumber. Every colony had a synagogue and at least one school. The JCA employed fifteen teachers in fourteen colonies and provided Hebrew teachers (who doubled as kosher butchers) as well.

The JCA was a stern but devoted parent to the Jewish farm colonies of the West and, like recalcitrant children, many of the colonists never repaid their loans. They cried poverty and ruined crops and often they were right. Sometimes they refused to pay on principle, saying that the Baron de Hirsch had left the money for their use (the

*The best-known were Wapella, 1888; Lipton, 1902; Edenbridge, 1906; and Sonnenfeld (later renamed Hoffer), 1906.

Baron had died in 1896). At bottom, however, they knew that their other creditors would be a lot harsher than the JCA — and, with ill luck and inexperience, they owed money in many places.

During its life-span of more than fifty years — from 1907 until the 1960s — the Canadian Committee of the JCA never collected on more than half its outstanding loans. For example, in 1917 the Association advanced a seed loan to Harry Fishtrom of Hirsch. Five years later, nothing had been repaid. By 1922 Fishtrom owed $337.47 to the JCA, $4,000 to Canada Life, and $2,000 to the Merchants' Bank. His crop was seized and his mortgage foreclosed by the bank. Then there was the case of John Hershburg, also of Hirsch. Hershburg made a homestead application in 1903. By 1915 he owed $2,990.18 to the JCA in outstanding loans and interest. The JCA wrote to him, and wrote to him again, then sent someone to talk with him, until finally, in desperation (not a penny had been paid on his account), it sold his land to another colonist. Hershburg was heartbroken. "Wer shel I go at my old age? I worket 23 years on this land and have no hom. Surely Baron de Hirsch didnt told you to do such a thing like this. . . . O God wer are you?" he wrote in plaintive, phonetic English.

> If I'll not get my land beck I will do this wot I never did, I will writ to King Jorg of London England and will adwertis in the English papers and will send copys to Paris. I will sell a cow and adwertis all over the world wot Baron de Hirsch Institute Canadian Committee hes don with me. Baron de Hirsch, Stend up, get awake, look wot your money is doing with people that workid so hart a life time to mik a hom and now are linge in the prery without a hom . . . I hop you will understend an old brooken heart. . . .
>
> very cincerily yours,
> John Hershburg.

To its credit the JCA did take steps to aid Hershburg, but its relationship to the colonists remained paternalistic, and the colonists responded by becoming dependent on their institutional benefactor. In 1922 A. Gorbach of Hirsch owed the JCA almost $4,000, but he had other debts as well — including $1,100 to the lumber company and $100 to the doctor. His creditors (all except the JCA) were eyeing his crop as repayment. But Gorbach turned to the JCA for protection and actually felt free enough to ask for another mortgage. Some time later, in the middle of a business letter, Gorbach asked the JCA administrator to look up his son in Winnipeg and ask why he hadn't written home. But the clearest example of JCA paternalism came in the 1920s when bootlegging became a major industry at one of the Jewish colonies.* When the JCA learned what was going on it threatened to evict anyone who was caught making money in this immoral way.

Louis Rosenberg

For twenty-one years one man personified the JCA for the Jewish farmers of western Canada. Between 1919 and 1940 Louis Rosenberg organized and supervised the co-operative farm unions, the teaching of Hebrew, the administering of loans, and the social services and immigration work of the JCA in the West. It was also his thankless job to try to collect money owed to the Association.

Rosenberg was like a camp counsellor with unruly charges in his care. He travelled continuously, visiting each colony at least once a year. In the early days he moved around by horse and buggy from Sonnenfeld, Hirsch, and Lipton in the south of Saskatchewan to Edenbridge in the north, then headed west into Alberta. At each settlement he would report on each individual farmer. How many acres had been broken and ploughed since the last visit? How

*Edenbridge.

many acres did he have planted in wheat, barley, and oats? What did he do with his crop? Had he increased his herd of cattle? Rosenberg was always forthcoming with advice. If the market for grain was poor, he would recommend a temporary emphasis on dairy farming. He settled boundary disputes, advised the homesteaders about their children, and found them teachers and Hebrew instructors. Rosenberg was a lifeline for isolated settlers; he was their link to other farm communities and to other Jews.

Louis Rosenberg emigrated to Canada in 1915 from Leeds, England, to teach in the Jewish farm settlement of Lipton, Saskatchewan. His information about the Canadian prairie was sketchy and, armed with a freshly earned doctorate in sociology from the University of Leeds, he was sure he would be the principal of a small school, at the very least. He was principal, as it turned out, *and* the only teacher, in a one-room schoolhouse in the colony. He lived at the back of the school—called Tiferes Israel (Pride of Israel)—and warmed himself and cooked on a tiny wood-burning stove; and on the High Holidays, when the colony imported a Torah from Winnipeg, Rosenberg (who could read Hebrew) became the conductor of religious services. He stayed for several years, working in exchange for room and board only. Crops were bad and there was little money around. But the first-hand experience Rosenberg scraped together at Lipton made him an ideal choice for the JCA when it began looking for a western supervisor for its colonies. He was an educated, English-speaking Jew who could mediate between the eastern-European colonists and the Anglo-Saxon world surrounding them. (When he got the job Rosenberg wisely undertook a crash course in Yiddish.)

Rosenberg was continually called upon to demonstrate that there really were Jewish farmers—that such a combination was not outside the realm of human possibility. By 1934 there were one thousand Jewish families farming in Canada (fifty per cent of them in the Prairies) and some of

them had been working the land for a half a century. But
the disbelief persisted. In 1933 the JCA presented an exhibit
at the World Grain Exhibition and Conference in Regina
which detailed the activities of Jewish farmers. Seventy
thousand people visited the exhibit, including one man
"whose dress and appearance marked him as no farmer," in
Rosenberg's opinion. "He looked at the grains grown by
Jewish farmers in Canada and the Argentine, the fruits,
nuts, oils and wine produced by Jewish farmers in Palestine,
and then came to a halt where I sat at my desk under a large
sign which read 'Jewish Farmers Cultivate By Their Own
Labour Over Five Million Acres Of Land'. He looked again
before leaving, and speaking to himself, without turning his
head towards me, he rapped out as if trying to convince
himself, 'Doch giebt's kein Judische farmer!—Neverthe-
less, there *are* no Jewish farmers!'"

Rosenberg was a man of diverse interests. He was a
trained statistician, cautious in his manner and attentive to
detail, and for twenty years he kept careful notes on the
farm colonies and other aspects of Jewish life in Canada.
The result was the publication, in 1939, of an astonishingly
detailed study called *Canada's Jews*. Eugene Forsey called
the book "a masterly piece of work", and a reviewer from
the University of Leeds described it as "a study in detail
unknown elsewhere". Rosenberg was also a closet socialist
—as an employee of the JCA he thought he should be
publicly apolitical. He had been influenced by the Fabian
Socialists in England, and in the 1930s he became a founder
of the CCF in Saskatchewan. Under the secret pen-name of
Watt Hugh McCollum (Watcha m'call 'im) he wrote hundreds of political pamphlets for the CCF, as well as a book
called *Who Owns Canada?* which exposed the concentration
of economic power in the country through interlocking
directorates.*

The Jewish farmers themselves had some difficulty fig-

Who Owns Canada? was first published by the CCF in 1936 and revised
in 1947.

uring out just what Rosenberg's Ph D stood for. They knew about doctors of medicine, and a few of the lawyers had become doctors of law. But a doctor of *tzotzialism?* "No," Rosenberg would explain, "not socialism, *sociology.*"

From time to time, well-meaning Canadian Jews with fashionable left-wing leanings would take up the cause of communal Jewish farm colonization, particularly during the Depression, when, to people living in the cities, anything looked better than urban poverty. These groups were a problem for Rosenberg, for they usually bypassed the JCA and proposed schemes the Association thought were harebrained and naïve. In 1932, for example, a group called the Co-operative Jewish Agricultural Society of Calgary suggested moving ten families of practically destitute Jews to an area of only 200 acres thirty miles out of Calgary. Each family would have to find $250, but the remainder would be raised by selling shares among the Jews of Calgary, Winnipeg, Vancouver, and other western centres.

Rosenberg was aware that inexperienced city people without capital could not succeed on an Alberta farm, especially in 1932, when many experienced farmers were on relief. He was also quite aware that local municipalities already providing relief to farmers would resent and possibly refuse to help city folk who suddenly popped up in their area as farmers. And in such hard times the JCA certainly could not afford to carry more people than it was already handling. Rosenberg published a piece under a pseudonym in the *Israelite Press* of Winnipeg in which he pointed out the weaknesses of the Co-operative Jewish Agricultural Society of Calgary. He advised Jews with some capital who wanted to move to farms to do so through the good offices of the JCA.

Crisis struck in 1938 when the Paris offices of the JCA closed. Colonization had to take a back seat to the urgent needs of European Jewish refugees. Budgets were cut drastically and the Canadian Committee was forced to become self-sustaining; in particular the budget for Hebrew instruction in the colonies was slashed. This was a serious blow to the colonists. Without the possibility of Hebrew and religious instruction for their children — part of the learning and tradition that kept them Jews — parents would not stay long on the farms.

During the 1930s the Canadian Committee of the JCA lobbied insistently for action on the part of the Canadian government. Immigrants were now refugees, but the only legitimate way they could enter Canada was as "farmers". Finally in 1938, after years of unsuccessful pleading on the part of Jewish leaders, the Liberal government of Mackenzie King decided to admit one hundred refugee families from Czechoslovakia under the aegis of the JCA. They were settled on farms in the Niagara Peninsula and near Montreal and Winnipeg. But the closing of the JCA in 1938 also closed the door on the last hope for a large-scale entry of "agricultural" refugees into Canada.

But hopes died painfully, and in January 1940 the Canadian president of the JCA, Rabbi H. Abramowitz, was still writing to the Paris office begging that they reconsider. "These decisions were [made] just at a time when Canadian Jewry has been aroused to its responsibilities and is yearning for the relief of distressed European Jewry," he wrote. "We may point out that the Jews of Canada are looking to the JCA to aid and guide them in the task of absorbing and establishing refugees in this country as you have done in the past. It is felt that if an appreciable number of Jewish refugees would be established on the land, we would be able to secure the government's consent to the admission of other categories of refugees...into this country...."

But the offices remained closed, including the western office of Louis Rosenberg in Regina.

After the German occupation of France in June 1940 it was clear that the Paris office would not reopen.* A promi-

*In 1947 the JCA reopened in London.

nent member of the JCA had been arrested in Amsterdam by the Nazis and only in 1941 was it learned that the director of the Association, Louis Oungre, had successfully escaped to New York.

The important role of the JCA in the lives of the Jewish farmers in western Canada diminished sharply.* Louis Rosenberg was hired by the Canadian Jewish Congress as executive director of its western region, and in 1945 he became national research director, a position he held until his retirement in 1968. In that job he was, once again, astonishingly productive. In his lifetime he wrote and published over 12,000 books and pamphlets.

But Rosenberg's most vivid memories lie elsewhere. They are of the years he spent riding across the Prairies a half a century ago, visiting Jewish colonists in the far-flung settlements they had built with their own hands.

---

*The Canadian Committee of the JCA was revived after the war with the settlement of refugees from Displaced Persons camps. In 1960, 120 families were still farming under the auspices of the JCA, but by 1970 only a handful remained.

CHAPTER SIXTEEN

Edenbridge

OF ALL THE JEWISH FARM COLONIES in western Canada, the most successful was Edenbridge. The name itself symbolized the attitude the immigrants brought to their new life. Painstakingly they had built a wooden bridge across the Carrot River and in a flush of pleasure decided to name it after themselves — Yid'n Bridge* — Jew's Bridge. But when they were offered the chance to have the local post office in their colony, they reconsidered. What would Canadians know about Yid'n Bridge, they asked themselves? So they rolled the word around on their tongues and came up with the similar-sounding "Edenbridge". *They* knew what it meant. Besides, they had every intention of turning this wilderness into paradise on earth, so why not name it such in the beginning?

The first settlers at Edenbridge were men and women who had escaped from Lithuanian pogroms to South Africa in the late 1890s. When they decided to move again, to the Canadian prairie, they did so entirely independently, unaware of the Jewish Colonization Association and the assistance of the Baron de Hirsch Institute. They came because they were young and adventuresome and because, although they had migrated to South Africa, "America" was never far from their thoughts. "America" was where most of the eastern-European Jews were heading.

*pronounced Yeed'n.

In Wynberg, South Africa, one evening in December 1904, twenty-one-year-old Sam Vickar read an article in the American Yiddish newspaper *Der Amerikaner*. The writer described his unhealthy life as a worker in a New York garment factory and how he had escaped tuberculosis and tenement poverty by moving to a homestead in North Dakota. He advised anyone who wanted a free, healthy life to settle on a farm. Since there were no more free homesteads in North Dakota, he recommended writing to the Department of the Interior in Canada.

Impressed and excited, young Vickar ran into the shop where his brothers were working and shouted, "I'm going to Canada." They thought he had gone mad, but he convinced them, and the next day they all sat down to compose a letter to the Canadian Department of the Interior. What they wanted to know most of all was whether, as Jews, they would be welcome. Six weeks later they received a reply. Canada was a land of religious freedom, they were told. Everyone was welcome.

Vickar and his brothers, David and Louis, formed a group of about forty prospective Jewish farmers, and everyone began to prepare for the journey to Canada. Their instructions from the Canadian authorities were vague indeed. They were to travel to Winnipeg. There they would receive information about where to take up their free homesteads.

In February 1906 Louis Vickar, his wife, and their two-year-old daughter, along with Louis's sister Fanny, and her husband Jacob Sweiden, left Cape Town along with nine other South African Jews. In April Sam Vickar and his brother David also set sail. A friend bade them goodbye. "You'll find nothing but wolves and Eskimos in your Winnipeg," he teased. "I'll see you back here in six months."

The Vickars promised him he was wrong. "You won't see us return," called Sam. "Not after six years."

In July they landed in Quebec. Two days and three nights later they reached Winnipeg, where they were met by Max Broudy, one of the original group. Star City, Saskatchewan, was the final destination, he informed them. "Bring high boots, for there is lots of water," he warned. "And household remedies. There is no drugstore in Star City...."

Star City was no city—just a stop on the railway line; but a team of horses was waiting and Sam and David Vickar were driven to the settlement. They followed a zigzag trail through bush and sloughs to the Carrot River, where, to their relief and surprise, they saw their sister Fanny waving at them from the far shore. The driver drove the horses into the water and the Vickars watched their baggage apprehensively as the river crept over the sides of the carriage, but before long they had arrived safely. Family and friends who had last seen each other five months earlier in Cape Town now clasped each other tightly in a strange wilderness. Happily they walked from the banks of the river to the log cabin that Harry and Eli Wolfovitz had built. It was made from poplar logs with walls about five feet high (both the Wolfovitz brothers were short men) and had one window. The ceiling was made of small poplar logs laid across poplar joists two feet apart. Sod and clay had been laid over the wood to keep the heat in. Eli Wolfovitz lit a fire to welcome the new arrivals and threw handfuls of green grass on the flames to keep the mosquitoes away. Fires, grass, and mosquitoes. "That was the first thing we learned about pioneering in Saskatchewan," Sam Vickar would say later.

It was a Friday afternoon, and before sunset the two Wolfovitz women lit and blessed the Sabbath candles. Supper was rice soup served on a table made from three poplar branches with a board from a grocery box nailed on top. There were no chairs, so they took their meal standing. Suddenly a chunk of mud fell from the ceiling and landed in Sam Vickar's soup. It was all too much; he began to cry and ran outside into the bush. It was raining. In his misery, Sam thought of returning to South Africa, but then he remembered that he had told his friend he would not return before six years had passed. That settled it. He dried his eyes and returned to the house.

Over the next few days, Sam and Dave Vickar and their brother-in-law Jacob Sweiden filed applications for homesteads, bought a pair of oxen and a plough, and built the first frame house in Edenbridge. Then, with happy optimism, they set out to plough a piece of land for a vegetable garden, only to discover that not one among them had the slightest idea of how to break virgin land. Harry Wolfovitz claimed *he* knew how. He had worked on a farm in Russia, he said. So Sam harnessed the oxen, Jacob Sweiden set the plough in the earth at the place they wanted to start, and they hooked up the oxen. "Away we go! Get up boys!" they shouted at the oxen. Miracle of miracles, the animals actually started to move and a furrow appeared in the earth. The problem was getting back. The oxen proceeded to cover up the furrow they had just opened.

They turned the oxen around a few times, but nothing seemed to work. Eventually a local farmer came to their rescue and showed them how to make a start when ploughing. "That was when we found out it was harder to be a farmer than a store clerk," Sam Vickar would recall.

Vickar took work as a handyman for a local pioneer called Wittig. He got up at 4 a.m., cleaned the barn, and fed and watered the animals. Then he ate breakfast with the family. They had fried pork on the table at every meal, so Vickar ate only bread and butter, potatoes, and tea.

One Sunday Mrs. Wittig asked young Sam to attend church with them. He refused.

"What church do you belong to?" she asked.

"I belong to the Jewish synagogue," he replied.

Mrs. Wittig drew in a small, short breath and looked angrily at Sam.

"You can't belong to the Jewish synagogue," she said coldly. "You're not a Jew."

"But I am a Jew," retorted Sam, wondering what was going to happen.

"Impossible," said Mrs. Wittig. "If you really are a Jew, where are your horns?"

When Sam looked astonished, Mr. and Mrs. Wittig led him into their bedroom where pictures of Moses and Aaron hung on the wall.

"Look at Aaron," Mrs. Wittig cried triumphantly. "*He* has horns."

Sam tried to explain that Aaron did not have horns. The picture showed him blessing the people. He was the High Priest and his arms were outstretched, his fingers spread to hold up his prayer shawl.

The Wittigs were surprised and shaken enough to forgo their trip to church. Instead, they talked with Sam — questioning him about Jews. He was the first Jew they had ever met. Sam was even able to tell them how surprised he was that although he had sat at their table for four weeks and eaten nothing but bread and butter and potatoes, they had never asked why he didn't eat pork. From that day on he was served eggs at mealtime.

Once Edenbridge was founded, people began to send for their relatives, and they, in turn, sent for others. They came from Poland, Galicia, Lithuania, Russia, and England. They were blacksmiths, shoemakers, tailors, carpenters, students, millers, unskilled labourers, storekeepers, peddlers, butchers, and electricians. Not one of them had ever been a farmer. By 1910, 138 people lived in the colony. They owned 7,610 acres, of which 614 had been broken and cleared and were under cultivation. They had 29 horses, 166 head of cattle, and $4,635 worth of farm machinery. They were succeeding, and they were justly proud.

But other problems plagued Edenbridge — social and political problems. Many of the incoming settlers were *Am Olam* believers whose ideological struggle was to prove that Jews, too, could successfully participate in the "noble labour" of agriculture. They were left-wing socialists,

Jewish nationalists who had transferred the ideals of Zion to the Canadian prairie. They were anti-religious and militantly opposed to the trappings of traditional Judaism.

The colony split into two physically separate parts. The "radicals" lived in the north section and kept pretty much to themselves, attending religious services only on the High Holidays of Rosh Hashanah and Yom Kippur. They were led by Mike Usiskin, who later became part of the Jewish communist movement and wrote a book called *Oksn Un Motorn* (*From Oxen to Motors*) celebrating the Edenbridge experience as a new pathway for the Jewish people. On the south side of the colony were the more traditional and conventional Orthodox Jews. They were led by the Vickars.

The disputes in the tiny colony of Edenbridge mirrored the conflicts that were taking place between the left-wing idealists and the Orthodox traditionalists in Winnipeg, Toronto, Montreal, and New York City—the difference being that the leftists of Edenbridge were ideologically committed to the back-to-the-land movement and the redemption of the Jewish nation through the pursuit of agriculture. The New York socialist Yiddish paper, the *Jewish Daily Forward*, found its way into the bush country of northern Saskatchewan and was read, avidly, by candlelight in log cabins beside the Carrot River. Eventually tensions became so unbearable that both sectors built themselves separate community centres. The synagogue was built in the south end in 1908 in a grove of black and white poplars (the Vickars headed the building committee) but the north end built its own structure—the International Hall and Free Library. When the Jewish Colonization Association began to bring aid to the Edenbridge settlement, its agent reported that "Socially, the farmers of Edenbridge are the worst people I came across....Their acrimoniousness towards each other [has] exceeded all bounds...."

From the beginning the Vickar family dominated Edenbridge. They went into business early, first selling farm implements, then opening a general store. They made

enough money to buy more land and soon they were
wealthier than the other settlers in the colony. This, of
course, left their friends and neighbours feeling ambivalent. On the one hand, the Vickars were respected and
deferred to because they were wealthier than anyone else.
On the other hand, they were resented and envied.

The north-enders (also known as the Londoners or the
Townshippers because they lived on the township line)
were mostly Russian Jews who had come to Canada via
the Jewish East End of London. They had read about
Edenbridge in an advertisement the Vickars and the other
colonists had placed in a London newspaper. All the colonists were anxious to attract more settlers to help with the
awesome task of clearing the land. Mike Usiskin (known
during his life at Edenbridge as Uncle Mike) and his friends
were eager to make a move. "We were ready to live in the
wilderness, among wild animals if need be," Usiskin
recorded in his book.

Usiskin was an intense, intellectual young man, an *Am
Olam* believer and a universalist. Like many socialists of his
day he was overflowing with optimism; hoping to improve
communication in the world he learned Esperanto; he also
became a vegetarian. Usiskin had been appalled by the
conditions of the London poor during the first decade of
the century, and when he transmitted his feelings to paper
more than thirty years later, his passion had not diminished:

> Dear friends, do you know what it means to be the slave
> of a slave? Have you ever met people who place less
> value on a whole human life than they do on the tiniest
> screw of a machine? Have you ever been witness to a
> tiny child whose mother was forced to send him out to
> work in a factory, run down and crushed by the wheels
> of a machine drawn by some drunken charlatan? Have
> you ever seen men fighting off dogs for a piece of
> bread, or over a bone in a garbage can? Have you ever

had to listen to kindhearted folk preach of the good things to expect in the hereafter while taking what they can for themselves in the present? Have you ever met fighters for peace with guns in their hands? Have you ever had to face the outrageous contrast that exists between the poor working classes who live in the dirty, smelly, noisy East End and the idle rich of the clean, quiet, and cheerful West End? Have you ever, dear friends, given any thought to the worries suffered by one class as opposed to the well-being of another class? Have you ever had to pass drunken women with babes at breasts lying in the gutters outside saloons?...Even the hardships endured by Robinson Crusoe sounded less difficult to overcome than those one had to endure in this society....

Although Usiskin was interested in the ad from Edenbridge, he was positively fascinated by a letter an Edenbridge settler had written to a family member in London who was also thinking about making the move across the sea. The letter read:

Flee my friends from the London fogs....Flee from the confusion of streets where some maniacal driver may cut you down. Flee from the tenements and the bosses who live off your blood, sweat and tears. Flee from the two-faced society where the politicians don't say what they mean and don't think what they say. Come to Edenbridge where the air is fresh and still...so peace-ful that you can lie down to rest in the middle of the road. No one would ever wake you, let alone run over you. The forest here is so vast that personal expansion has no bounds. You can live here by your own resources, but our people are all eager to help you and will greet you with open arms. Come, help us tame this wild land...help us settle our colony....We need your energies....You will not regret it.

Usiskin's brother David left first; Mike followed later, in May 1911. Like the Vickars who had come to the same place five years earlier, Mike Usiskin's first impressions of the countryside that would be home for the rest of his days were ambivalent, to say the least. Star City was a misnomer. "I was in the middle of a vast, uninhabited country with only the tiny rooftop of the railway station as evidence of civilization.... I was alone at the final stop...and I had mixed feelings.... I had joy...but [also] great loneliness. It was 4 a.m. and I stood alone in this 'Star City' not knowing where to go. I had expected to find a city of a few thousand inhabitants, but from where I stood no city was even in sight."

His brother arrived, however, and before long the horse and wagon were lurching back towards the Edenbridge colony. "No one need envy the trip back," wrote Usiskin. "The mud came up over the wheels, the horses could barely drag their legs forward, and we, splattered from top to bottom with mud, lay in a bare, open wagon, not so much as straw to lie on, and dozed off and on with each lurch forward. From time to time we'd wake up to find that a wheel was stuck, or some tree had fallen across the road, and we'd have to get out and push the tree out of the way and get the wagon back in the proper ruts.... [Then] the sudden halt of the wagon awakened us. Our bones ached from the all-night jarring of the bare wagon. I'm sure if it wasn't for our clothes, our bones would have fallen right out of our bodies on the wagon floor...."

In the early years of Edenbridge, the post office was the centre of social activity; the colonists were isolated, not just from the outside world, but from each other. To visit a neighbour (or to get to the post office, for that matter) one had to push through uncharted bush and swamps. Usiskin tells of one man who was lost in the bush for two days, although he was only a mile or so from his own house. To visit the post office was something of an occasion, and most of the settlers fought their loneliness by trying to get there as often as possible. Shortly after his arrival, Mike Usiskin wrote:

> The post office was about the size of a bedroom.... You could put the entire building on a sleigh [and have] room for a few extra passengers.... In the middle was a box stove around which everybody huddled like geese on a cold day.... There was no furniture in the place, not even stoves to sit on. Very rarely would one see a woman.... It was too difficult for them to cross over the deep swamps.... There I encountered several Jews whom I could not distinguish as having come from many familiar parts of Europe. Instead there seemed to be a mixture of Europeans, Africans and Americans.... The African wore a light shirt, the Lithuanian had on tall boots, the American wore a leather jacket, the Canadian a fur cap with the flaps pulled down over his ears and Edenbridge style overalls—a virtual checkerboard of patches. All of them had one thing in common—beards—some short and some long....
>
> The room was as smoky as a local bar. The firewood was too long for the stove and stuck out. It would have been too much trouble to start chopping all the wood by hand to fit the stove, so no one bothered.... So what if some of the pieces were short and the others too long! We weren't, after all, keeping up with Parisian fashions here, so why be fussy about it? In addition, nearly everyone had a cigarette dangling from his lip.... But what other solace did these lonely parts of the country offer?...
>
> In the small gathering of people I overheard four separate discussions...."The revolution would not have been lost if all the leaders had united!" shouted one man. "If all of Russia would have risen up in one day, you would have seen some great changes. It would have been the end of Nicholas and then all the Russian people along with the other racial groups... would have

been able to live like brothers!" He was interrupted by a young woman. "Why do you say, like brothers? What about us women? Aren't we people, too? Our men are brave here in Edenbridge, standing around a warm fire. Here they can talk of overthrowing monarchies or of reclaiming Zion where they can all live like kings... using their wives as handmaidens. No thank you sir. I would not want to live in a land where you would be king."...

The next man to speak was a small, thin, blond, quiet-spoken Jew. "What good does it do you to argue over the merits of the Holy Land when none of you has ever been there?...It's quite possible that the people who live there are anxious to leave...."

"And come to Edenbridge," added another. "Yes, to Edenbridge. Let's talk about our own land. How long are we going to have to live like wolves in the forest before we can begin to see where we are heading? How long will it be before we can read a newspaper like civilized people?"

Then the blond man began to speak "Brothers, the whole capitalist system is at fault. The politicians inch forward only to place themselves nearer the largest pile of money. This is a country where you get things for yourself by learning to become shrewd and clever in grabbing the things you want out of the hands of others....But the honest and just man who considers it an injustice to live off the hard work of others...he is considered to be unproductive...and undesirable... not worthy to stand on so rich a soil!"

The young man was just beginning to...launch into a new lecture...when the crowd's attention...directed itself to an open door through which they saw an unusual sight. A man of average height with a goatee and childlike, gleaming eyes was dancing around...and as he danced he sang:

> Yidl plays the fiddle
> Jackie the bass does play
> Me, I sing a song
> In the middle of the road way

...He made it difficult for others to complain. They were ashamed to grumble when they saw a fellow, close to sixty years of age, jump with glee and begin to dance a jig.

It wasn't easy to adjust to isolation and the still, unnerving quiet of the virgin forest. The Edenbridge pioneers had arrived in the wilderness from London, New York City, Cape Town, and the noisy, bustling shtetls of Lithuania. To combat the eerie solitude and to keep in touch with each other, they devised a human telephone. Once a day each person would visit his closest neighbour carrying news that had been brought by the person who had just visited him. And they held meetings—three and four of them a week. Many of the meetings broke down in argument, but to communicate, even under the pressure of conflict, was better than not to communicate at all. Meetings lasted until one and two o'clock in the morning, as though the Edenbridge farmers hesitated to return to the isolation of their shacks. But eventually the constant bickering became hard to take. Usiskin despaired, though he was possibly as responsible as anyone for maintaining the tensions.

> We had developed our own civilization....We had nearly everything we needed...but we were missing one thing—unity. And because of this, we really couldn't get ahead. If one person said "day", sure as anything the other would say "night". If one said it was winter and very cold, the other would point out very clearly with good examples to fortify his proof, that it really was summer and very hot. That this was the

situation was not the fault of the common folk, but of our leaders. Our leaders were robust, clean-blooded idiots with loud voices and big mouths who could and would shout down any opposition. Battles, hostilities, arguments and disagreements—but only God knows why we had to disagree. Everyone had more work than he could handle, building shacks and barns and clearing the one-thousand-year-old bush a few yards at a time so that no amount of work seemed to make a dent it it...but somehow, the squabbling became part of the life....

Life in Edenbridge was hard work from sunrise until well into the evening. The area around the settlement was thickly covered with a light poplar and red-willow forest and every inch had to be cleared before crops could be planted. Each tree was taken down individually with an axe. The base was chopped and then, with a team of horses, the tree was pulled down with a chain. The branches would be "limbed" and burned, but the tree itself was saved for firewood in the winter. It might take several men a whole hour to get one tree down. Then the roots had to be pulled out of the ground before they could break the ground with plough and oxen in preparation for planting.

The Edenbridge farmer rose between 4 and 5 a.m. to feed and curry the horses, milk the cows, and clean the barn. He ate a good breakfast—in the family of Cecil Gordon, who was born at Edenbridge in 1912 and farmed there until 1965, it was oatmeal, two eggs, fried potatoes, three slices of toast, and coffee—and he was out in the fields by 7 a.m. At noon he would eat heartily again—meat, potatoes, bread, and fruit—before returning to the fields until sundown. At night, Gordon's mother would make borscht—Russian style. There were also three eggs per person, potatoes, cheese with cream, and herring. Herring cost seventy-five cents a barrel and even the poorest Russian Jewish farmer could treat himself to that old-home delicacy. After supper he'd feed the horses and bed them down for the night. By 9 p.m. he'd be ready for sleep. His wife would raise chickens, turkeys, ducks, and geese, milk the cows, and grow a vegetable garden. She washed clothes, churned butter, baked bread, and sewed. (At age twelve, Gordon got his first combination overalls made from cloth remnants from Eaton's.) She made warm comforters with chicken and goose feathers. They were needed. Winter nights on the Carrot River in uninsulated houses were so cold that the water in the pail in the kitchen would freeze solid and the children would wake to see icicles hanging in the room.

To succeed on a pioneer farm, a man needed to be married. Some of the north-enders married gentile men and women from the surrounding farms and towns, but for the Orthodox faction in the south the question of finding a Jewish bride or groom presented a serious problem. The most likely place to meet someone was in Winnipeg.

Early in 1912 David Vickar (who was by then thirty-five years old) went to Winnipeg to look for a bride and returned, several weeks later, to announce that he was engaged to Sophie Gelman. They were married in Edenbridge just before Christmas, and before Sophie's mother and sisters left the colony to return to Winnipeg, Sam Vickar asked Gella, the older sister, to marry him. She replied that she already had a boyfriend, but Sam, the girl's mother, and her sister (who was now Sam's sister-in-law) persuaded her to change her mind. So she stayed two more days, and they had an engagement party.

In July 1913 Sam went to Winnipeg to visit Gella and to arrange for her to come to the colony to help with the threshing. They were expecting a big crop. In March 1914 they were married in Winnipeg and returned to live in Edenbridge.

David Vickar and his wife and Sam Vickar and his wife built a house together, with a partition down the centre. There was a common living-room and a common kitchen, but the two families ate separately. Gella Vickar would scrub her half of the kitchen floor to the half-way mark. Sophie Vickar was expected to wash the other half. Upstairs there was a central hallway with two bedrooms on each side — one for the parents, the other for the children. The David Vickar family eventually had five sons and one daughter, and the Sam Vickar family had five sons.

As children were born into the colony, the ideological divisions, the feuding, and the bickering between the north- and south-enders focused on the issue of teachers. For at least twenty years the factions argued over school taxes, over who should choose the teacher, and about the worth of the various teachers (who came and then left with disconcerting rapidity). The community built two schools, one for the north and one for the south, and had two sets of secular teachers, two Hebrew teachers, and two boards of trustees. Feelings over ideological differences became so bitter that in 1921 the Jewish Colonization Association considered removing both teachers, uniting the school boards, and engaging only one teacher for the colony. Finally they removed one of the teachers, whom the Vickars disapproved of, to the Lipton colony in south Saskatchewan.

By the early 1920s the colony was doing well financially. There were now 218 settlers — including men, women, and children. In 1923 the net equity of the community was $256,004 and the average equity per farmer was $5,818. Each farm had an average of five horses and three milk cows.

During the winter the men worked in neighbourhood lumber camps cutting and hauling firewood for sale in the local villages. Some hauled grain for farmers or storekeepers who were far from the railway line. As a group they felt prosperous and magnanimous enough to form the Edenbridge Immigrant Aid Society and to take in several refugees from the Romanian pogroms of 1923. North and south also co-operated long enough to create the Hebrew Farmers' Literary Institute of Edenbridge, which planned

Abandoned hut at the failed farm colony of Moosomin (Jewish Historical Society of Western Canada)

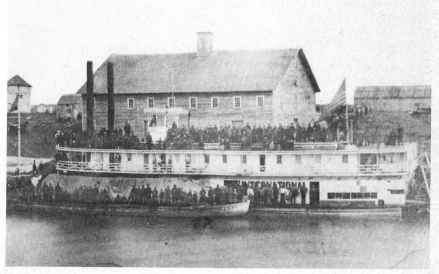

Immigration reception centre in Winnipeg, 1874 (Manitoba Archives)

The stones seemed to grow in the fields at the Sonnenfeld/Hoffer colony in the Northwest Territories (Saskatchewan). (Public Archives of Canada)

Felling the trees at the Edenbridge colony in northern Saskatchewan (Courtesy of Marcia Basman)

In 1916 Louis Rosenberg was the teacher in a one-room schoolhouse, called Tiferes Israel, in the Lipton colony. Rosenberg later became the western agent for the Jewish Colonization Association. (Jewish Historical Society of Western Canada)

A Hebrew class at the Sonnenfeld colony in 1934 (Jewish Historical Society of Western Canada)

Mr. and Mrs. A. Gorbach were pioneers at Hirsch, Saskatchewan, in the 1890s. Hirsch was the first successful Jewish farm colony in western Canada. (Multicultural History Society of Ontario)

Graves on permafrost. Because it was impossible to dig deep enough, graves were built on top of the ground. (Public Archives of Canada)

Jews' Bridge, or Yid'n Bridge, became Edenbridge when the young colony was offered the chance to run the local post office. The bridge joined the north and south parts of the colony. (Jewish Historical Society of Western Canada)

Mike Usiskin as a young man in London and in Edenbridge in 1933 (Courtesy of Marcia Basman)

Edenbridge girls all dressed up and sitting in the forest (Courtesy of Marcia Basman)

Usiskin and two friends in his wagon (Jewish Historical Society of Western Canada)

The Edenbridge synagogue was built on the south side of the colony by the Orthodox settlers. (Jewish Historical Society of Western Canada)

Friends and officials came from as far away as Winnipeg to celebrate the twenty-fifth anniversary of the colony. (Multicultural History Society of Ontario)

Pioneer Sam Vickar, pointing to a poem called "The Vickar Story" that was written for him and his wife by a nephew on the occasion of their fiftieth wedding anniversary.

Sam's son, Norman Vickar, now a cabinet minister in the Saskatchewan government, and his wife, Florence.

Norman's son, Larry Vickar, his wife, Tova, and their children (Preceding three photos courtesy of the Vickar family)

dramatic evenings at which adults and children performed. They bought books, for which the Jewish Colonization Association contributed fifty dollars. And they formed a "morals" committee to try to control the activity they were most worried about—bootlegging. A colonist by the name of Zalmen Golden was manufacturing stills for the entire region and seven Edenbridge farmers had been either fined or imprisoned in the Prince Albert jail for terms of one to three months. The morals committee decided that

> ...if a farmer is breaking the law which causes shame and blasphemy on the Jewish name, the offender shall be first warned to discontinue. If he still continues the shameful work or disgraceful dealing and if he is con-nected with the JCA, the Committee shall approach the JCA on behalf of the Association to sever all connections with him, *viz.* to foreclose on him. If he still continues, action shall be taken to hand him over to law....

However, as Louis Rosenberg, the JCA agent, noted: "As long as the present prohibition laws are in force...no amount of moral persuasion will make the farmer or the city man give up the chance of making an easy dollar."

But conditions in the Carrot River district began to change, and after 1923 the tide of success turned. Soon most of the saleable timber had been cut and people in the villages had begun to heat with coal. The new railway line brought transportation closer, and merchants and farmers had no further need to have their grain and merchandise hauled from a distance. That meant that all yearly expenses had to be met from the always unpredictable proceeds of the farm harvest. Relations with neighbouring farmers began to deteriorate as well. In the early years there had been little if any anti-Semitism. Co-operation was vital among those pioneering on the cold flats of Saskatchewan and, although prejudice remained a reality, it was in no one's best interests to act on it. But the old-country

antipathies between Jews and Ukrainians had been transported across half a world—they had lived together in the
Ukraine and emigrated together to the Canadian Prairies
—and, when life settled into an easier pattern, old irrita-
tions occasionally erupted into new conflicts. In 1924 several locals occupied the north-enders' International Hall
and Free Library and broke the windows. The farmers of
Edenbridge felt intimidated; they were afraid to start an
open quarrel. So one day, when the Hall was empty, they
simply carried it to a new location, closer to the centre of the
colony, where it continued to serve as a place for Hebrew
instruction, a library, and a meeting-hall.

There were financial strains on the community's
resources as well. As the 1930s progressed and more and
more immigrants entered Canada, general public protest
against "foreigners" grew louder and more virulent in tone.
The Canadian Committee of the JCA had instructions from
Paris not to provide new arrivals with money for living
expenses or medical aid. Immigrants were supposedly
screened in Europe to make sure they had enough capital to
cover these costs; but still many of them arrived penniless.
The established Jewish colonists were aware that if the
newcomers became dependent on the municipality they
would be deported, and the JCA and Jews in general would
be the targets of angry criticism. So the farmers of
Edenbridge and of the other colonies carried the load of
cash loans and guarantees at a time when they could afford
it least.

Those who hoped that the pressure of these economic
and social problems would diminish the internal rancour in
the community were disappointed. One typical story illus-
trating just how uncompromising the feuding parties could
be dates from around 1930 when the left-wing north-
enders formed their own branch of YCOR, the Yiddish
Colonization Organization. One of YCOR's major aims was
to make the area of Biro-Bidjan in Russia an autonomous
Jewish region where Soviet Jews could prove that a new

synthesis of Jewish life and socialism was possible through the uplifting, noble labour of agriculture.

The leftists of Edenbridge thought of themselves as an important forerunner to the Biro-Bidjan experiment, and the Jewish section of the Communist Party of Canada agreed. In 1932 a representative from YCOR headquarters in New York was sent to Edenbridge to speak at a meeting that had, for some reason, been arranged to take place in the colony's synagogue. Rather than compromise their principles by wearing a skull-cap in the synagogue (as the Vickar brothers insisted they do), the north-enders cancelled the meeting and the YCOR representative went home.

In 1930 the whole of western Canada was struck by crop failure. Low market prices scarcely justified the work of stacking and threshing what little there was, and in Edenbridge they burned what was left of the crop after the season's growth. In 1931 the province was hit by drought. In 1932 ten families left the colony. By 1933 net equity for the community had dropped to $177,849 and the average equity per farmer had dropped to $3,952. But most ominous of all for the future of Edenbridge was the fact that out of sixty children over the age of nineteen, only fourteen were working as farmers. The others were teachers, merchants, clerks, students, and plumbers. One was an engineer and one was a lawyer.

The pattern of change had begun.

Still, they were optimistic, especially the Vickars. Sam and Dave had added to their original 160-acre homesteads until eventually they owned and cultivated more than 1400 acres between them. The brothers were founders of the Edenbridge Public School Board, and alternated as commissioner of oaths for the province and reeve of the municipality of Willow Creek. They also took turns as president and secretary of the Edenbridge congregation (naturally their families had the best seats in the synagogue), and Sam was president of the cemetery committee.

In 1931 the colony celebrated its twenty-fifth anniversary with a parade headed by children bearing flags followed by a band and an ox-cart carrying the surviving original pioneers. The rest of the colonists paraded on foot. The parade stretched over two miles of road, and almost a thousand visitors came from Saskatoon and from as far away as Winnipeg to join in the celebrations. All the right people sent greetings: the Premier of Saskatchewan, the federal Minister of Agriculture, the local member of Parliament, the western commissioner for the federal Colonization and Immigration Department, the manager of the Colonization Department of the CNR. Lyon Cohen, then head of the Canadian Committee of the Jewish Colonization Association, sent a telegram from Montreal, as did Sam Jacobs, MP. Louis Rosenberg represented the JCA and, in his sober and somewhat humourless way, celebrated by preparing a table of the loans disbursed to Edenbridge settlers since 1910 showing how much of the money had been repaid. The Edenbridge record was fairly good, if not quite banquet fare for a happy day.

But in typical Edenbridge fashion, the wrangling between factions almost spoiled the occasion. The north-enders felt that the planning committee had placed too much emphasis on the role of the original settlers (i.e. the Vickars) and not enough on the contribution of the colonists who had come in later years. They decided to boycott the entire event and were only convinced to participate at the last moment by Louis Rosenberg. But if this small dispute shook Rosenberg's confidence a little, it was not for long. "There is no doubt that as soon as the present economic situation improves the Edenbridge colonists will forge ahead and will rapidly liquidate their indebtedness to the Association and to their outside creditors. The spirit and attitudes of the Jewish farmers of this colony...augur well for the continued success and emancipation of the Jewish farmers of the neighbourhood," he wrote in a report on the occasion to his superiors in the Montreal office of the JCA.

Although at the time only Argentina and Palestine had a higher percentage of Jews farming the land than Canada, the passage of years ultimately proved Rosenberg wrong, at Edenbridge and at the other Jewish farm colonies of western Canada. Children were educated in Winnipeg and Saskatoon and stayed on to work in the cities. Where else could they find a Jewish boy or girl to marry? their parents asked each other as they nervously eyed their dwindling farm populations. Jewish farm parents were faced with a major decision. Should they keep the kids on the relatively isolated farms, or educate them in the cities where there were Jewish religious and social institutions and a Jewish community?

In the long run the parents made their choices. Finally, like the Jewish communists of the 1930s and 1940s, the farm colonists of the West did not encourage a second generation to repeat the experience of their own lives — in spite of their protestations to the contrary. Like other Jews of their era they believed in education as the key to their children's future. They educated their children and the children never returned to the farm. Eventually the parents grew too old to work the land. They sold out and moved to the cities to finish their lives near their newly urbanized children and their grandchildren, for whom the pioneer farm was no more than a place for Sunday picnics in the summer.

In the mid-1950s only fifteen families remained in the Edenbridge colony, and Cecil and Jennie Gordon, who had thought they would stay forever, sold their stock of animals and left for the winter. Until 1965 they farmed grain in the summer and wintered in Saskatoon. Then they left for good, to be near their sons who were at high school in the city. Now the sons are both doctors and live far away. Cecil Gordon is sixty-eight and he putters in a vegetable garden behind his modest house. There he can close his eyes and feel close to the soil again.

In the late 1970s the colony rattled in the wind like a deserted ghost town. The old frame houses had been torn down by new owners or had simply toppled over in sad capitulation to age and the elements. All that remained along the banks of the Carrot River was the fine house for two families built by the Vickar brothers in 1917. In that house, called B'nai David (Sons of David), lived the last Jewish farmers at Edenbridge, Charlie and "Little" Vickar.* Charlie and Little are unmarried, getting on in years, and a bit grumpy. Together they tend the old synagogue (which has been designated a historical site) and the willow-shaded graveyard alongside where the old pioneers lie buried. Charlie is reeve of the township, carrying on the Vickar tradition of public service.

Sometimes during quiet moments, the brothers gaze thoughtfully out the window of the old house that once shook with the sharp vitality of fifteen lives. They look past their own cultivated land to the deserted ruins of pioneer dwellings where their old friends used to live. Then they turn to each other — puzzled — and ask why young Jews no longer come to colonize and farm the land at Edenbridge.

*Norman Vickar the younger was called "Little"to distinguish him from his cousin who was also called Norman.

CHAPTER SEVENTEEN

Generations of Edenbridge

Sam Vickar and Gella Gelman

Ed... Norm(m. Florence Zeitlin)...Morris...Harry... Joe

Larry(m. Tova Superman)... Reva... Fay

Samuel... Stephen

LIVING ON THE SOUTH SIDE OF EDENBRIDGE, one never needed to wonder about such modern dilemmas as one's Jewish identity in a gentile society. It was enough to attend synagogue regularly, to educate one's children in Jewish tradition, and to live one's life according to the dictates of Jewish law. It was enough to know that one was not godless or otherwise sinfully misguided like the heathen socialists on the other side of the colony. It was enough to impart a legacy of public and private success and, finally, to die thankful to a Queen in England whose government embodied humane ideals — ideals that had allowed you citizenship and brought you and your children happiness in a new land.

The Vickar children have not forgotten, nor have the grandchildren two generations down the line. But the inevitable questions are beginning to emerge. The presumed indelible ink of yesterday's certainties has begun to fade a little. And the process of adaptation and readaptation has begun.

Norman Vickar

Norman Vickar, MLA and Minister of Industry and Commerce in the NDP government of Premier Allan Blakeney, has his constituency office in an old house on Main Street in Melfort, Saskatchewan (population: 5,000). As a Cabinet minister, Vickar now lives in Regina, but he still comes to town often to do business and to "mainstreet", as he calls it. Shaking hands is ever the politician's chore.

Norman was born in the Edenbridge colony in 1916, the second son of Sam Vickar. He is outgoing, convivial, not given to introspection, and conservative; and he is proud to think of himself as a carrier of tradition—Jewish tradition in general and Vickar tradition in particular. His values are Vickar values—ambition, hard work, and determination (the Vickars like to call it "drive")—and Norm considers these qualities the bedrock of the family's success. "My dad and my uncle did well because they were aggressive," he noted, using another favourite Vickar word.

And successful they are. Norm is in politics, finally, after his older brother, Ed, tried and failed to become mayor of Melfort three times. Ed lives in Winnipeg and is the owner of one of the largest car dealerships in the West. His nephew estimates that he's a multi-millionaire. Ed's daughter Elaine, married and living in Saskatoon, is past president of every possible existing committee to do with Jewish life in the city; and Larry, Norm's son, is now an enterprising young salesman in Uncle Ed's car business. Larry also uses the word "drive" a lot and his father describes him as "aggressive".

The generations of Vickars are proud to be conventional pillars of the community, and an easy confidence swishes about some of them in almost palpable waves. Norm is direct about his father's achievements at Edenbridge and blunt about his influence. "Whenever a decision had to be made at Edenbridge, my father or my uncle made it. And that was that. If people resent it when we say the Vickars were the stalwarts of the community, maybe it's because the truth hurts," he said, implying that the old rancour between the north-enders and the south-enders in the pioneer colony has not yet been laid to rest. "They had lots of ambition," his brother Ed said simply. "They were self-made people.... And as a married man, a father, and a grandfather, I, too, can say that I am a self-made man. When I got married in 1940 I didn't have forty cents to my name. Nobody gave me anything or did anything for me. The opportunities were there and I took them."

Norm and Ed Vickar's self-confidence may come from the fact that Edenbridge, where they were raised, was a totally Jewish environment where no one ever felt the need to question or feel self-conscious about his or her origins. In the two schools in the colony, at least ninety per cent of the class was Jewish, including the teacher. The community was surrounded by a gentile world, but most of the time that world was not hostile. Jews and gentiles alike brought their legal and their personal problems to Sam and Dave Vickar, who offered carefully considered and highly respected advice. If anything, the message conveyed to the Vickar children was not that Jews were less, but that Jews were more. Some of that childhood perspective is still present in Norm's speech. "Around Edenbridge, people generally looked to the Jews as the guiding light or the Moses in the community," he said.

Norm Vickar didn't particularly like farming, so when he finished high school he moved into the family implements business at Gronlid, a village near Melfort. He married Florence Zeitlin in 1947, and in 1955 they moved to Melfort, a few miles down the road from the colony. Ed had a car dealership there, and when he decided to move to Winnipeg in 1963, Norm and two of his other brothers took over the business.

As a boy, Norm accompanied his father on his frequent official jaunts into the larger community. He listened to Sam talk to people about local concerns and he learned to appreciate the obvious perks of leadership — the respect his father enjoyed and the way a good reputation swelled and swept over the countryside.

So in 1962 Norm became president of the local board of trade in Melfort and head of the band association, a move which "started Melfort on its band history and put me in the limelight," he claims. In 1966 he was elected alderman and in 1968 he ran for mayor of the town.

He was defeated — by anti-Semitism, he believes. ("If I wasn't Jewish I would have made it.") There were indications that he was right. A local church supported the other candidate to keep a Jew from becoming mayor, and friends whispered reported slanders into his ear. But he ran again in 1970. Ed and the rest of the family asked him why he bothered. Why stir the pot of race antipathy and risk humiliation? But Norm replied, "They said I was Jewish two years ago. What else can they say? People get tired of listening to the same story."

He won — and was mayor until 1976. In 1975 he ran provincially for the NDP and won that too. In 1976 Allan Blakeney offered him a Cabinet post.

Still, traces of bitterness from the past remain. The Vickars of Edenbridge were respected by the gentile population who came to them for advice and did business with them, but there remained a distance between them. "When it came time to give the Jew a little glory, a little extra, it was hard for the community. It was okay for Ed to be president of the Chamber of Commerce or president of this or that community organization, but mayor . . . that was too much. Ed would have done big things for Melfort. But he was never given the chance.

"But that kind of anti-Semitism doesn't exist any more in Melfort. I proved that even though I'm Jewish, I could still do a job for the community."

Norm and Florence no longer keep a kosher home because they had to fly their meat in from Winnipeg and eventually that became expensive and impractical. But, otherwise, Norm is convinced that the values taught him by Sam Vickar need no altering or compromise. "I will always put my Jewishness first," he said emphatically. "I will never hide it, no matter where I go. I don't mind telling you that I eat no pork and everybody knows this. And if it is served in Cabinet circles someone will holler, 'Well, Norm, they're serving chicken today,' you know, in a joke, and that's just fine. I don't eat it, that's all."

One area, however, remains as dangerous and fraught with taboo as it was three-quarters of a century ago in the sod houses along the south side of the Carrot River. Inter-marriage. Norm dated gentile girls knowing in the back of his mind that he could never become seriously involved with any of them. And, when the time came, like his father and his uncle, he went to Winnipeg to find a bride.

Norm and Florence had three children, one boy and two girls. When they finished high school in Melfort, it was important to get them off to university in Winnipeg as quickly as possible. The Vickars decided that, socially, prospects were better in Winnipeg. "We thought there was more chance for them to meet Jewish friends there than in Saskatoon," said Norm frankly. But pressure to make the "right" choice was always subtle. "I don't remember myself or Florence telling any one of our children that we didn't want them to marry a non-Jewish person, but in a roundabout way they knew what we meant all the time," said Norm. "They knew what we were talking about."

The careful legacy of Sam and Dave Vickar also was not left to chance. "I had several talks with my son, Larry, and I told him, 'Your first involvement has to be with the Jewish community,'" Norm stated candidly. "And today I am proud. I am proud that my kids have accepted the values of my family."

Larry Vickar

For Norm's son, Larry, life is at once more complex and less navigable. Larry is in his early thirties and the father of two small children. He and his wife, Tova, an Israeli, live in a modest house in a solidly Jewish district of Winnipeg. Larry isn't quite sure why he lives there, since he feels in conflict about it, but finally settles on what he self-mockingly calls his favourite rationalization. He plans to send his children to a parochial school and it is in the neighbourhood.

Larry Vickar is a good man and he tries to do the right things. He works hard as a sales manager in his uncle Ed's car business, sometimes putting in twelve-hour days. And he has taken his father's admonition seriously. He has been vice-president of his B'nai Brith lodge and chairman of the Israel bond drive. He has been chairman of the UJA campaign and a member of the community council of the YMHA. He pays his membership to the synagogue (although he rarely attends services) and contributes to the UJA and to Israel. These are not empty gestures. Larry Vickar cares deeply about all things Jewish. They permeate his life and he claims, in a modest way, to be as knowledgeable as anyone in the West about Israel and current events that affect Jews.

So perhaps it is the predictability of his life that has begun to make him feel uneasy about things he has never questioned. There is much about being a Jew that is deeply attractive. Through it he feels a sense of continuity with his grandfather, Sam Vickar, and with the struggles of the early years at Edenbridge; through it he feels a connection to the land, and through the land strong roots in Canada itself; through it he feels the taut strength of an umbilical cord that links him to generations stretching back into eastern Europe. This continuity he wishes to maintain. For this reason he and his wife will send their children to a parochial school where they will learn the substantive material that connects Jews to their past elsewhere—the languages of Hebrew and Yiddish, the history of war and subjection—and also those moments of triumph that blink light into the darkness of Jewish history like an occasional firefly in the night.

What Larry Vickar admires most about his grandfather and his father is the way they have refused to compromise. "Grandfather stuck to his values and did as his conscience led him, not as he felt others wished him to do." That's where Larry has trouble. What do you do in a world where you don't really want to make waves or cause trouble? Do you call attention to your differences and perhaps get looked at strangely and whispered about behind your back? That may be all right for some people, but it's hard for Larry Vickar. "Sometimes I feel I'm trying to hide my identity, especially with customers. If something is arranged and it falls on an important Jewish holiday, I don't like to make a point of the fact that I'm Jewish and ask them to change the date. I tend to say nothing and that makes me feel guilty. But for my father and my grandfather, I'm sure there was never any question...."

Some while ago Larry overheard a secretary at the office refer to someone as a "Jew doctor". He had been serving a customer and had slipped into the office to get a piece of information from a file when he heard it. "I stopped. I was going to say to her, 'You use the word Jew like there was something wrong with it; was he not a good doctor? Did he do something wrong?'; but I was busy and I thought, well, I'll do it later. But I didn't, and then two or three days went by. Why did she have to do that? Why, in the office of a company owned by Jewish people? My grandfather or my father would have sat down with her and had a proper discussion, nicely, but I didn't, and I couldn't stop thinking about it for the longest time. You know, when you think of a Catholic or a Protestant or whatever, you think of them first of all as Canadians, but with Jews I think people think we are always Jews first. Maybe it's this self-consciousness that keeps me from speaking out. Maybe I'm just a coward."

Unlike his father, Norm, Larry was not raised in the protected Jewish environment of Edenbridge where ninety per cent of the school kids were Jews like himself. He was a town kid, joining in the schoolyard ridicule of the country kids who were bussed in daily. Being Jewish in Melfort was not a problem, for him or his gentile friends, but when he arrived in Winnipeg after high school the world as he knew it turned upside down. There was an unspoken social code that everyone else seemed to know about. "I couldn't understand why Jewish kids had so little contact with non-Jewish kids or why their parents wanted them to socialize almost entirely with other Jews. It surprised me that the jokes I heard made about the gentiles were the same sort of jokes I had heard the gentiles make about the Jews. The stereotype joke can be applied to everyone. And I wondered, here we are in a free country, in Canada, and yet we choose to live in little groups in certain parts of the city. We strive to live there. Now *I* strive to live here, it is true. And most of my friends now are other Jews. . . . "

Larry Vickar was taught to serve the community and to be proud of the Jewish traditions of language and law, although, confusingly for him, both the latter were honoured more in the breach than in the observance as the years went by. Yiddish was a language he heard only when his parents talked with his grandparents. It was the language parents spoke when they didn't want the children to understand. The colour, humour, irony, and earthiness that characterized it and carried the cultural cement that bound the Jews of eastern Europe to each other was lost to him — except in translation, which was not the same. Hebrew remained a "dead" language, something to suffer through while preparing for a bar mitzvah at age thirteen, when such study would mercifully cease. Keeping kosher was becoming a joke for some — two sets of dishes at home, but pork ends at the Chinese restaurant on Sunday nights. In Larry's own childhood his grandmother would secretly give him a glass of milk during a meat dinner — breaking the kosher laws that forbid the mixing of milk and meat. Grandfather, sitting at the same table, would be duped. No one thought this disrespectful, just amusing. Besides, this was Canada, and everybody knew that modern nutrition required healthy children to consume a quart of milk a day, regardless of the make-up of the meal on the table.

Larry was also taught to treasure Israel, that Israel is a buffer against a repetition of the most dreadful event of our time — an event that is carried, an unhealed wound, in the hearts of all Jews. But above all he learned that he was not to sever the bond with the past. Intermarriage was plainly and simply out of the question.

Every summer, Norm and Florence Vickar sent their children to a Jewish camp in Alberta. Larry went there for five or six years and loved it. Then, when he was thirteen, his father learned that there was a B'nai Brith Jewish fraternity in Saskatoon and drove him there in the car so he could attend a meeting. After that Larry took the bus or the train to attend a few yearly meetings, but the highlight was always the week-long convention that was held at Christmas or Easter, both times when friends from Melfort were busy and the Jewish child would feel most lonely and excluded.

There was always a sense at the back of Larry's mind that the friends in Melfort were not the people with whom he would spend his life. They might stay in Melfort; Larry knew he would not. He would be sent to school in Winnipeg where he would meet a Jewish girl to marry. So dating in high school remained slightly remote — as it had been for his father before him. Once, though, in Grade Twelve, Larry became involved with a girl in his class. One night he found his father waiting for him when he came home. "A nice girl and a nice family," said Norm, "but don't you think you might be moving in a direction it might be hard to come back from? Don't you think you should look at the situation clearly now and analyse things a bit?"

"He didn't say it. He didn't have to say, 'I don't want you to continue seeing this girl because you may want to marry her and she is not a Jew,'" recalled Larry. "I understood and I respected his feelings. I knew his values and those of my mother. I stopped seeing her. And you know what? I think I was relieved."

The sanction against intermarriage was not an idle threat. One of Larry's cousins married a gentile and her own parents refused to attend the wedding.

Larry Vickar still doesn't believe in intermarriage, and his arguments are all familiar: Marriage is difficult enough without adding problems; it is a terrible thing to raise children without a sound religious identity; it is foolish to celebrate the holidays of two religions.

But he remains confused. He is embarrassed by a perception of clannishness among Jews, yet he lives by choice in a solidly Jewish neighbourhood of Winnipeg. When he came to Winnipeg he was appalled and surprised that young Jews socialize only with each other, yet he is planning to send his own children to a parochial school where they will not have the opportunity to make friends from other backgrounds. And from the safety of this cocoon he is still embarrassed to remind the gentile world that he is a Jew.

Always there is the annoying certainty that neither his grandfather, Sam, nor his father, Norman, would have harboured such doubts. Larry Vickar would like to say with his father and his grandfather and with his ancestors, men and women who lived and died in Russia for hundreds of years, that the fact of being a Jew is the most important thing in his life. But he can't. And so far nothing, not even an impressive list of personal service to the causes of the Jewish community, has filled the growing void.

Epilogue

IT TAKES A LONG TIME to move from one part of the world to another. It takes even longer to decide to unpack your suitcase. The first generation of Jews to come to Canada brought the habits and the practices and the superstitions and the hopes and the fears and the quarrels with them. Like immigrants everywhere, they recreated the look, the sounds, and the feel of "home" as best they could; then they huddled closely together to ward off the icy chill that sprang from the strange new world surrounding them. Many were Orthodox Jews, tied to ancient traditions and ways of being. Some came from long lines of scholars who had rocked back and forth in suffering and in joy intoning the eternal prayers, or who had argued their days away over interpretations of the Talmud. Some were rebellious and idealistic. Their political battles were easily transported to the New World, and there are still men and women alive today, communists and socialists, who are quick to warm to their favourite subject — each other — and who are never happier than when they are railing against their erstwhile and beloved enemies.

The question of Jewish identity was not an issue for this first generation of immigrants. The devout knew exactly who they were and what they were doing — they were fufilling the God-given covenant between Moses and his people. The secular political activists knew, as well, that central to

273

Judaism itself was the notion of living inside and not outside history; that the object of the ethical Jewish life was to create a climate of goodness on earth. Rabbis had been known to sermonize that that was, indeed, what being the "Chosen People" actually meant. So the socialists and the communists knew who *they* were and what *they* were doing. By struggling to make the world a more just place in which to live, they were also fulfilling an ancient covenant of the Jews.

The new immigrants spoke to each other in Yiddish, the cultural glue of millions of eastern-European Jews. In Yiddish the devout believer and the militant Marxist on the picket line communicated (if they chose to) with ease and intimacy. Brothers and sisters, sharing a language and a culture, they looked out at the gentile world through the same thick-paned window. And, side by side, they looked over their shoulders to see what the gentiles were up to. Was it time to unpack the suitcase?

The second generation looked into the suitcase, but were embarrassed by its contents. If "settling in" meant setting up house with that baggage, they preferred to leave the case shut and buy a new one. All that ethnicity made them squeamish and self-conscious. The children of the communists thought their parents were a little bit crazy to be dreaming of Russia when they were in a great new land of opportunity; the children of the Jewish socialists found the ideology of their parents irrelevant. But the second generation did not abandon the idealism that was by then ingrained in their bones. They modified it, instead, and it emerged as a deeply felt reflex liberalism and sense of social concern. Liberalism emerged in across-the-border support for the black civil-rights movement in the United States in the 1960s and in a generally sympathetic response to the aspirations of Quebec nationalists in the early days of that movement. The good intentions occasionally led to ludicrous consequences. In the case of the civil rights movement, middle-class Jewish liberalism persisted long after rumours of anti-Semitism among radical American blacks began to be whispered in shocked, disbelieving tones. In the case of the Parti Québécois, widespread liberalism persisted until the election of 1976, when, terrorized by the spectre of a separatist as premier, Jewish Quebeckers began to leave the province in droves. The following paragraph appeared in a Toronto magazine in 1972:

> ...In the Sixties, Stokely Carmichael came to Toronto to raise money. In an enormous Forest Hill home he talked to a sympathetic audience about growing black anger. Rumours of militant black anti-Semitism hung in that room, heavy and unspoken. White uniformed catering ladies passed tidbits; Carmichael passed a hat ("cheques will be fine"). Then someone asked for the mike and said "it". Everyone looked embarrassed. The men signed the cheques. Last year I listened to René Lévesque tell a Holy Blossom audience why the Québécois must separate. A hundred hearts beat in sympathy. Rumours of Québécois anti-Semitism hung there, heavy and unspoken. Someone took a floor mike and said "it". The audience murmured a bit, and many hissed the questioner. Liberalism is a fine tradition that no one wants to abandon.

The second and third generations have not abandoned liberalism as such. In the autumn of 1979 they rallied vigorously to support the boat people of Viet Nam — innocent and despised cast-offs who (unlike their own people some thirty-five years earlier) still had a chance to survive. But when it came to big-"L" Liberalism and voting, they were no longer as sure as they once had been. Sir Wilfrid may have welcomed Jews into Canada, but that was a long time ago. And the record of the King government had been disillusioning, to say the least. Furthermore, it took the Liberals until 1969 to name a Jewish Cabinet minister, Herb Gray, and everyone knew that David Croll had been named to the Senate in 1955 (significantly, after the death of Mackenzie King) so as not to have a Jew in the Cabinet.

The second and third generations began to vote along other than ethnic lines, and when the upper-middle-class, significantly Jewish riding of St. Paul's in Toronto voted Conservative in the election of 1972, a notable change in voting patterns had occurred.

But the second generation experienced a continuing dilemma as it peered into the heritage bag of its immigrant parents. If Yiddish was a part of the contents of that suitcase, then the second generation didn't even want to look. Yiddish was the language you understood because your greenhorn mother and father spoke it, but *you* always answered in English, thank you very much. *You*, after all, were a Canadian and not a foreigner. Hadn't your parents scrimped and saved so you could become just that? So you could share in the great North American dream of success?

There was, however, one central fact that made the contents of that immigrant bag irrevocably distasteful. By the 1950s the second generation had plainly and simply moved into another economic class and the Jewish proletariat, so central to the lives and the thinking of the immigrant generation—including the immigrant institutions that represented them—had virtually disappeared. The Labour Zionists, the Workmen's Circle, the UJPO—all were populated by retired, aging needle-workers whose children had moved into another universe. While continuing to love their parents, vast numbers of these children snubbed their culture, shuddered at the sounds of the old-country language, abandoned their religious orthodoxy (some sneered bitterly that God had died in an oven at Auschwitz), and derided their parents' politics. But still the parents were proud. Maybe the young folk didn't speak Yiddish or Hebrew, but they were doctors and lawyers and accountants and independent business people. The promised dream of the good life would be theirs.

The children moved out of the immigrant quarter and took their parents with them. In Montreal they moved from downtown into the plusher districts of the west end; in Toronto they moved from the streets surrounding Kensington Market up Bathurst Street, the central corridor of the city;* and in Winnipeg they moved from the famous North End to West Kildonan, then to Garden City, then to River Heights.

In Toronto, those who settled in the well-to-do community of Forest Hill became subjects of one of the first sociological studies of an upper-middle-class neighbourhood in North America. *Crestwood Heights*, published in 1956, analysed the habits of Forest Hillers with a scrutiny usually reserved for South Sea Islanders and caused a mild sensation (not to say scandal) in "Big City"(Toronto) and elsewhere.

The dream of material success which had reached its zenith in post-war Canada and the United States in the 1950s was symbolized by the move north to The Village.

[Crestwood Heights represented] a dream of a material heaven in the here and now, to be entered by the successful elect. . . . What is envisioned is a material abundance to be achieved and maintained only by unremitting struggle and constant sacrifice. No citizen of Big City or its hinterland, casting a longing and covetous eye towards Crestwood Heights, could easily envisage a life of leisure there. Should he, by some stroke of fortune or through his own exertions, enter the promised land, he will fully accept continuing work and increasing anxiety as the price he must pay if he does not wish to be cast out of his paradise. His character will have been so firmly structured by the time he finally arrives in Crestwood Heights that leisure and inactivity are now his greatest threats. Once there, the grandchild of Irish

*Between 1951 and 1961 the Jewish population of North York increased from 4,000 to 49,000.

peasants propelled towards North America by the
dream, could no more freely shed his cultural inherit-
ance of thrift and industry, hoarding and frugality,
than could the Jewish child of ghetto parentage cast off
completely his age-old fear of segregation and persecution.....

Another price exacted by the North American success
god was a dampening of the intellectual and emotional
passions the immigrant parents had felt. The second generation may have been uncomfortable with the distinctive
contents of their parents' suitcases, but they didn't quite
know what to fill their own with. They, in their turn,
glanced over their shoulders to see what the gentiles were
up to, but now they also yearned for acceptance. Suddenly
they had disconcerting choices to make, as well. In the old
ghetto they never had to tell anyone who or what they were.
It was obvious from where they lived or from the accented
English their parents spoke. But with the move into new
districts they had to decide, as Irving Howe put it, "whether
or not they wanted to declare themselves as Jews." They
had to decide how they would transmit their traditions to
their children. And what traditions (if any) they wanted to
transmit.

They did, as it turned out, still want to have a
synagogue, but not the old shtetl-type shul of their parents.
The majority abandoned orthodoxy as irrelevant to modern North American life and became affiliated with Conservative or Reform temples.* The trend in Canada was
similar to that of the United States. The new temples were
more like community centres than houses of worship and

*In a Toronto survey in 1961, only fifty per cent of the families were
connected with a synagogue. In another study carried out from
1967 to 1970, nineteen per cent said they were Orthodox, forty-five
per cent said they were Conservative and twenty per cent said they
were Reform. Sixteen per cent said they had no religion. All, however, were similar in their positive expressions of feeling about their
Jewish identification, which was not based on religious practice or
synagogue affiliation.

their main function was education—in particular, the education of the children.

There is a widespread feeling among Crestwood Heights parents that the child should be exposed to *"some* religious training" from which the parents may, or may not, hold themselves aloof. This theory holds that the child, when he reaches adulthood, may then make his own choices.... A Jewish mother, in discussing the pressure brought to bear on her by her children to conform to Orthodox ritual, made the following remarks: "My husband's family were Orthodox and observed all the rituals. We only observed what seemed to us significant.... R. finds out about the rituals from her friends and at religious school. When she asks why we don't observe, then I just tell her the plain truth— that some people believe in them, but we don't. If she wants, she can grow up to have the other rituals, if she likes them....

"...The children have religious school from three-thirty to four-thirty. It gives them a chance to get their homework done, if nothing else...."

Thus the religious activities of the Crestwood Heights family...serve to gird the child with the minimum of spiritual armour, which may be shed easily in favour of other defences, should it be experienced as obsolete or cumbersome. For the runner of the Crestwood Heights race needs, first and foremost, to be *free* for the course he has to follow. He cannot afford to be held back by old-fashioned beliefs any more than he can allow himself to be tied to old-fashioned people or material objects. Like a new and finer house, a new and advanced religion can be a powerful source of reassurance to the Crestwooder that he has escaped his hampering past and can now grasp at a more alluring and dazzling future.

The choice of what to put in the new heritage suitcase looked unpromising. Even worshippers at the shrine of material success might feel uneasy about replacing the contents of their parents' bags — the Yiddish language, culture, religion, memories of the old country, and deeply felt political ideology — with something as inappropriate as, say, a new car, or a swimming-pool in the backyard, or a television set. After all, to move into the middle class and absorb its values was not exactly a "Jewish" occupation. Forest Hill itself was an ethnic mix of people whose backgrounds were diametrically different, but who shared a point of view and wanted the same things. So if the old contents of the immigrant suitcase were unsuitable, what in the name of Moses (and Abraham and Isaac and Jacob for that matter) might go into the new heritage bag? The generation born after 1940 could not even pack the scars of a collectively remembered Canadian anti-Semitism, which might have bound them to each other and to their traditions. They had known only peace and security; they had grown up during a time when it was no longer fashionable or even socially permissible for Canadians to be overtly anti-Semitic, whatever private thoughts they may have entertained.

The solution to the dilemma came in 1948 and was definitively stamped and packed into the suitcase in 1967 during the Six Day War between Jews and Arabs. In 1948 Canadian Jews rejoiced at the creation of the State of Israel, not primarily as believers in the traditional ideology of Zionism, but as partakers in a historic feast. The political reality of Israel caught the imagination of the Canadian Jewish community, coming as it did just after the war as the terrors and humiliation of the Holocaust were seeping through their pores to take up permanent residence in their hearts.

Israel had practical needs; Israel needed money; and Israel needed support — which often meant unquestioning allegiance to the policies of the ruling party, whatever they might be. Now the bond drives began to take place in the synagogue, acquiring a quasi-religious significance. The

author of an autobiographical article in a Toronto magazine recalled his personal experience in synagogue on Yom
Kippur.

> The Rabbi addresses what his predecessor addressed in
> each and every year of his tenure: the survival of Israel.
> If it is difficult to believe firmly in God or even to
> question Him about His role in the modern Jewish
> world, it is a simple and automatic matter to take this
> opportunity, when there are more Jews gathered
> together than at any other time, to define our responsi-
> bility as the support of Israel. . . . We are then given the
> opportunity to raise our pens and pencils in unison and
> pledge money to buy Israeli bonds. . . . Our religious
> heritage has been ceded to our role as funders of the
> state, and the amount of our contribution seems the
> barometer of what kind of Jews we are. The decision is
> private; it is personal, the way our relationship with God
> used to be. . . . I find it impossible to imagine our lives
> without Israel and her imperilled existence.

Like their immigrant parents, the second generation
remained fearful about the threat of intermarriage. The
philosopher and theologian Emil Fackenheim has said that
Jews should not allow Hitler a posthumous victory of this
sort, and he has also suggested that young Jewish women
ought to produce as many children as they can to coun-
teract the losses (to the horror of many who cringe at the
idea of social engineering). But the young people of the
third generation do not seem to be listening. Although
Jewish-studies programs flourish in universities and more
children are enrolled in religious schools than at any time in
the recent past, the rate of intermarriage has never been
higher. Research in Toronto in the early 1970s found that
the vast majority of young Jews (including thirty-three per
cent of the Orthodox) approved of intermarriage without
qualification.

But there are other, different sorts of changes taking place. Although the old suitcase was never unpacked, the third generation has been taking a curious, interested look at its contents. Classes in Yiddish language and literature are springing up, and although Canadian children will never actually speak to each other in that language, they are at least learning to understand the sounds and traditions of east-European Jewry. Sometimes their grandparents, the emancipated second generation that shuddered in shame at their own parents' strangeness, watch with furrowed brow and listen in bewilderment. It's hard to understand why the ethnicity they sloughed off at such personal cost is actually being cultivated in some quarters. But the third generation, and in some cases the fourth, is no longer embarrassed by the contents of the old suitcase. As Irving Howe put it, "They [have] moved far enough into the pleasures of assimilation...to feel ready for the pleasures of nostalgia."

It is one hundred years since the first refugees from Russian pogroms began to arrive in Canada. Generations have died and generations have been born, yet the immigrant experience is still within touching distance. The fear and the breath-catching excitement of the young man who is about to leave his home and his family—perhaps forever—is a memory that lives only just beneath the skin. His words can still touch a throbbing nerve and shrivel the half-century that lies between the telling and the hearing. A prayer is whispered across the decades—and heard:

> Light me, Holy Spirit,
> On the trackless way I roam,
> Full with terrors infinite,
> And far from hearth and home.
> Holy light, O guide me
> Where waves on the sea shore moan,
> Oceans part me from friendship:
> Night, storm—I am alone.

Bibliography

The following books, articles, and other sources have been of most value to me in the preparation of this book.

Books:

Avakumovic, Ivan. *The Communist Party in Canada.* McClelland & Stewart, 1975.

Belkin, Simon. *Through Narrow Gates: A Review of Jewish Immigration, Colonization, and Immigrant Aid Work in Canada (1840-1946).* Canadian Jewish Congress, 1966.

Betcherman, Lita-Rose. *The Swastika and the Maple Leaf: Fascist Movements in Canada in the Thirties.* Fitzhenry and Whiteside, 1975.

Buck, Tim. *Yours in the Struggle: Reminiscences of Tim Buck.* Edited by Phyllis Clarke and William Beeching. N.C. Press, 1977.

Caiserman, H. "History of the First Jewish Congress in Canada." In *The Jew in Canada*, edited by A. Hart, 1926.

Chiel, Arthur. *The Jew in Manitoba.* University of Toronto Press, 1961.

Eayrs, J. *Appeasement and Rearmament.* University of Toronto Press, 1965. (Vol. 2 of *In Defence of Canada*)

_____. "A Low, Dishonest Decade: Aspects of Canadian External Policy, 1931-39." In *Growth in Canadian Policies in External Affairs*, edited by H. Keenleyside et al., 1960.

Figler, Bernard. *Lazarus Cohen.* Published by the author, 1968.

_____. *Louis Fitch, Q.C.* Published by the author, 1969.

_____. *Lyon Cohen.* Published by the author, 1968.

_____. *Rabbi Dr. Herman Abramowitz.* Published by the author, 1968.

_____. *Sam Jacobs: Member of Parliament.* Published by the author, 1959.

Groulx, Lionel. *L'Appel de la race*. Éditions Fides, 1956. (1st pub. 1922)

Gutkin, Harry. *Journey into Our Heritage: The Story of the Jewish People in the Canadian West*. Lester & Orpen Dennys, 1980.

Hart, Arthur D., ed. *The Jew in Canada*. Toronto Jewish Publications, 1926.

Howe, Irving. *World of Our Fathers*. Simon & Schuster, 1976.

Hutchison, Bruce. *The Incredible Canadian*. Longman, 1970.

Kage, Joseph. *With Faith and Thanksgiving: The Story of Two Hundred Years of Jewish Immigration and Immigrant Aid Effort in Canada, 1760-1960*. Eagle Publishing Co., 1962.

Kallen, Evelyn. *Spanning the Generations: A Study in Jewish Identity*. Longman, 1977.

Kay, Zachariah. *Canada and Palestine: The Politics of Non-commitment*. Keter Publishing House, 1978.

Keenleyside, H., et al. *Growth in Canadian Policies in External Affairs*. Duke University Press, 1960.

Lipton, Charles. *The Trade Union Movement of Canada, 1827-1959*. N.C. Press, 1973.

McGregor, F. A. *The Fall and Rise of Mackenzie King, 1911-1919*. Macmillan, 1962.

Neatby, H. Blair. *William Lyon Mackenzie King*. Vol. 3 of *The Prism of Unity*, University of Toronto Press, 1932-9.

Newman, Peter C. *The Bronfman Dynasty*. McClelland & Stewart, 1978.

Rhinewine, A. *Looking Back a Century*. Kraft Press (Toronto), 1932.

Richler, Mordecai. *The Street*. McClelland & Stewart, 1969.

Rodney, William. *Soldiers of the International: A History of the Communist Party of Canada, 1919-1928*. University of Toronto Press, 1968.

Rosenberg, Louis. *Canada's Jews*. Canadian Jewish Congress, 1939.

Sack, B. G. *History of the Jews in Canada*. Canadian Jewish Congress, 1965.

Seeley, J., et al. *Crestwood Heights*. University of Toronto Press, 1956.

Speisman, Stephen. *The Jews of Toronto*. McClelland & Stewart, 1979.

Teboul, Victor. *Mythes et images du Juif au Québec*. Éditions de Lagrave, 1977.

Whitaker, Reginald. *The Government Party: Organizing and Financing the Liberal Party of Canada, 1930-1958*. University of Toronto Press, 1977.

Articles:

Abella, Irving. "Portrait of a Jewish Professional Revolutionary." *Labour/Le Travailleur*, vol. 2, no. 2, 1977.

———, and Troper, Harold. "'The Line Must Be Drawn Somewhere': Canada and the Jewish Refugees, 1933-9." *Canadian Historical Review*, June 1979.

Arnold, Abraham J. "Jewish Immigration to Western Canada in the 1880s." *Canadian Jewish Historical Society Journal*, vol. 1, no. 2, Fall 1977.

Belkin, S. "Forty Years of JCA Work in Canada." Public Archives of Canada, Rosenberg Papers, vol. 22.

Carrothers, W. A. "The Immigrant Problem in Canada." *Queen's Quarterly*, Summer 1929.

Draper, Paula J. "The Accidental Immigrants: Canada and the Interned Refugees, Part I." *Canadian Jewish Historical Society Journal*, vol. 2, no. 1, Spring 1978.

Hurd, W. Burton. "The Case for a Quota." *Queen's Quarterly*, Winter 1929.

Jungfer, V. "Être Juif au Québec." *L'Actualité*, October 1978.

McIntyre, L., and Jeffries, J. "The King of Clubs: A Psychobiography of William Lyon Mackenzie King." Unpublished paper.

Rosenberg, L. "There *Are* Jewish Farmers." *The Jewish Standard*, March 30, 1934.

Rudin, A. James. "Crisis at the Bronfman Centre: The 'Man in the Glass Booth' Controversy." *Midstream*, vol. 20, no. 10, December 1974.

Sarner, M. "Beyond the Candles of Chanuka." *Toronto Life*, December 1978.

Stern, Beverly. "The ILGW in Toronto, 1900-1935." Uncatalogued material in the archives of the Multicultural Society of Ontario, Toronto.

Usiskin, M. "Oksn un Motorn." 1945. (Unpublished translation by Marcia Basman.)

Vickar, S. "Zimbale to Edenbridge." *Congress Bulletin*, January 1966.

Yarosky, M. "Quebec's Jewish Community: Bridging the Past and the Present." Paper presented in Toronto, June 1979.

Manuscript Collections and Periodicals:

Bennett (R. B.) Papers, Public Archives of Canada (PAC), MG 26 K, Reel M1482

Canadian Jewish Archives, New Series, nos. 1-13, compiled by David Rome

Canadian Jewish Chronicle

Canadian Jewish Historical Society Journal (CJHSJ)

The Canadian Tribune

286   *Jews: Their Experience in Canada*

Clouds in the Thirties: On Anti-Semitism in Canada, 1929-1939, Sections 1-6
  by David Rome

Hart Family Papers (1724-1800), PAC, MG 24 D 40

Jacobs (S. W.) Papers, PAC, MG 27 III C 3

Jewish Colonization Association, PAC, MG 28 V 83

Jewish Daily Eagle (Kanader Adler)

The Jewish Standard

The Jewish Times

Kenney (R. S.) Collection, Thomas Fisher Rare Book Library, University
  of Toronto

King Papers, Immigration — Jewish, 1933-39, PAC, MG 26 J 4, vol. 193,
  pp. 122619-122681

King Diary, PAC.

L'Action Nationale

Mail and Empire (Toronto), Sept. 25, Oct. 2, and Oct. 9, 1897

Macdonald (Sir John A.) Papers, PAC, MG 26A

Public Records Division, PAC, RG 76 and RG 25 G 1

Rosenberg (Louis) Papers, PAC, MG 30 C 119

Royal Commission on Espionage, King's Printer, 1946

Schomberg, A. *Diary*, PAC, MG 18 N 18

Vochenblatt

Notes

35   "Dear Organization...": Undated MS, CJA, no. 1, p. 2.
35   "Tens of thousands...": *Ibid.*, p. 4a.
36   "The Canadian Jews...": H. Caiserman, "History of the First
      Jewish Congress in Canada", in Hart, *The Jew in Canada*, p. 465.
36   "We Zionists...": Quoted in Caiserman, p. 468-9.
37   "It is not true...": Quoted in Z. Kay, *Canada and Palestine: The
      Politics of Non-commitment*, Keter Publishing House, 1978, p. 22.
37-42 Caiserman, pp. 465-82.
44   There were now...than Protestants: CJA, no. 3, p. 6.
44   "Remember you are...": *Jewish Daily Eagle*, September 17,
      1923.
45   "The Jew is...": Rev. Dr. Barclay, quoted in CJA, no. 3, p. 15.
45   "We are determined...": Rev. R. T. Overing, quoted in
      Canadian Jewish Chronicle and in CJA, no. 3, p. 25.
46   Rabbi Cohen wrote...: CJA, no. 3, p. 29.
46   "Do you wish...": Bram de Sola, quoted in CJA, no. 3, p. 30.
47   "I [am]...Protestant leanings": Peter Bercovitch, quoted in
      B. Figler, *Louis Fitch, Q.C.*, published by the author, 1969, p. 4.
47   "These Jews...": Louis Fitch, *ibid.*
48   "Westmount men": *Montreal Star*, April 24, 1930.

CHAPTER THREE

49   "Arcand made...under the law": L.-R. Betcherman, *The
      Swastika and the Maple Leaf: Fascist Movements in Canada in the
      Thirties*, Fitzhenry and Whiteside, 1975, p. 9.
50   *Montréal Juif: Dessins Gais*: Published by Imprimerie Bilaudeau
      Limitée.
51   Adrien Arcand...fascist Italian state: Betcherman, p. 35.
52   "The problem posed...": Anatole Vanier, "Les Juifs au
      Canada", *L'Action Nationale*, September 1933. (Translation by
      Erna Paris.)
53   "Jews aspire...": André Laurendeau, *Politiciens et Juifs*, n.p.,
      1933. (Translation by Erna Paris.)
53   Betcherman, p. 10 ff.

CHAPTER FOUR

56   One doctor in the...: J. Kage, *With Faith and Thanksgiving: The
      Story of Two Hundred Years of Jewish Immigration and Immigrant Aid
      Effort in Canada, 1760-1960*. Eagle Publishing, 1962, p. 88.
56   W. A. Carrothers, "The Immigration Problem in Canada",
      Queen's Quarterly, Summer 1929.
56   W. B. Hurd, "The Case for a Quota", *Queen's Quarterly*, Winter
      1929.

57   "warned...against the consequence...": Vice-Admiral E. A. Taylor, quoted in *Glasgow Herald*, July 12, 1938. Clipping in PAC, Bennett Papers, MG 26 K, Reel M1482, p. 529051 ff.

57   "we [in Canada] think...": Senator Raoul Dandurand, quoted in J. Eayrs, "A Low, Dishonest Decade", in H. Keenleyside et al., eds., *Growth in Canadian Policies in External Affairs*, Duke University Press, 1960, p. 62.

57   "to rely on force...": *Ibid.*, p. 63.

58   "one of studied neglect": W. A. Riddell, quoted in Eayrs, p. 67.

58   "Never was Mackenzie King...": *Ibid.*, p. 76 ff.

58   The total number of Jews...: Quoted in Betcherman, p. 103.

58   When Auschwitz...: Terence Des Pres, *The Survivor*, 1976, p. 106, quoted in P. J. Draper, "The Accidental Immigrants: Canada and the Internal Refugees, Part I", *Canadian Jewish Historical Society Journal*, vol. 2, no. 1, Spring 1978, p. 7.

59   Opinion poll, 1946: Nancy Tienhaara, *Canadian Views on Immigration and Population: An Analysis of Post-War Gallup Polls*, quoted in Draper, p. 11.

59   In 1935, 880 Jews...: Kage, p. 259, 260.

61   La Fédération des Clubs Ouvriers...: Betcherman, p. 36.

61   La Ligue de l'Action Nationale...: PAC, Public Records, Immigration Branch, RG 25 G 1, vol. 166, file 342, part 1.

61   The St. Jean Baptiste Society...: *Ibid.*, letter from Bernard Benoit, June 16, 1933.

61   In May, the Jewish...: Cable from HICEM to JIAS, May 24, 1933, in Jacobs Papers, PAC, MG 27 III C 3, p. 2677.

62   On November 6, 1933...: PAC, King Papers, W. J. Egan to O. D. Skelton, p. 541782.

62   Skelton had already...: PAC, RG 25 G 1, vol. 166, file 342, part 1, L. Kempff to O. D. Skelton.

63   Magladery claimed...: PAC, King Papers, Magladery to Skelton, May 30, 1934.

63   By July 1934...: *Ibid.*, Magladery to Skelton, July 30, 1934.

63   Although Frederick...all the opportunities": I. Abella and H. Troper, "'The Line Must be Drawn Somewhere': Canada and the Jewish Refugees, 1933-9", *Canadian Historical Review*, June 1979, pp. 183-5.

64   A poignant set...: PAC, Bennett Papers, pp. 529095-529113.

66   Before the war's end...: Interview with Sam Lipshitz, Toronto, 1979.

CHAPTER FIVE

68   "We cannot bring all...": Sir Wilfrid Laurier, quoted in Kay, p. 32.

68   Before the election...: A. K. Cameron, quoted in Figler, *Sam Jacobs*, p. 45.
68   But before offering him the nomination...: A. K. Cameron, quoted in *ibid.*, pp. 50-1.
68   "I can safely say...": Jacobs to Laurier, December 20, 1916, *ibid.*, p. 52.
69   Jacobs admired Laurier...: Interview with Senator H. Carl Goldenberg, Montreal, 1979.
69   The esteem was...as well as our defender": Figler, *Sam Jacobs*, pp. 58-61.
70   "Should this government...": PAC, Jacobs Papers, vol. 1, Jacobs to Herbert J. Samuel, October 20, 1921.
71   "The sight of Jacobs'...": Quoted in F. A. McGregor, *The Fall and Rise of Mackenzie King, 1911-1919*, Macmillan, 1962, p. 82.
71   Jacobs was re-elected...: Figler, *Sam Jacobs*, p. 118.
71   "The addition of the name...": *Ibid.*, p. 119.
72   By 1922...: *Ibid.*, pp. 128, 149, 152.
72   "Should this be...family is enough": *Ibid.*, pp. 132-3.
73   According to Jacobs' friend...: *Ibid.*, p. 263.
74   During the election...to Chevrier": PAC, King Diary, October 30, 1925.
75   A week later...: PAC, Jacobs Papers, p. 2126, January 15, 1930.
75   "...I said I personally...": PAC, King Diary, June 28, 1933.
76   A. A. Heaps...: PAC, Jacobs Paper, vols. I-II, Heaps to Jacobs, December 13, 1929.
76   "I wish I were in your place...": *Ibid.*, Jacobs to the Hon. J. H. King, June 10, 1930.
77   Around the same time...: *The Western Producer* (Saskatoon), December 2, 1926, in PAC, Jacobs Papers, vols. I-II, p. 1493.
77   "Dear Mr. Egan...": PAC, Jacobs Papers, vols. I-II, p. 1990, Jacobs to Egan, September 4, 1928.
78   He gave R. B. Bennett...one of them: PAC, Jacobs Papers, vols. I-II, November 1929.
79   "The future is very dark...": *Ibid.*, Paul Nettelier (signature illegible) to Jacobs, May 1, 1933.
79   The Quebec City Council...: *Ibid.*, unidentified newspaper clipping, May 1, 1933.
79   "In the period covering...": *Ibid.*, Jacobs to Dr. Harry Friedenwald, December 26, 1933.
80   In 1936, Jacobs...: Kage, p. 101.
80   "I am seriously...": PAC, Jacobs Papers, vol. 3, Jacobs to Hector Hughes, Esq. K.C., October 28, 1935.
80   "Mr. King gave me...": Quoted in Figler, *Sam Jacobs*, p. 228.
80   "My dear King...Casgrain's formal reply: PAC, Jacobs Papers, vol 3, September 8, 1936–December 3, 1936.

81   "Jewry rests...": *Montreal Star*, March 31, 1937, quoted in Figler, *Sam Jacobs*, p. 211.

81   "From the front pages...": PAC, Jacobs Papers, vol. 3, p. 3486, Senator Thomas Cantley to Jacobs, April 1, 1937.

82   "To represent Canada...break your heart": Figler, *Sam Jacobs*, pp. 217-18.

82   "Sir Wilfrid Laurier...": PAC, Jacobs Papers, vol. 3, p. 3687.

CHAPTER SIX

84   Canada couldn't possibly...: PAC, King Papers, Blair to Skelton, January 18, 1938.

84   Blair and Skelton prepared...a committee": *Ibid.*, Skelton to King, April 21, 1938.

85   It was to be...practically everyone: Abella and Troper, pp. 193-6.

85-6 "The Évian conference...": *Danziger Vorposter*, quoted in *The Guardian, ibid.*, p. 196.

86   "By the time...": *Ibid.*, p. 196.

86   In 1938 Saul Sigler...: Interview with Saul Sigler, Toronto, 1980.

88   A memo was prepared...: PAC, King Papers, J. A. Gibson to King, November 29, 1938.

89   "The sorrows...": PAC, King Diary, November 12, 1938.

89   The delegation suggested...: PAC, King Papers, A. D. P. Heeney, Memorandum for Fyle (*sic*) re Entry of Refugees into Canada, November 23, 1938.

90   "Since most of...": PAC, RG 76, vol. 440, file 670224, June 16, 1939.

90   Postscript number one...: PAC, RG 76, vol. 440, file 671224, Hugh E. Arnold to W. L. M. King, August 6, 1939.

91   PEQ...FF...: *Ibid.*, November 29, 1965.

91   As early as...: PAC, Bennett Papers, letter from North Battleford Board of Trade, February 14, 1936.

92   The following year...: PAC, Bennett Papers, British Immigration file, 1620, Saskatchewan Immigration and Settlement Convention, 1937.

92   He spoke of "freedom...": *Ibid.*, from the *Prince George Citizen*, August 18, 1938.

93   As C. P. Stacey...: C. P. Stacey, *A Very Double Life: The Private World of Mackenzie King*, Macmillan, 1976.

93   As a student...: In 1897 King wrote four articles for the *Mail and Empire*: "Crowded Housing: Its Evil Effect" (Sept. 18); "Foreigners Who Live in Toronto" (Sept. 25 and Oct. 2); and "Toronto and the Sweating System" (Oct. 9).

292 _Jews: Their Experience in Canada_

93   "There is something...": PAC, King Diary, February 3, 1900, quoted in L. McIntyre and J. Jeffries, "The King of Clubs: A Psychobiography of William Lyon Mackenzie King", unpublished paper.

93   "For the most part...": PAC, King Diary, May 26, 1900, quoted in McIntyre and Jeffries.

94   A. A. Heaps...: Leo Heaps, _The Rebel in the House_, quoted in D. Rome, _Clouds in the Thirties: On Anti-Semitism in Canada, 1929-1939_, section 6, p. 83.

94   "to save the wrong class...": PAC, King Diary, June 2, 1935.

94   "as a man of deep sincerity...its borders": PAC, King Papers, memorandum prepared for Chamberlain and Eden, June 29, 1937, quoted in J. Eayrs, _In Defence of Canada: Appeasement and Rearmament_, University of Toronto Press, 1965, p. 231.

95   "hypnotized": PAC, King Papers, letter from Violet Markham, June 15, 1937, quoted in Eayrs, p. 231.

95   "did not appear to be...": Quoted in Eayrs, p. 231.

95   At the end of...can say": PAC, King Papers, memorandum by King on interview with Hitler, June 29, 1937, quoted in Eayrs, pp. 226-31.

95   "[Please] let them know...": PAC, King Papers, King to Windels, Hitler, and Ribbentrop, quoted in Rome, _Clouds_, sect. 6, p. 94.

95   "Force is not...": Quoted in B. Hutchison, _The Incredible Canadian_, Longman, 1970, p. 249.

96   "look glum": PAC, King Diary, November 24, 1938, quoted in Blair Neatby, _William Lyon Mackenzie King_, University of Toronto Press, 1976, p. 305.

96   "My own feeling...": _Ibid._, March 29, 1938, quoted in Neatby, p. 304.

96   Of that number...: Estimation of four thousand refugees in Abella and Troper, p. 181.

CHAPTER SEVEN

97   ...a poll taken...: V. Teboul, _Mythes et images du Juif au Québec_, Éditions de Lagrave, 1977, p. 14.

98   By 1971...: Canada Census.

98   ...more than fifty per cent...: M. Yarosky, "Quebec's Jewish Community: Bridging the Past and the Present", paper presented in Toronto, June 1979.

99   "the central character...in his commentary: A. J. Rudin, "Crisis at the Bronfman Centre: The 'Man in the Glass Booth' Controversy", _Midstream_, vol. 20, no. 10, December 1974, p. 49 ff.

100 "The survivors put on..." (ff.): Interview with Sam Shriar, Montreal, 1978.
104 "Cabinet solidarity..." (ff.): Interview with Victor Goldbloom, Montreal, 1978.
105 "Goldbloom [is] putting in...": Interview with Max Wolloch, Montreal, 1978.
106 One week before... Union Nationale: P. C. Newman, *The Bronfman Dynasty*, McClelland and Stewart, 1978, pp. 271-3.
107 "Don't vote with your heads... out of Quebec: Privately held tape recording of meeting, November 1976.
110 By November 1978...: Interview with Victor Goldbloom, Montreal, 1978.
110 Between 1971... they will not be back": Interview with Jack Kantrowitz, 1980.
111 "What does a middle-class...": Interview with Jean-Claude Lasry, Montreal, 1979.
114 "My educated...": Interview with Saul Hayes, Montreal, 1978.
115 "This notion...": Interview with Michael Yarosky, Montreal, 1978.
115 "The Jewish community...": Interview with David Rome, Montreal, 1979.
115 "When we have crossed...": Interview with Victor Goldbloom, Montreal, 1978.

CHAPTER EIGHT

121 "Construction was dense..." (ff.): S. Speisman, *The Jews of Toronto*, McClelland and Stewart, 1979, pp. 83, 85.
121 "We lived in a cellar...": Interview with Becky Lapedes, Toronto, 1980.
124 "My father and..." (ff.): Interview with Joe Salsberg, Toronto, 1979.

CHAPTER NINE

128 Between 1900 and 1914...: C. Lipton, *The Trade Union Movement of Canada, 1827-1959*, N.C. Press, 1973, p. 98.
128 ...pretext that they were "learners": *Whyte Report on the Sweating System in Canada*, CJA, no. 9, p. 66.
130 ...by 1932 there were... (ff.): B. Stern, "The ILGW in Toronto, 1900-1935", uncatalogued material in the archives of the Multicultural Society of Ontario, Toronto, p. 6.
130 But wages were...: CJA, no. 9, p. 53.
131 In 1898, when carpenters...: W. L. Mackenzie King in the *Montreal Herald*, April 16, 1898, CJA, no. 9, p. 45.

131   Some women...: Testimony of L. Gurofsky in the *Whyte Report*, CJA, no. 9, p. 77.
131   King estimated...: *Montreal Herald*, April 16, 1898, CJA, no. 9, p. 77.
131   He was appalled...: King in the *Mail and Empire*, September 25, 1897.
131   "What a day...": King Diary, quoted in *Toronto Daily Star*, December 26, 1964.
132   "scandalous conditions": Quoted in Lipton, p. 110.
132   ...(in 1912...): Stern, p. 8.
132   Hours in the Eaton's...: CJA, no. 9, p. 75.
133   "a state of...": Quoted in Stern, p. 6.
135   Between 1900 and 1914...: Lipton, p. 110.
138   "a frail teen-aged girl...": I. Howe, *World of Our Fathers*, Simon and Schuster, 1976, pp. 298-9.
138   In 1909...: Stern, p. 20.
140   "[Posluns] had no love...": Harry Clarmont, interviewed for Multicultural Historical Society of Ontario.
142   In Winnipeg...(ff.): A. Chiel, *The Jew in Manitoba*, University of Toronto Press, 1961, pp. 118-20.

CHAPTER TEN

144   "to prepare...": W. Rodney, *Soldiers of the International: A History of the Communist Party of Canada, 1919-1928*, University of Toronto Press, 1968, p. 38.
145   In November...: *Globe and Mail*, November 15, 1937, quoted in Betcherman, p. 103.
145   A former Party official...: Estimate by Sam Lipshitz.
146   It was advertised...: *The Needle Worker*, November 1951.
147   "That made an...": Interview with Morris Bederman, Toronto, 1979.
151   "wrote declamatory odes...": Howe, p. 420.
154   "The Party Program..." (ff.): *The Struggle Against Jewish Bourgeois Nationalism: Outline of Report to the Jewish Conference*, Toronto, 1951 or 1952 (undated).
154   The Jewish National Committee...: 1955.
161   "When he spoke...": Howe, p. 340.
168   "I wasn't very much...": Interview with Sam Carr, Toronto, 1979.
170   "The Canadian people...": Sam Carr in *The Clarion*, June 8, 1940, quoted in the *Royal Commission on Espionage*, 1946.
171   When the news...(ff.): *Royal Commission on Espionage*, 1946.
173   The following instructions...: *Ibid*.

174   "What's going on...": Buck, p. 350.
175   "One black, thundering...": Richler, p. 31.

CHAPTER ELEVEN

182   In answer to the charge...: Editorial in the *Vochenblatt*,
        December 19, 1952.
185   "pooh-poohed the whole idea": Interview with Salsberg, 1979.
186   "I, too, believed...": Salsberg in the *Vochenblatt*, October 25,
        1956.
188   There he was told...(ff.): Interview with Salsberg.
189   "If there was...": Interview with Jerry Bain, Toronto, 1979.
190   "Those who speculate...": Tim Buck in the *Canadian Tribune*,
        April 23, 1956.
191   "Some are asking...": Leslie Morris, *ibid*.
191   "Socialism, the system...": Norman Freed, *ibid*.
191   "It is possible...": J. Gershman in *Vochenblatt*, April 12, 1956.
192   "I refuse to...": Fritzie Rose in *Vochenblatt*, April 26, 1956.
192   As a gesture...: Salsberg was reinstated in July 1956.
194   "When people [became aware of]...": Al Hershkovitz, inter-
        viewed for the Multicultural History Society of Ontario, 1977.
200   "They're killing them...": Interview with Joe Salsberg.
201   "One time...": *Ibid*.
201   "remain inside, no matter what..." (ff.): I. Abella, "Portrait of a
        Jewish Professional Revolutionary", *Labour/Le Travailleur*,
        vol. 2, no. 2, 1977, p. 211.

CHAPTER TWELVE

207   "I am a capitalist...": (ff.): Interview with Jerry Goodis,
        Toronto, 1980.

211   "A false impression...": L. Rosenberg, "There *Are* Jewish
        Farmers", *The Jewish Standard*, March 30, 1934.

CHAPTER FOURTEEN

215   "The Mansion House Hall...": Chiel, pp. 26-7.
217   As Irving Howe...: Howe, p. 27.
217   "I am discussing...": PAC, Macdonald Papers, MG 26 A,
        vol. 219, pp. 93321, 93324, and 93327, January 25 and
        February 3, 1882.
217   "The 'Ole Clo' move...": PAC, Macdonald Papers, Macdonald
        to Galt, quoted in A. J. Arnold, "Jewish Immigration to Western
        Canada in the 1880's", *Canadian Jewish Historical Society Journal*,
        vol. 1, no. 2, Fall 1977, p. 86.

296   *Jews: Their Experience in Canada*

218   "Such a timely measure...": PAC, Governor General's corre-
       spondence, John Taylor to Marquess of Lorne, February 13,
       1882, p. 44, quoted in B. G. Sack, *History of the Jews in Canada*,
       Canadian Jewish Congress, 1965, p. 195.
218   "A large and influential...": Colonel I. de Winton to Mac-
       donald, February 18, 1882, quoted in Sack, p. 195.
219   Winnipeg in the 1880s...God of their ancestors": Chiel,
       pp. 31-7.
223   "The government has made..." (ff.): Quoted in Arnold,
       pp. 89-90.
223   Finally, in 1884...(ff.): Chiel, pp. 44-5.
224   "From the outset...": Alexander Galt, quoted in Arnold, p. 94.
225   "adopt all of Israel...": Quoted in Chiel, p. 48.
226   ...when the immigration agent...: PAC, Rosenberg Papers,
       MG 30 C 119, vol. 12, P. Doyle to H. B. Small, August 26, 1891.
226   "The government has no vote...": *Ibid.*, J. Lowe to Baron de
       Hirsch, September 11, 1891.
226   "I have learned...": *Ibid.*, Hugh Sutherland to Harris
       Vineberg, December 26, 1891.
227   Also in December 1891...: PAC, Rosenberg Papers, December
       10, 1891.
228   "It was the first...": Chiel, p. 51.

       CHAPTER FIFTEEN

230   "God help the...": *Canadian Gleaner*, May 20, 1892, quoted in S.
       Belkin, "Forty Years of JCA Work in Canada", PAC, Rosenberg
       Papers, vol. 22.
230   ("Some have never...: PAC, Rosenberg Papers, vol. 22, Asher
       Pierce to Vineberg, May 1892.
231   "All hands arrived...": *Ibid.*, McDiarmid to Vineberg, May
       1892.
231   "[Every day...]": *Ibid.*, June 16, 1892.
232   "peaceful, honourable...": PAC, Rosenberg Papers, vol. 13,
       Constitution and By-Laws of the Agricultural Society of Baron
       de Hirsh (*sic*) in Philadelphia, May 24, 1892.
232   "condition and progress"...: PAC, Rosenberg Papers, vol. 16.
233   "There is no destitution...": *Ibid.*, vol. 21.
234   "To make the Jew..." (ff.): *Ibid.*, vol. 22, quoted in Belkin,
       "Forty Years".
235   ...Harry Fishtrom...: PAC, Rosenberg Papers, vol. 7.
235   ...John Hershburg...: *Ibid.*, vol. 9.
236   ...A. Gorbach...: *Ibid.*
238   "whose dress...": Rosenberg, "There *Are* Jewish Farmers".

238 "a masterly piece of work": Canadian Jewish Congress Archives, Rosenberg, Correspondence and Records, Western Division.
238 "a study in detail...": *Ibid.*
240 "These decisions were...": PAC, Rosenberg Papers, vol. 1.
241 "The important role...": *Ibid.*, vol. 22.

CHAPTER SIXTEEN

243 In Wynberg...eggs at mealtime": S. Vickar, "Zimbale to Edenbridge", *Congress Bulletin*, January 1966.
246 Once Edenbridge was...: PAC, Rosenberg Papers, vol. 21.
247 "Socially, the farmers...": *Ibid.*, vol. 18, E. Guilaroff, July 1, 1914.
248 "We were ready...squabbling became part of the life": M. Usiskin, "Oksn un Motorn", 1945. (Unpublished translation by Marcia Basman.)
254 The Edenbridge farmer...(ff.): Interview with Cecil and Jenny Gordon, Saskatoon, 1977.
257 "if a farmer...": PAC, Rosenberg Papers, vol. 18.
257 "As long as the present...": *Ibid.*
259 In 1930...(ff.): *Ibid.*, vol. 21.
260 "There is no doubt...": *Ibid*, Rosenberg to JCA.

CHAPTER SEVENTEEN

264 Interview with Norman Vickar, Melfort, 1977.
268 Interview with Larry Vickar, Winnipeg, 1977.
275 "In the Sixties...: E. Paris, "Growing Up a Jewish Princess in Forest Hill", *Toronto Life*, October 1972 (cf. Paris, "Ghetto of the Mind", in W. Kilbourn, *The Toronto Book*, Macmillan, 1975.)
277 "[Crestwood Heights represented]...": J. Seeley et al., *Crestwood Heights*, University of Toronto Press, 1956, p. 6.
277(n) Between 1951 and...: E. Kallan, *Spanning the Generations: A Study in Jewish Identity*, Longman, 1977, p. 61.
278 "whether or not they...": Howe, p. 614.
278(n) In a Toronto survey...: Kallen, p. 64.
279 "There is a widespread...dazzling future": Seeley, pp. 214-16.
281 "The Rabbi addresses...": M. Sarner, "Beyond the Candles of Chanuka", *Toronto Life*, December 1978.
282 "Light me, Holy...": Nathan Horowitz, *Canadian Jewish Chronicle*, vol. 16, no. 17, September 21, 1928 (translated).

Index